SUCCESSFUL
SPORTS OFFICIATING

Second Edition

American Sport Education Program

Human Kinetics

Library of Congress Cataloging-in-Publication Data

Successful sports officiating / American Sport Education Program. -- 2nd ed.
   p. cm.
 Includes bibliographical references and index.
 ISBN-13: 978-0-7360-9829-8 (soft cover)
 ISBN-10: 0-7360-9829-1 (soft cover)
 1. American Sport Education Program. 2. Sports officials.
GV735.S94 2011
796--dc23

                      2011022660

ISBN-10: 0-7360-9829-1 (print)
ISBN-13: 978-0-7360-9829-8 (print)

The web addresses cited in this text were current as of June 2011, unless otherwise noted.

Acquisitions Editor: Aaron Thais; **Developmental Editor:** Anne Hall; **Assistant Editor:** Tyler Wolpert; **Copyeditor:** Patsy Fortney; **Indexer:** Dan Connolly; **Graphic Designer:** Joe Buck; **Graphic Artist:** Tara Welsch; **Cover Designer:** Keith Blomberg; **Photographer (cover):** © Human Kinetics; **Photographer (interior):** © Human Kinetics, unless otherwise noted. Photo on page 117 © Dale Garvey and page 149 © AP Photo/Willis Glassgow; **Photo Asset Manager:** Laura Fitch; **Visual Production Assistant:** Joyce Brumfield; **Photo Production Manager:** Jason Allen; **Art Manager:** Kelly Hendren; **Associate Art Manager:** Alan L. Wilborn; **Illustration:** © Human Kinetics; **Printer:** Sheridan Books

Copies of this book are available at special discounts for bulk purchase for sales promotions, premiums, fund-raising, or educational use. Special editions or book excerpts can also be created to specifications. For details, contact the Special Sales Manager at Human Kinetics.

Printed in the United States of America   10 9 8 7 6 5 4 3 2 1

The paper in this book is certified under a sustainable forestry program.

Human Kinetics
Website: www.HumanKinetics.com

United States: Human Kinetics
P.O. Box 5076
Champaign, IL 61825-5076
800-747-4457
e-mail: humank@hkusa.com

Canada: Human Kinetics
475 Devonshire Road Unit 100
Windsor, ON N8Y 2L5
800-465-7301 (in Canada only)
e-mail: info@hkcanada.com

Europe: Human Kinetics
107 Bradford Road
Stanningley
Leeds LS28 6AT, United Kingdom
+44 (0) 113 255 5665
e-mail: hk@hkeurope.com

Australia: Human Kinetics
57A Price Avenue
Lower Mitcham, South Australia 5062
08 8372 0999
e-mail: info@hkaustralia.com

New Zealand: Human Kinetics
P.O. Box 80
Torrens Park, South Australia 5062
0800 222 062
e-mail: info@hknewzealand.com

E5239

SUCCESSFUL
SPORTS OFFICIATING

Second Edition

CONTENTS

FOREWORD

The first edition of *Successful Sports Officiating* was published in 1998. In the ensuing years the landscape of officiating has changed. Today fresh skills and techniques are needed. This second edition provides those for you.

In the foreword for the first edition, I wrote about the demands that come with being a sports official, and I wrote about the psychic income each of us receives every time we officiate a contest. Those words hold even more meaning today.

Sports officiating is rewarding. It is also challenging. The most common image people have of officials involves a player, coach, or fan yelling at an official. Yes, that can and does happen, but overall, the experiences you will have as an official will be exhilarating and positive. The skills you develop will serve you well throughout your life.

To be a good official, you need a blend of certain qualities: courage, self-confidence, determination, and decisiveness, to name just a few. In each game you work, you will be faced with many situations. Collectively through these situations you will be asked to demonstrate the fairness of a judge, the skill of a diplomat, the authority of a police officer, and the understanding of a parent. All in all, much will be asked of you.

So, then, if you will have people yelling at you and you will have to make quick decisions and get sweaty doing it, why would you officiate? That's easy. You officiate to give back to the game and because you believe sport is a valuable component of the educational process. You officiate because you want the challenge of keeping order and fairness when chaos lurks at every turn of events. You officiate because you relish the opportunity to undertake a tough assignment and win at it. When the game is over and you know you have done a proper job, a fair job, you will have a special feeling of accomplishment, even though there might still be boos ringing in your ears. By the way, learning to love those boos is just one more ingredient of becoming a good official!

Learning to be a good official has never been easy. Today those who play, coach, and watch the games have vastly different perspectives and expectations than they did five years ago.

Technology now plays an integral role in officiating. Sometimes, as in the professional level, technology is used in recasting plays. In other levels, technology is used in holding officials accountable for their performances. Suffice it to say that officials have joined the ranks of public persons, absorbing all the burdens that come with such status.

To be an effective and well-accepted official today, you need to understand the totality of the sport experience, to understand that sport is life with the volume turned up. That understanding provides the basis for the development of your personal philosophy of officiating. You also need to study, absorb, and turn into action the training materials that give you a proper base of knowledge.

What does a sports official need to know? The easy answer is this: the rules and proper positioning—the mechanics. Without doubt, those two bodies of knowledge are critical to any official. Today, though, you need to know more. For example, you need to have a basic understanding of your legal rights and responsibilities, proper nutrition and conditioning, time management, the techniques of game management, and defining and maximizing your personal officiating style.

Successful Sports Officiating is comprehensive, authoritative, and practical in its approach to officiating. It presents a blend of techniques that speak to the commonality of all officiating. I know within its pages you will find answers to the questions you most often ask yourself about becoming and succeeding as an official. The book is written and edited by a team of experts who are practitioners of the art and science of officiating. Their experiences and knowledge will serve you well in your quest to understand what's involved in successful officiating. You will be able to take from this book the principles, practices, and policies and apply them in each game you work. You will be a better official, and a more successful official, through the knowledge presented in this book.

Barry Mano
Founder and publisher of *Referee* magazine
President of the National Association of Sports Officials

Part I

Building Your Sports Officiating Career

Chapter 1

Officiating: Past and Present

Jerry Grunska

The perfect game hasn't been worked yet.

But that's no reason to give up trying.

Jerry Markbreit, former NFL referee

This chapter addresses the following:

- A brief history of home-grown American sports and how officials' roles have changed over time

- The root of gender issues in sports and officiating, and legislation designed to eliminate discrimination

- Officiating shortages and methods of acquiring sufficient officials

THE EVOLUTION OF OFFICIATING

The progress of sports and their development into today's recognized games are easily traced. Although the evolution of officiating is sketchy, it is known that from the beginning, competitions required rules monitoring. Several uniquely American team sports started with a prominence in the East. As a result of modifications and adjustments that occurred over the years, some of them look much different now than they did at the start. Lacrosse, a genuinely American sport that Native Americans played before colonists arrived, took place without officials monitoring the rules. This chapter provides a look into the development of sports officiating and its progress through the American-born sports of basketball, football, and baseball.

BASKETBALL

Basketball is a game that was invented on demand. The way it started is both amusing and the source of rich lore.

In a sense, it is possible to attribute the impetus for basketball's birth to physical training clubs in Germany called *turnvereins*. These widely prevalent clubs relied on invigorating apparatus work and tumbling for bodybuilding: tossing Indian clubs and medicine balls; swinging from rings; swiveling on the pummels of the bulky, leather-encased horse; squirreling through parallel bars—what would be called gymnastics today. Exercises included military drills and marching. The purpose of this training was to prepare youth for combat.

In 1891, the six-year-old School for Christian Workers in Springfield, Massachusetts, had essentially adopted the German system, extending it to promote an ideal of strong minds in strong bodies with a nonsectarian ethic of wholesomeness. This was the birth of the Young Men's Christian Association (YMCA).

When students at the Springfield institution, later called a college, were forced indoors in November after a balmy autumn in 1891, they balked at the shift to the old-school routine. Dr. Luther Gulick, dean of physical training, dismissed one instructor who couldn't cope with the malcontents. He then tried to take over the program himself but gave up when he couldn't get the students to cooperate either. In exasperation, he called on a second-year graduate student to solve the problem. Gulick ordered the young man, James Naismith, to try something completely different.

Naismith, a graduate of McGill University in Montreal, had coached football for six years and had just finished work at a Presbyterian Theological Seminary. According to historian Edward Steitz (1976), Naismith "felt that teaching young men through sport was a better way than preaching—especially if one could work through their love for athletics."

Naismith asked building superintendent Alfred "Pops" Stebbins to locate a pair of boxes and hang them from the gallery in the gym. Stebbins couldn't find boxes, so he nailed two half-bushel peach baskets 10 feet from the floor. The revolutionary thing about the baskets was that they provided a horizontal overhead target. As a result, players had to develop completely new skills for moving the ball on the floor (passing and dribbling), and they had to shoot at the baskets. The challenge became an instant sensation. Because the class had 18 members, there were 9 players on a side at first.

The players ran into a problem almost at once: People watching from the balcony could bat away shots or guide errant tosses into the basket. Also, at first, a helper had to lift the ball out of the basket after a score. That problem was solved when a cloth sleeve was attached to the baskets after holes had been sliced in the bottoms. Officials pulled a cord to help the ball slip through (metal hoops replaced the baskets in 1893). A year later, backboards were used to thwart unruly onlookers.

The first official basketball game began at 5:15 p.m. on March 11, 1892, in the Springfield gymnasium. It pitted the secretaries against the faculty, and the secretaries won, five baskets to one. Amos Alonzo Stagg, the future Grand Old Man of football, put in the lone field

goal for the faculty. Naismith, doubtless the referee, thought Stagg's style was too rough.

The first female basketball game took place the same week. Stenographers and secretaries took on the faculty wives. Because the ladies wore bloomers, no male spectators were admitted. Inventor Naismith must have refereed the match, but history has not recorded the score. One of the stenos was a lass named Maud E. Sherman, and she became Naismith's wife.

Thanks to a conscientious chronicler named Edward S. Steitz, we know that two officials oversaw the action from the start of the sport because the respective duties were defined along with the original rules. The referee was responsible for the ball going in the goal, for the ball going out of bounds, and for player conduct in relation to the ball. The referee also timed the game, although we don't know the length of quarters or halves. The umpire, evidently a subordinate figure, was solely in charge of calling fouls. He probably was not allowed to have a whistle. Authorities were reluctant at the start—as they were in other sports as well—to give too much or even equal responsibility to all judges on the floor or field. (In all sports, historically, authorities feared giving so-called "extra" officials too much authority. Therefore, a head referee was designated, and the likelihood is that another official used hand signals to indicate decisions—not a whistle.)

Because referees were physical educators, they probably sported white duck trousers, the prevailing uniform at the time. The umpire doubtless wore the same, as well as a shirt and tie, perhaps even a black bow tie. (Early football referees sported white shirts and black bow ties, plus a drab gray tam on their heads.) Like the players, they wore knickers.

In 1904-1905, expectations for making all calls were divided equally between the two basketball officials, and scorekeepers and timers on the side of the court became adjuncts to games. We don't know how floor markings came about or when free throws were introduced, but we do know some things about player freedoms and restrictions because they were spelled out from the onset.

In some respects, basketball was derivative, adopting aspects of other sports. The original outline described how a player could move by bouncing the ball (the term *dribble* was carried over from soccer). It was a goal game, with goals at either end of a flat indoor surface. Players who fouled were sent to the sideline,

A Little League Case Study

Side-by-side suburbs Deerfield and Highland Park, north of Chicago, started Little League baseball programs some time ago, but they went separate ways in terms of style. Deerfield ordered complete uniforms, acquired all the equipment, signed up parents as coaches, and groomed the fields, but they forgot about securing umpires. Parents volunteered, and their performances were rather lame, even though a few courageous chaps donned masks and held Styrofoam chest protectors for behind-the-plate duty. One positive result was that spectators held their tongues at missed calls, offering friendly jibes instead of harsh catcalls. Before long, an enthusiastic man named Dick Cavanaugh took an umpiring course and started a training program for willing parents. Cavanaugh was so inspired that he applied to work games for the Chicago Cubs when Major League umpires went on strike.

By contrast, Highland Park recreation directors adopted a no-parents policy, no uniforms either. Youngsters were their own coaches, and one man, jovial and knowledgeable Chuck Shramm, stood behind the diminutive pitchers calling balls and strikes at every game, advising fielders where to throw the ball and helping runners tag up on fly balls. For the participants it was a very cheerful experience, devoid of tension.

The results of these cases of makeshift and make-do arrangements, measured later in the way baseball was performed at the high school level, were pretty even. Highland Park did send one player, Jim Panther, to the major leagues, and he pitched briefly for the Atlanta Braves and the Chicago White Sox.

---

temporarily disqualified, and their team had to play short-handed until a goal was scored. This is similar to the penalty box in hockey. The dribbler, allowed to dribble only *once* with two hands, could not be tripped or struck legally, although he could bull his way on a path anywhere on the court with impunity, elbowing and shouldering opponents out of the way, as in rugby. The dribbler wasn't originally allowed to shoot for the basket, however. He had to pass the ball to a teammate for that opportunity.

Basketball players used soccer balls to begin with. A larger inflated sphere with leather covering and stitches (like football laces) was introduced in the early 1900s.

If a player was running when he received a pass, he was allowed to take several steps to control momentum. The referee determined how many steps he could take.

The popularity of basketball spread so fast that it was being played in California by the end of 1892. Also, students from the Christian Workers' school quickly took the game abroad, where it was played in Turkey, India, Japan, France, Persia, and Greece.

Clearly, basketball took some time to be perfected. Elements were adjusted to give it the appearance it has today. Opening the bottom of the goal was an early adjustment that facili-

tated game play. Another was discarding the requirement of a center jump after every goal. Very few officials—even today—have been able to master the toss for a jump ball; invariably, it is hoisted either too high or not high enough. The toss should rise to the maximum height of the players' jump. The after-goal jump was abolished in 1937. Now, the team scored upon inbounds the ball from under its own goal after an opponent's score.

The National Federation of State High School Associations (NFHS) issued a formal basketball rule guide in 1937, in conjunction with the Amateur Athletic Union (AAU). Previous to that, players used the guidelines created in 1915 by a rules committee formed by the YMCA and other interested groups, which refined Naismith's original stipulations. One Naismith prescription that was abandoned was the awarding of a goal to a team that did not commit a violation while its opponent piled up three transgressions.

A six-foot-wide key in front of the basket was introduced in 1932. This is a lane in front of the basket that is topped by a semicircle, resembling a keyhole. This area was restricted; players could be in it for only three seconds at a time. This kept extra-large players from camping under the basket so they could score easily. The key was widened to 12 feet in 1975.

Handling Official Scarcity

In the Chicago suburbs, football officials have traditionally been scarce at the high school underclass levels because schools field so many teams. The varsity and sophomore teams play doubleheaders on Friday nights and Saturday afternoons, but they also field JV squads for midweek games and freshman teams for Saturday mornings. There are over 120 high schools in the greater Chicago area. Many schools have A and B freshman teams, and some even have C-level players. It is very easy to predict the cycle. When the NFL's Chicago Bears have a good year, the following autumn will see a surge in football participation at the freshman level. Therefore, officiating associations have developed training programs for two-person officiating to cover the huge array of weekly contests.

A fascinating offshoot of such dedication is that a few C-level players, not in full development at age 14, become solid contributors to their high school teams later on. Here is one memorable example: A C-level player at Proviso East High School in Melrose Park, Illinois, went on to be awarded Linebacker of the Mid-Century when he played for the Green Bay Packers. His name was Ray Nitschke.

In 1932, a rule was adopted to avoid close guarding of offensive players. If a defender guarded a player with the ball, either while dribbling or stationary, for more than five seconds, a referee called a jump ball. Today, instead of having a jump ball, the ball is awarded to the other team for a throw-in.

In the 1950s, floor officials adopted the diagonal system of floor coverage. In this system, the lead official moves under the offensive basket, and the trail official hovers near the half-court time line on the opposite side of the court.

Colleges introduced three-person officiating crews in 1969, and the NBA adopted the practice in 1975. This is one case in which colleges developed a policy before the professionals. Many other practices, in all sports, have been handed down from the highest level to the amateur ranks.

In today's game, a possession clock forces teams to shoot within a certain time frame (professional and college only). Also, goals scored from a considerable distance from the basket are awarded three points. These two elements alone have changed the way basketball games are played, with skillful three-point shooters able to turn games around in a short interval, from a half-circle arc beyond the top of the key.

Officiating duties have increased in basketball, along with the pressure to make accurate calls. The observations of Professor Steitz are as valid today as they were a generation ago: "The game of basketball is one of the most difficult sports to officiate. . . .The complex maneuvers, the rapid rate at which it is played, the near hysteria that prevails, and the proximity of spectators to . . . the action are just a few of the factors" (Steitz, 1976, p. 36).

In essence, Dr. Steitz understated the issues. The game has indeed changed radically over the years, and officiating has been hard-pressed to keep up. Other major sports have not changed as significantly, although the officiating has undergone some critical adjustments.

FOOTBALL

An outgrowth of the English sport of rugby, football was first played in the United States at the college level. Rutgers beat the College of New Jersey (later, Princeton) 6 to 4 on November 6, 1869, in the first recognized game.

"The first game resembling present-day football was played in 1874, when a team from McGill University in Montreal, Canada, visited Harvard University. The Canadians wanted to play . . . rugby . . . running and tackling" (*World Book Encyclopedia*, 2010, p. 367). Harvard wanted to play a new version that featured mostly kicking, like soccer (they agreed on a round ball). The schools played two games, one McGill's style and one Harvard's. Running with the ball and the customary rugby scrum became more popular than trying to kick a ball over a crossbar, and the "most influential figure in modernizing football was Walter Camp, who had played for Yale University from 1876 to 1882." Camp was responsible for setting up such standard practices as the scrimmage line; the center snap; the measuring chains; the four-downs-for-a-first-down system; and scoring designations for touchdowns, conversions, field goals, and safeties.

Like basketball, football spread quickly, and soon high schools and town teams began to establish rivalries throughout the nation along with colleges. As far we know, just a pair of officials administered the games in the beginning.

The early football contests were extremely violent. Many games were more like organized fights than athletic contests. Players wore no pads and no helmets at first. A few wore stocking caps, which offered little protection. By 1900, many players had been severely injured, and a few had died, causing much alarm across the nation. The situation grew into a crisis, and President Theodore Roosevelt gathered college presidents together in 1905 to address changes in the rules for player safety. Safety issues have been primary in football ever since.

First came stipulations about protective gear, and next came restrictions on the types of blocking players could use. Blocking below the waist was permitted, but upright blocking required closed hands (fists) to the blocker's chest (only shoulders with pads could deliver a blow), and contact had to be in front of an opponent. Fists extending more than 45 degrees constituted an illegal use of the hands. The flying wedge was also forbidden, a tactic whereby players locked arms and formed a human buttress to secure the advance of a ball carrier. In the beginning, blockers were restricted in the use of hands, but about 35 years ago NFL players began pushing moves with open hands when executing pass blocking. The rules were then rewritten to allow pushing, which is what is in place today. Today, blocking is actually pushing—at all levels, high schools and colleges included.

For a long time, professional football was considered a renegade activity, frowned on culturally and disparaged by sportswriters as impure because it violated accepted standards of amateurism—meaning that players were being paid to play. Some sportswriters implied that only outlaws or, at best, men of questionable character were eager participants. College players performed in professional leagues under assumed names on Sundays so as not to jeopardize their amateur standing. Professional football (using three referees) became a formal entity in 1920 when a group of businessmen calling themselves the American Professional Football Association gathered in an auto dealer's garage in Canton, Ohio. They renamed it the National Football League in 1922, and they planted teams in medium-sized towns such as Canton; and Pottstown, Pennsylvania; Decatur, Illinois; and Racine and Green Bay in Wisconsin.

In the early days of football, professional and college teams used three officials in a game. Colleges had their officials line up down the middle of the field: a referee, an umpire, and a back judge. Covering the sidelines could not have been easy, and it's possible that they received help from the chain crew. In the 1930s, the professional game added a fourth official, and the colleges followed suit, reluctantly. This added person was obliged to kneel on the sidelines while the ball was alive. In that isolated spot these officials likely did not make many calls (maybe offsides on jumpy linemen).

All officials before World War II had limited roles. Only the referee, for instance, could signal a touchdown or field goal. He could look to the other officials for help, but the most they could do was give a thumbs-up or thumbs-down, with a hand held near the belt buckle, as though sending a signal surreptitiously. Auxiliary officials had to signal a touchdown by pointing the index finger and offering an almost imperceptible nod of the head.

In the 1930s and 1940s, substitutions were limited at all levels. A player who left the game could not return until the next quarter. Officials had to keep track of players coming and going on a clipboard. Consequently, players had to play both offense and defense. Many

Officiating Transparency

Mike Pereira, former NFL vice president of officiating, offered this view of the zoom-lens spotlight: "Officials have gotten to the point that they realize they are in a transparent business. They know when they are right or wrong. . . . [They] have gotten to . . . where they understand criticism and that the criticism can lead to a better understanding of the job" (*Referee*, September, 2010, p. 34) resisted the wide open free substitution in the 1950s, because it was a point of pride to be considered a 60-minute man.

Free substitution, though, had the salutary effect of turning players into specialists. Today, highly skilled players make the game exciting with their superb talents of passing, catching, and running.

Five-person officiating crews came about in the 1960s to help handle the increased emphasis on the forward pass. Early in the century, college teams eschewed the forward pass, even though Teddy Roosevelt's commission codified the legitimacy of a back's heaving the nearly round ball to either an end or another back. In a captivating scenario, Notre Dame quarterback Gus Dorais threw passes to his end Knute Rockne in a 35-13 upset of a favored Army team in 1913. By the 1920s, passing attacks were common in football. But the idea of putting more officials on the field to increase the scope of coverage was slow to take hold.

In the 1930s and 1940s, in addition to having to operate under restricted movements, football officials were equipped with small handheld horns, which they blew when declaring a foul. Radio announcers said, "There was a horn on that play," and then the penalty was addressed. In the 1950s, small red and white flags about the size of handkerchiefs were used to designate fouls. The color was changed to solid gold in the 1960s with the advent of television (gold was easier to spot on color TV). Beanbags were an added implement in the 1970s. Prior to that, officials marked spots on the field by dropping their caps, such as when a member of the kicking team touched a kick beyond the line of scrimmage. But caps were dirtied in inclement weather, and beanbags were substituted.

After they were introduced, beanbags posed unexpected problems. At first they were filled with real beans, which tended to sprout when the bags got wet. Next, the NFL tried buckshot in the bags, but these set off alarms when officials tried to go through airport security. They finally settled for simply packing the small bags with fabric and attaching a flap so that the devices could be tucked in the belt and plucked out swiftly when needed.

In the 1970s, the professional game became too sophisticated for five officials to handle adequately, and it moved to seven people, which colleges quickly copied. The idea was to have each eligible receiver guarded by a particular official, because rules stipulated restrictions on how defenses could attack pass receivers running downfield. The turn of the 21st century saw many teams open up the game by deploying receivers all across the field, putting more pressure on officials.

In the 1930s and 1940s, before the Super Bowl era, one NFL referee worked all the big games and handled the final championship games for more than a dozen years in a row. Ron Gibbs, a widely respected banking executive from Springfield, Illinois, traveled to all his games by train, just as the teams did.

Such a string of lofty assignments would not be possible today, given the practice of merit in selecting play-off and Super Bowl officials. The NFL has a referee's organization (not exactly a union), which evaluates officials. Video technology allows for much more elaborate and precise game assessments. In fact (and this is true for bowl game selections of major college conferences as well), intense, comprehensive video analyses permit evaluators to grade officials on every play in each game.

One element of football that has remained the same for officials is the necessity to inspect player equipment before and during the game. Face masks are standard now, and knee and hip pads (to protect the kidneys) are also mandated. Some players try to lighten the load by slipping pads out of the sleeves in the shells that cover their legs, which is illegal. By rule, safety is a prime concern of officials.

Health professionals and fans—plus professional and college athletic administrators—recognize that playing football has wrecked many performers' lives. After their playing days have ended, many experience ongoing debilitating leg and back injuries and, most seriously, head trauma as a result of battering.

Officials can't do much about the pile driving that takes place in the modern game other than guarding against action in which deliberate blows are inflicted, called spearing. The game is indeed violent, and the only way officials can serve as protectors is to apply the rules of contact as they are expressly defined.

BASEBALL

Baseball had a trio of recorded beginnings, only two of which have been substantiated. The sport is clearly an offshoot of the British game of rounders, played since the 1600s overseas and in the 1700s in the American colonies. Its main feature was that runners were put out by soaking or plugging. That is, fielders threw the ball at them (almost like dodgeball). When the game changed (most likely in the 1830s or 1840s in New York City) to having runners put out by being tagged or forced out by touching a base, America's pastime was born.

The second version of baseball's birth is that it was invented in Cooperstown, New York, in 1839 by Abner Doubleday, who became a Civil War general and died in 1893. It is a myth, however, that he originated the game.

Someone reported that Doubleday laid out a diamond and specified how the game was to be performed, but research has proven this claim to be specious. Doubleday is just an amorphous figure in the origin of baseball. Alexander Cartwright was known as, "a New York City sportsman, and called *the father of organized baseball* because he started a club called the Knickerbockers in 1845 whose sole purpose was playing Base Ball" (World Book, "B," op. cit. p. 134). He wrote out a set of rules,

to which supplements were added in 1848 and 1854.

Some of Cartwright's rules have since been changed. For instance, he decreed that the first team to score 21 runs won the game; pitchers had to throw underhanded 45 feet from home plate; a batter was out if a fielder caught a lofted ball on the first bounce (changed in 1864); and a strike was called only when a batter swung and missed. Early baseball did not have walks, and called strikes were introduced in 1868.

By 1900, both major leagues were formed, although since that time, many teams have changed cities, and teams have been added. Most of the rules were the same at the turn of the 20th century as they are today.

Compared to basketball, which has undergone many significant changes since its inception, and football, in which officiating changes have been relatively modest, baseball has remained a relatively staid sport. Rather than evolving, baseball officiating (umpiring) has been adapting. Baseball was a "punch-and-slice" game in its early stages until Babe

Curtis Woodcock

Umpires have to learn to work heel-to-toe in the slot, a proper positioning that allows the viewing of an entire pitch.

Ruth broke it open with a huge accumulation of home runs (using lively, tightly wound balls) in the 1920s. Today it is a combination of long-ball and short-ball at the professional and collegiate levels, but power distances in batting are not so prevalent at the teenage levels (although metal bats at all levels make long hits possible).

Major league games had just one umpire in the 1880s and 1890s, and in the early part of the last century they moved to a two-man system. A third umpire was added in the 1930s and 1940s, and four umpires per game has been the standard for decades, with two more along the foul lines beyond first and third bases in all-star contests, end-of-season play-offs, and the World Series. At other levels the number of umps on a given game varies. High schools usually use just two umpires, one behind the plate and one on the bases. At very low levels, in educational settings anyway, games are often handled by just one umpire for cconomic reasons.

Like the football referee, the baseball umpire's major role is to ensure the safety of all players. Even though major injuries are rare in this sport, current rules are spelled out to lower the risk of injury. At all levels, down to Little League, all personnel on the field are required to wear helmets. Because thrown or batted balls can be lethal, pitchers are monitored closely for perceived viciousness. Even softball, the so-called diminutive version of baseball, is not played with a ball that has give to it, which was once the case with 12-, 14-, and 16-inch pillow-type spheres. Nowadays, softballs are of solid kapok-cork-polyurethane composition and have a tight leather covering.

In 1887 a Chicagoan named George W. Hancock inaugurated an indoor game of soft-ball. This sport, after moving outdoors, has also undergone numerous manifestations. First, the ball was a 12-inch round lump of truly resilient stuffing, and then versions of the game employed 14- and 16-inch heavier samples. The game was often played by men (sometimes without gloves) in small parks. But fast-pitch softball caught on quickly, and by 1933, the American Softball Association was formed to standardize playing conditions. By 1952, the game was being played in 125 countries.

Softball is mentioned here because at present 90 percent of the games throughout the United States are seven-inning slow-pitch affairs, often played with an hour-and-a-half time limit. Hundreds of communities support men's, women's, and co-ed recreational leagues. Fast-pitch softball (with balls that have a hard inner core, as mentioned) is also a popular women's sport, sponsored by many schools and colleges. Few colleges presently administering athletic programs are without women's softball teams. Consequently, many umpires are needed, and they are largely trained by local organizations.

Slow-pitch softball games are often worked by a single umpire, without a mask, who is supposed to move out from behind the plate to cover plays at the bases when the ball is alive. One must know the rules, of course, but it is relatively easy to learn slow-pitch umpiring.

OTHER SPORTS

Other sports that have risen rapidly in popularity and require expert officiating are soccer and lacrosse. At times lacrosse can be very rough because players are permitted to hit one another below the waist with their sticks. The women's game, also played on a wide scale, has rules against striking opponents. Both soccer and lacrosse are very old.

A form of soccer was played in ancient China in 400 BC. In 1848, U.S. schools drew up rules for both women's and men's versions. Because of its international popularity, its rules have been standardized for some time, as has its officiating practices. Countries throughout the world play the same game. The first World Cup (men) was played in Montevideo, Uruguay, in 1930. The first Women's World Cup was played in China in 1991. In 2000, soccer was the fastest-growing sport in U.S. high schools.

An Umpire's Biography

Bill Klem was the longest-tenured umpire in the major leagues, working from 1905 until 1940. He declared, "In my heart, I never missed a call," but he would have been hard put to support this contention if he worked under the pinpoint video screening of today's games. Klem also umpired a record 18 World Series, which would be impossible in the rotation system of modern times.

At the upper levels, soccer is officiated by a referee and two assistants; the assistants' role is primarily to call offsides. At youngster levels, below high school ages, usually one person officiates. Teenagers often serve as referees for very young children, from ages six or seven and up.

The movement of lacrosse, from the East Coast and into the Midwest and beyond, is little short of a phenomenon. Many high schools and colleges now sponsor teams. Like soccer, lacrosse is a professional sport in the United States, and qualified officials are in high demand. The sport can be claimed as 100 percent American because it originated with the Iroquois.

GENDER ISSUES: YOU GO, GIRL

U.S. society boasts female firefighters and police officers, as well as long haul truck drivers and school bus drivers. Women serve as city mayors, state governors, college presidents, members of Congress, Supreme Court justices, and cabinet appointees.

But it wasn't always this way.

True, "There has never been a time when girls and women were wholly excluded from sports" (Guttman, 1991), but until recently, their engagement has been limited and minimal. Dates and numbers tell a significant story. Although women competed in the Olympics in 1900, they were limited to certain events in track plus swimming races and tennis. At that time, women were definitely considered second-class citizens. Consider that, in 1869, black men were allowed to vote, but women weren't, regardless of race. In 1848, a cluster of 300 women gathered in Seneca Falls, New York for the first women's rights convention. After many speeches, demonstrations, and marches on Washington, D.C., the 19th amendment to the Constitution was passed in 1920 (amid the protestations of numerous short-sighted elected officials and societal naysayers) giving women the right to vote. A few people went on record asserting that the demise of Western Civilization was sure to follow.

Many behaviorists from the first half of the 20th century claimed that the female constitution could not function under the pressure of competitive team sports. Others asserted that

playing sports beyond puberty endangered girls' future reproductive capabilities.

Today, in addition to the burgeoning of women's sports and the subsequent involvement of thousands of women in officiating, some women have even broken the barrier of officiating men's sports. A few women have umpired minor league baseball games, although none have reached the major leagues. Each state doubtless has a few females officiating high school football, and in 2009, the first female referee worked a college bowl game. The NBA

Unlike past sporting events, female officials are an integral part of today's athletics.

has a single female referee, Violet Palmer of California, who has been a widely admired performer for more than a half dozen seasons.

When colleges first began forming women's basketball teams in the late 1970s, the refereeing was done mostly by men. Then, in the 1980s, when national college championships were instituted for women in basketball, cross country running, field hockey, gymnastics, swimming, tennis, track and field, and volleyball, the approximate ratio was two male officials for every female. Today that ratio is reversed: it is now two women to every man.

Title IX's Legacy

In 1971, John Erlander, a member of the U.S. House of Representatives from Illinois, declared, "[Title IX] will plant the seed of destruction for our system of higher education (Guttman p. iv)."

No person in the United States shall, on the basis of sex, be excluded from participation in, be denied the benefits of, or be subjected to discrimination under any educational program or activity receiving Federal financial assistance.

The Title IX law

Every time a girl plays Little League, every time a father assumes his daughter is as likely to go to college as his son, every time no one looks twice at a female cop or balks at a female surgeon, it's a moment in history, radical and ordinary, both at the same time.

Columnist Anna Quindlen, 2002

Hoop Dreams, 1904. Ten Montana and Idaho Indian girls from the Fort Shaw Indian Boarding School headed to St. Louis for the World's Fair, where they earned the moniker Champions of the World, beating the Missouri All-Stars in a best-of-three basketball series.

Wild West Magazine, October 2010, p. 8.

At Coolidge High School in Washington, D.C., Natalie Randolph is making history—as one of the nation's only female football coaches [head coach].

Parade, August 22, 2010, p. 6.

The way this all came about—"no shots were fired, but a revolution followed" (Blumenthal, 2005)—can be traced to a single legislative edict. President Lyndon Johnson signed the Civil Rights act in 1964, and President Richard Nixon signed an extension of that act in 1972. The 1972 legislation included a clause with a Roman numeral, Title IX, which stipulated that no one should be subjected to gender discrimination under any educational program that received federal financial assistance. In other words, if colleges received funds from the government, they had to equalize much of their funding for many of the activities they ordinarily supported. The huge disparities had to cease. If there was a baseball team at a school, for instance, and a women's group petitioned for a school-backed softball team, with scholarships included, the school had to ante up a sum larger than 1 percent of the baseball budget, which was the case at many institutions. Schools could not side-step the issue by dropping a so-called minor (non-revenue-generating) sport in exchange for adding a women's sport. A school couldn't abandon men's tennis to build a women's field hockey squad, for example. It had to be tennis for tennis and field hockey as an add-on.

The NCAA, a bastion of entrenched male athletics, sued to stop the stipulations of Title IX in 1976. It lost the case.

A 17-year-old high school student named Donna DeVarona was on the cover of *Sports Illustrated* in 1964 because she had won two Olympic gold medals and recorded an international record in the individual swimming medley. Her career was over. There was nowhere for her to go for competition after high school.

In 1971, there were 20,000 boys' basketball teams in the United States and 5,000 girls' squads (usually playing a truncated version of the real thing, with split court restrictions). Girls' participation in sports tripled from 1971 to 1973, from 300,000 to 900,000. Today, three million girls play organized sports.

Here are some more impressive facts. In 1982, more women than men earned bachelor's degrees for the first time. Title IX used the term *activities*, not just sports. In 2004, Harvard admitted more female undergraduates than male undergraduates.

In 1970, Billie Jean King received $600 for winning the Italian tennis championship; the male winner got $3,500. She boycotted the next championship tourney. In 1973, the U.S. Open awarded $25,000 to both the male and female winners.

There is no question that Title IX ensured the emancipation of women in U.S. society, breaking the so-called glass ceilings in all walks of life, not just sports. In 2002, Patsy Mink, a member of the U.S. House of Representatives, said, "We must teach each generation that there was a time when Title IX did not exist." Representative Edith Green, Oregon, a crusader for women's rights during her entire several-decades-long political career, added, "The trouble with every generation is that they haven't read the minutes of the last meeting" ("Women's Sports," p. 217).

SHORTAGE OF OFFICIALS

A phone survey of eight states reveals a picture that is both reassuring and somewhat troubling. On the positive side, high school varsity sports are comfortably covered with adequate to superior officiating. There are surprises here for several reasons, including the fact that some states are experiencing a growth in the number of schools. In a five-year span, from 2005 to 2010, Colorado has gone from 310 to 340 schools with the addition of charter schools and private schools, some church sponsored, which have added sports to their programs. "Fresh officials are not really trying hard to enter the field," CHSAA Officials Liaison Tom Robinson said. "In many instances officials who do boys' sports also work the girls," he added. The crossovers include basketball, soccer, and lacrosse. In other words, instead of new officials entering the fields, veteran officials are taking on new sports.

States sampled	Officiating director
Colorado	Tom Robinson
Georgia	Dr. Ralph Swearngin
North Carolina	Mark Dreibelbis
North Dakota	Matt Fetsch
New Mexico	Dana Sanchez
Oklahoma	Mike Whaley
Oregon	Jack Folliard
Utah	Mike Petty

Officials' supervisor Mark Dreibelbis of North Carolina reported that registration of new officials has remained high despite the fact that the state has been adding about five schools a year. "Several seasons ago we had 365 schools, and now we have 390." The one sport that is a little short of experienced officials is lacrosse, which is in its second year. "For a few years it was a club sport, and now the schools have taken it over. The problem is that few adults have actually played the sport. For us it is an embryonic program." Colorado also reported a slight shortage of lacrosse officials.

The worry about widespread shortages of sports officials is more an anticipation than a reality. It's been assumed in some quarters that a down economy would stimulate unemployed people to seek officiating opportunities as a source of part-time income. For the most part that has only happened in small degrees and only in large cities. "What has happened," one state clerical person said, "Is that a few retired officials have decided to register once more." But that could be a limited trend; it certainly isn't a flood of desperate individuals.

"We always have enough varsity officials," said Colorado's Robinson. "It's at the underclass level that we're hurting. We don't have enough younger officials signing up for training."

North Dakota's Matt Fetsch was the lone representative to admit having trouble finding sufficient numbers to cover games. Hockey has been an entrenched sport in this state immediately south of Canada, and the need to attract new officials in that sport is evident. "Every year the available pool of officials seems to go down," he said. He also said that some schools are scheduling football games on Thursdays instead of Friday nights, to make sure they can secure officials. "This despite the fact that there is a strong movement toward school consolidation in our state. Districts with two schools—because of enrollment shrinkage—are combining into one," Fetsch added.

Several states besides North Dakota reported huge gains in popularity as reasons for slight shortages in soccer. Schools that haven't traditionally fielded the sport are adding it in large numbers in Georgia, Utah, Oregon, and Oklahoma. "We're a little thin in volleyball too," said Oklahoma's Mike Whaley. "But the problem is most pronounced in rural areas." In the West, distances are often stretched out between small towns. Sometimes schools are obliged to use locals (teachers or citizen volunteers who may not even be registered) to handle underclass high school and middle school games.

"It's an economic factor," said Mike Petty of Utah. "Soccer is a low cost investment. Just a ball, a field, and a pair of goals are all schools need for soccer, and the facilities are already there. Kiddie programs have risen all over and that naturally has led to an increase in high school involvement." Few adults have played soccer under the auspices of public schools (the same is true of lacrosse and wrestling), which means that recruiting referees has to be an active affair. The implication here is that former athletes may be the best candidates for continuing in their sports as officials.

"It helps to live in a college town," said North Dakota's Matt Fetsch. He has advertised for new officials on radio and television, but the best route has been to contact college physical education instructors and ask them to make persuasive announcements in their classes. He didn't say it, but college students are also candidates for working subvarsity contests in sports. "We work through high schools to locate former athletes and extend invitations to officiate," said Utah's Petty.

Jack Folliard of Oregon said that he has relied on the 100 local associations to bring in and train new officials. "We have used a DVD on the appeal of officiating and put it on our state website, plus sent it to TV outlets and newspapers. That has helped pull in fresh faces," he added. Folliard also reported that a small cadre of Portland officials set up a kiosk in a shopping mall. "Fellows with uniforms passing out brochures. A lot of people seemed intrigued, but of course there's no way to assess the possible quality in passersby," he concluded. "Then too we got 10 people signed up as prospects when they responded to our Internet come-on, craigslist," Folliard laughed.

Dana Sanchez of New Mexico said that she too sent a recruiting DVD to recreation centers and colleges. The state has had a small explosion (13 percent) in registrations, but they are still short of officials in the eastern part of the state (where there are few large cities) in softball and baseball. "We're also slender statewide in wrestling officials," she said. But Sanchez tried something special in Albuquerque. First, she executed what she called a media blitz through television and newspapers, accompanied by an offer of free training. "We doubled our numbers in baseball and softball," she said, very pleased.

Dr. Ralph Swearngin of Georgia may have had the best answer of all. "We've increased our registrations dramatically," he said. To achieve this, he has been persistent in his recruiting campaign. "After every Friday night sports events, a 60-station television network reports scores of all statewide games (football and basketball). We have a DVD promo that we supply the stations, featuring basketball sportscaster Dick Vitale. We also run it during commercial breaks on live coverage during state championship games," Swearngin explained. He believes that such an approach has definitely offset a dreary economy.

Finding the Right Instructor

Dennis Markusson, an attorney in the Denver suburb of Evergreen, has taught a beginners football officiating class during a high school district's evening school program for several years. He conducts eight sessions in July and August—one night a week—then holds an on-field clinic when high school teams start autumn preseason scrimmages. The district has six high schools, and their night school bulletins promoting classes are sent to thousands of recipients.

Markusson also plants an announcement in a sports column in *The Denver Post* daily paper. He has a well-known sports radio talk show host, Irv Brown, recite several promos (his show is during the late afternoon commuter drive time). Dennis posts more announcements on bulletin boards at recreational centers, local exercise facilities, and YMCAs. He also has placed his notices in sporting good stores and on supermarkets' flea market and garage sale registers.

Markusson gets anywhere from a dozen candidates to 40 prospective officials every year. Other instructors in metropolitan areas in many states have operated similarly through community colleges, trying to obtain rookies in baseball, softball, and basketball. In many cases, success depends on the strength of the instructor's reputation. But these techniques are probably limited to large cities. Small rural communities are not likely to raise substantial numbers of potential officiating candidates.

SUMMARY

With the rise of modern sports, we've seen the beginnings of sports officiating and its progress. From the early years to the present, officiating has seen tremendous changes in its evolution. Today's officials look much different from their predecessors—especially considering their responsibilities, mechanics, and appearance—but their development is far from over. From changing demands in games to an increasing need for transparency, officials will have to continue adapting their skills and practices to be successful.

An important change to officiating is occurring today with the inclusion of females to the profession. Until recently, female engagement in sports officiating has been limited and minimal. Because of legislation and changing perspectives, women are becoming an integral part of officiating. Their continued inclusion will only help the officiating world continue its growth.

Finally, a shortage of properly trained officials is perhaps the most pressing issue facing amateur officials. Most school districts report always having enough varsity officials; however, the problem lies in not having sufficient numbers to cover underclass events. In addition, the increasing popularity of some sports—such as soccer or lacrosse—has led to some shortages at all levels. Regardless, it's important that substantial efforts are made to actively recruit and train young people interested in officiating.

REVIEW QUESTIONS

1. Popular sports in the United States are largely
    a. violent in nature
    b. home grown
    c. foreign imports
    d. sedentary activities

2. Shortages of officials are most pronounced in
    a. poker
    b. basketball
    c. softball
    d. soccer

3. The one major sport that has undergone the most modifications over the years is
    a. gin rummy
    b. wrestling
    c. basketball
    d. baseball

4. The purpose of the key on a basketball court is to
    a. help officials make calls on fast breaks
    b. enhance the flow of the game
    c. give players a border for shooting three-point goals
    d. prevent tall players from gaining a special advantage

5. To some extent, football at the beginning was based on some elements of
    a. karate
    b. field hockey
    c. polo
    d. rugby

6. Before the 1950s, football officials had to
    a. wear protective clothing
    b. keep track of substitutions
    c. use blue beanbags
    d. announce all penalties on microphones

7. A principal duty of football officials is to
    a. have only two captains from each team present at the coin toss
    b. identify the location of concession outlets
    c. inspect the pads of players before the game
    d. be sure that passers throw the ball forward

8. In 1905, President Theodore Roosevelt called college presidents together for the purpose of
    a. striking a balance between offense and defense in football
    b. selecting officials to work games
    c. curtailing mayhem in football
    d. agreeing on academic standards for college graduation

9. Authorities who govern football at this time are very concerned about
    a. which bowl games should establish the number one team in the nation
    b. head injuries that result in postcareer trauma for many players
    c. how the public can be squeezed for more revenue
    d. which sections of the country produce the best players

10. Before Title IX was enforced, one myth that authorities embraced about women's participation in competitive sports was that
    a. Soviet women's gender had to be verified clinically
    b. their marriageability would be jeopardized
    c. black athletes were superior to white athletes
    d. their reproductive organs would be harmed

Answers on page 187

16

Chapter 2

Officiating as a Lifetime Career

Jerry Grunska

This chapter addresses the following:

- How to get started as an official
- How study and experience can lead to expertise
- Ways to acquire and improve officiating skills
- Ways to derive continued satisfaction

STARTING AS AN OFFICIAL

Starting out to officiate sports involves making connections with organizations that train and assign officials, and in the case of scholastic sports, places that register officials and supply instructional materials. For high school officiating, that means contacting the state office that oversees officiating. Usually the first step is to pay a registration fee and then successfully pass a test after studying the rule book of the sport in which you wish to participate. School athletic administrators can provide the contact information of the state office; YMCAs, local town headquarters, fitness centers, and workers in recreational facilities may also provide information about sports teams and leagues. Many youth leagues under high school age are sponsored by clubs or groups in charge of handling the sport. State organizations as well as local and regional entities are mostly interested in promoting rules and policies for various sports at the high school level.

The purpose of sports officiating is customarily thought of as helping opponents play a game, monitoring the action, and enforcing the rules. Some sporting events are team sports, whereas others are individual events. Individual sports include tennis, gymnastics, wrestling, and golf, as well as many other sporting activities that do not require officials. Some individual sports such as swimming, wrestling, golf, and track can be transformed into team competitions by comparing the collective scores of performers; in such competitions, judges may simply be volunteers offering to help run the meets. Starters in track need to have training, but track administrators who use stopwatches and measure such things as distances or jumping heights require only basic instruction before a meet begins. Someone who conducts the high jump in track, for instance, need only be aware of what a foot fault is or how many aborted approaches to the bar are permitted before disqualification. Judges of gymnastics events and aquatic diving, as well as figure skating, however, must have sophisticated knowledge of the activity to make legitimate assessments.

Soccer has risen to extreme popularity among youth because fundamental skills can be learned at an early age, and little equipment is necessary for playing the game—just a ball, a playing surface, and goals. Other sports have also drawn much interest within one generation, including ice hockey, field hockey, volleyball, and lacrosse.

Volleyball and ice hockey have been around a long time but have risen in popularity as they have become more available. Ice hockey requires a special rink to be played in a temperate climate, and many such facilities have sprung up all over the country. Volleyball had been a recreational sport in clubs, on beaches, and in YMCAs for some time. With the national impetus for girls' sports, volleyball has enjoyed a rapid rise in popularity as a school-sponsored sport.

Sports that have increased in popularity have often migrated from the East Coast; field hockey, rugby, and lacrosse have proliferated to the point at which many schools and colleges are now sponsoring them. The three basic American sports, though—football, baseball, and basketball—still draw the most people to officiating, because television brings them regularly and almost continually into our homes. These sports have millions of dedicated followers because their seasons are lengthy and individual performers frequently become cultural headliners. And let's not forget

softball. Every community dot on the map has slow-pitch softball competitions: men's, women's, and co-ed. Thousands of umpires are needed across the nation.

With the exception of baseball and softball, most widely popular sports are goal activities in which two teams on a rectangular surface (or in a pool, in the case of water polo) strive to score by propelling an object into a goal or across a line. All of these sports have large followings of participants, spectators, and faithful followers. Hence, they appeal to people who want to officiate.

An element that periodically comes into play and demands an official's attention is conflict between players. Except for baseball and softball, each field sport, as well as basketball, features regular physical contact between opponents. In fact, they are often referred to as contact sports. Legendary football coach Vince Lombardi purportedly said, "Football is not a contact sport. Dancing is a contact sport. Football is a *collision* sport!" When player flare-ups occur, officials are obliged to deal with them, sorting out which acts are punishable and which are merely incidental. Officials must also be alert for unseemly talk between

The official standing on the left watches on as players are locked in a scrum for the ball.

opponents. These potential actions require that officials exhibit a fine-tuned alertness.

Equipment

The uniform you wear and the accessories you have are often determined by the level at which you work. For instance, if you'll be handling junior high or pee-wee football games, you may be free to limit yourself to a striped shirt and a whistle, with a red bandana tucked in a pocket serving as a flag. Footwear can be ordinary gym shoes, and you can wear jeans or shorts and a hat with a John Deere logo. No one expects you to have a standard uniform. On the other hand, if you intend to serve high schools as an official, the organization that trains and hires you will identify the proper apparel and tools. Rule books do not always specify the nature of officials' uniforms: Baseball does, but football does not. Therefore, you must learn the expectations and requirements of those with whom and for whom you will be working.

In many instances, tradition is a governing factor, and when tradition changes, officials are obliged to follow along and purchase up-to-date supplies. In football, for example, striped socks have varied over the years. Recently, a new item has emerged: black trousers with a white strip; these were introduced by the NFL and have been widely adopted by high school officials. The people you work with will let you know their apparel expectations.

Of all sports, baseball and softball plate umpires require the most equipment. Because of pitching speed, baseball and fast-pitch softball umpires need proper buffering gear, from footwear with reinforced toe plates to shin guards, genital cups, firm chest protectors, and full face masks with attached throat shields, plus a jacket to wear in inclement weather. To be fully outfitted to call swift pitching (even in Little League), you may have to spend several hundred dollars. (Some leagues furnish this equipment to umpires.)

Slow-pitch softball umpires need only an indicator—a handheld ball-and-strike device. Thumbing the wheel on the indicator keeps track of balls, strikes, and outs. Most organized leagues, though, ask umpires to wear a specific stylized shirt and trousers (or shorts), and perhaps even a distinctive cap.

Officials who handle fast-moving team sports such as soccer and lacrosse may need only shorts and a whistle, but they can also don specialized garb depending on the level at which they are working. An eager teenager doing a children's soccer game, for example, may need only a whistle. A swim judge may be expected to bring only a whistle, or may be required to show up in white duck trousers with a stopwatch and a starter's pistol.

Officials who have to run will want footwear to fit the court or field conditions: nonskid soles, black shoes for basketball officials, black shoes with rubber cleats for field games. Many field games require officials to wear striped shirts (a style with a long tradition), and they may also have to carry items in addition to whistles, such as yellow and red cards, notepads and pencils, and stopwatches in the case of soccer referees.

Football officials probably have the most specialized equipment of all—white knickers; unique striped socks; penalty flags; beanbags; a clip for the chains; whistles; and cards for keeping score, for denoting which team kicks off, for recording time-outs, and for identifying special penalties such as player ejections. Football officials also usually carry a timing device in case of scoreboard failure (or a lack of one). The total outlay for a football officiating kit may be several hundred dollars or more.

Advice for New Officials

Perhaps the most important advice for new entrants into the officiating ranks, regarding game action, is not to make decisions in haste. "Hustle, but don't hurry" is one of the favorite maxims. "See the whole play" is another. Often, the action unfolds so quickly that you may have trouble following the entire sequence. Sorting out sequences in your mind is one skill you must work on diligently to master your role. Also, be sure to make calls with proper timing. Action should carry through before you make the call. Making calls too quickly will result in errors. Being too close to the action is sometimes detrimental also, and securing a clear angle can be impossible if you are too close because of your over eagerness.

The following suggestions are important if you are just starting out as an official:

- Read the rules.
- Keep the terms *borderline* and *spirit of the rules* in mind when exercising judgment.
- Watch other officials perform.

- Seek out mentoring by asking questions of fellow officials.
- Learn the game from the players' standpoint; discover how strategy operates.
- Master the mechanics
- Ignore spectators.
- Listen to coaches' questions and objections.
- Develop a soft, diplomatic system for dealing with conflict.
- Subdue any explosive or retaliatory tendencies you may have in your personality.
- Carry yourself with dignity and assurance.
- Avoid arrogance and self-righteousness; never be supercilious.
- Always be willing to learn.

Nearly every official who has risen in the profession is grateful for someone who supplied help at a critical time. Some local associations arrange to have veterans work with newcomers in formal mentoring programs, though such programs may not be well organized or operating when you need them. You can benefit considerably by seeking the advice of experienced officials on an informal, personal basis. Casual conversations with officials who are widely respected may prove even more beneficial than a formal program. Most highly regarded officials are flattered to be asked their opinions about tactics. They may also furnish advice on how to move up the ladder to prominent games and college opportunities.

Quest for Games

If you are just starting out as an official, you may simply notify a school or recreation center that you want to work games under that organization's auspices. If you are in a training program, the people administering it are likely to be in a position to assign games. If an outside administrator is in charge of game assignments, which is the case in many scholastic leagues, obtain that person's contact information and inquire about the opportunity. A short note describing your age and experience, availability, contact information, and a resume may be all that is necessary to get started. Assigners are often the best contacts for additional information about training, too.

An Official's Checklist

Following are actions every official should take before working a game:

1. Contact people in charge of the contest before leaving home, preferably several days in advance. They want to know you'll be there on time, and this gesture can be considered common courtesy. Some organizations and leagues insist on prior notice from officials because game sites and times may be switched for reasons such as field light malfunctions.

2. Be sure to secure directions to the school or game site. Because sites may not be adjacent to the school that furnished the contract, you should contact the organization you are working for to confirm the location of the game site.

3. Once at the site, either indoors or a playing field, complete a site check to be sure that no dangerous conditions exist, such as equipment from previous games littering the site. Occasionally, a gym may have objects such as volleyball standards carelessly positioned too close to the floor. A field may actually be unplayable because of severe weather.

If you are not in a formal program, consider an informal mentoring arrangement. You might ask an experienced official to observe and comment on a game that you work. If you are eager to pick up new ideas, you can also benefit by observing a veteran in action and discussing philosophy afterward. An ideal situation is to work a game or two with a veteran so you can observe that person and practice more sophisticated on-field or on-court approaches. These opportunities often occur in preseason scrimmages, when experienced officials are mixed with those who are learning.

When you are ready to work, acquiring a full slate of games may not be possible because there are so many variables. One factor is need. Are schools or recreation organizations experiencing a shortage of officials? If so, opportunities may be plentiful. Another factor is time. Are you contacting people for game assignments after they have already been made? Your chances of landing assignments are best if you pursue them three to six months before a season starts. A third factor is your location. Are there multiple schools and sports clubs nearby that need a lot of officials? If so, your chances of getting started with ample game assignments are good. But if you live in a small community with only a team or two engaged in your sport, opportunities will be limited. Therefore, you may have to enlarge your search. If you're willing to travel 15 or 20 miles to work games, make contacts in outlying locales. Even if you're hired, however, games may be scheduled sporadically, offering just a few openings per season.

Clinic Opportunities

Learning to become an official can best take place in a training program, and the availability of such programs varies widely according to geographical location. If you live in a metropolitan area, chances are there will be one or more associations dedicated to orienting newcomers and supporting veteran officials in popular sports. But if you live in a rural or outlying area where communities are small and connecting routes long, there may be no organization available for educating prospective officials. Consequently, you may have to gather start-up information from a book or from conversing with someone who already works the sport. Usually, officials obtain game assignments through officiating associations, but games may also be obtained by contacting schools directly.

Even small towns, though, often have a few introductory classes to provide new officials for youth sports with basic information. They may even have supervisors that watch officials perform and issue game assignments.

Many seminars, camps, and clinics are available for officials on a yearly basis; some are arranged by state associations, and some are set up by colleges, leagues, college commissioners, and private individuals. A few certified camps are conducted each winter by Major League Baseball umpires before their season starts. *Certified* means that organized professional baseball leagues depend on these camps to supply them with candidates for Minor League umpiring (which has a high

rate of yearly turnover). Directories of camps are published regularly in *Referee* magazine (P.O. Box 161, Franksville, Wisconsin 53126, 262-632-8855, or at www.referee.com). Also, state offices send out notices to officials about sport camps, either via mailed brochures or Internet sites.

Officials for football, basketball, baseball, softball, soccer, and volleyball are ordinarily served by overnight camps on college campuses. These clinics, some of which are a weeklong, often include the opportunity to work games, because they are combined with athletic participation by high school students. If scrimmages and games are part of the experience, videotaping of officials at work is also usually offered, as are personal evaluations by college officials and college commissioners.

Such camps have another value: an opportunity to network with people who can advance your career. The college officiating directors conduct some camps. They use camps to scout prospective officials for their leagues. Often, officials from the college conference are the camp instructors, and they also evaluate prospects if a college commissioner is not present. This is a rich opportunity for learning a great deal about how to officiate at a level higher than you may be working at present. Keep in mind that some of the best information may come your way during off-hours, when officials gather in dormitories or at meals.

Some state organizations sponsor overnight camps, and most of them conduct their clinics on weekends before the sport season begins. Again, these clinics offer the opportunities to meet officials at a higher level because generally the state associations rely on college officials to impart their advice and philosophies to aspiring officials. State or regional clinics may invite professional officials to deliver presentations, providing valuable information about how officiating takes place at the highest levels of sport. An important dimension of professional officiating is dealing with pressure and handling vast public exposure. Professional officials also have advice to offer about how to relate to players and coaches. Once more, these camps and clinics offer the opportunity to learn from one another in an informal atmosphere. Sharing experiences may be the most noteworthy part of such gatherings.

Discussions with other officials also are helpful in solidifying the rules in your mind. This is a major function of some officiating associations; many associations make it a point to address every rule during the course of a season. Rule books are accompanied by case books, which are published by the National Federation of State High School Associations. These publications portray game situations in which rules have to be applied in special ways. These texts can help you master the intricacies of a sport. When officials get together, they often pose game-situation problems to one another, much as the case books do, to reinforce their grasp of fine points.

Studying the Rules

Each sport has comprehensive rules governing player behavior and describing how games can proceed. These rules vary somewhat in terms of limits and adjustments according to the levels and skills of performers. Young athletes at grade school levels are likely to have different regulations for play than high school and college athletes have, and they, in turn, have rules that differ from those for professional athletes.

In addition to rules, you will also need to be familiar with the special vocabulary of the sport you officiate. Definitive terms govern each sport, and you are obliged to memorize these to administer a contest fairly.

An exciting aspect of officiating is that you can feel part of the action while policing it, as long as you understand the rules and strategies of the sport. It helps to have played the game, but that is not a necessity. You can learn a game's framework by watching it, internalizing its movement, and absorbing the rules.

Consider the case of umpiring slow-pitch softball. You may surmise at first that all you need to know are the differences between a ball and a strike, safe and out, and fair and foul. Knowing the rules will help you differentiate between a ball and a strike; there may even be a mat behind home plate to indicate a strike (i.e., a ball hitting it indicates that the pitch was in the batter's strike zone). However, there are other intricacies to take into account. A pitch can be too high, for instance, and an illegal pitch could also have a trajectory that is too low. Moreover, you will also have to know whether a runner can bowl over a catcher in

trying to score. Likewise, you must know the requirements for a legal catch, and the rights and prohibitions runners and fielders have regarding interfering with each other. A study of the rules will reveal the game's complexities, which you must master before you can be considered an expert. Polish takes a lot of buffing, and working many games may be required to reach a high point of mental skill.

Officiating is often a fun athletic endeavor. But a lot of study and extended experience are required to be a superior performer.

Applying the Rules

Learning the rules and staying abreast of changes are vital to your growth as an official. Some officials pride themselves on being experts at rule interpretation, whereas others coast along on perfunctory knowledge. Beyond learning the rules, you must take the impor-

Auxiliary officials, such as a chain crew, can serve vital roles during sporting events.

tant next step: applying the rules in a reasonable way. Rules can be applied to the letter or in a spirit that upholds the primary purposes of the game. All officiating manuals urge that officials apply the spirit of the rules in making judgments. Experience and consultation with other officials will help you understand how to apply the rules in keeping with the spirit of the game. This is the basis for a healthy sport philosophy.

Superior officials study the rules continually. Many set aside a time of day to read a segment of the rule book. It is almost impossible to pore over page after page of rules and retain what you have read; studying only a small section of the rule book at a time is a better use of your time.

Improving Skills

As in many other fields, you can work toward a certain goal in officiating (e.g., obtaining a satisfactory high school varsity schedule) and then take your skills for granted and not seek to improve. Many officials become self-satisfied once they reach a certain level of expertise. They often don't take constructive criticism well, nor do they seek evaluation from experts. In fact, they may not acknowledge that anyone could critique their work fairly, and they close their minds to the prospect of altering their habits. Faulty habits sometimes hold officials back at one level, preventing them from improving and advancing.

The gratification of a full schedule is one factor that may stifle improvement, but other factors operate as well. Once you reach a certain level, you will seldom get a critical review from an objective person who can identify your strengths and weaknesses. Also, you will seldom have opportunities to witness techniques that are more advanced than your own. You may be too busy working games to be on the lookout for ways to get better.

The first requisite for improvement is to acknowledge that you are not a polished expert, that some ingrained habits and personal tendencies may be detrimental to your officiating, and that you could benefit from advice for readjusting your techniques. Superior officials know that there is always more to be learned. The key ingredient to becoming better is to admit your fallibility and seek ways to expand your knowledge.

Self-Assessment

In addition to seeking advice from respected veterans, you can also engage in a deliberate self-assessment after each contest. A danger for many officials, as mentioned earlier, is to become self-satisfied, which means not questioning your own judgment and not evaluating the way you dealt with difficult situations. A reasonable way to start a self-assessment is to identify which calls seemed to be controversial and how you reacted to objections. Write this in a journal. Another area for introspection is the way you deal with coaches and players. If your explanations were unsatisfactory, recall what was said, and mentally develop an alternate way of responding that is more appropriate. Ask yourself the following questions:

- Did I resolve conflicts satisfactorily?
- Did I anticipate team strategies accurately and in a timely way?
- Was my judgment on given plays emphatic and correct?
- Did I overlook anything, either elements of play or player behavior?
- Was I influenced by crowd reaction or by verbal attacks from participants?
- Did I hustle at appropriate times?
- Was my game coverage consistently sharp?
- Did I communicate effectively with my partners?

Another form of review is asking for an honest response from partners or crewmates. Ask those with whom you work whether any of your habits seem to have negative outcomes—for example: "Is my strike zone consistent? Am I moving into position to make calls correctly? Have I been too loose in calls or too tight? Am I letting the players play the game? Am I intruding too much on play? Am I calling undue attention to myself?" These are all legitimate issues that are correctable if you concentrate on improving.

Another way to observe yourself at work is to ask coaches or game administrators for videos of games you have officiated. Nowadays, teams record many of their games and sometimes even their practice scrimmages. Officials often take blank DVDs along and ask game administrators to record the game and return the DVD, which most schools are willing to do. There is perhaps no better way to see how you really look in a game than to view a video of yourself in action.

ADVANCING TO THE NEXT LEVEL

If you want to rise in the profession, seek opportunities for exposure beyond your normal operating circles. For instance, if you aspire to work at the college level, it is important to be seen working college scrimmages or off-season practice sessions. Working at various levels provides a broader perspective of how games should be handled. Sometimes this chance to work at more advanced levels may occur at camps or clinics, as previously discussed, but you generally must seek out these opportunities by inquiring when such practices take place and by asking to be involved. To rise above your current level, let it be known that you are entertaining such ambitions. The advanced leagues will not send someone to scout you unless you tell them that you are interested.

"The cream rises to the top" is a saying that can readily be applied to sports officials. If a person shows exceptional promise, someone above usually notices. However, just as it is rare for a teenage athlete to become a standout college performer, so do officials experience difficulty advancing. The reasons for this are that opportunities are few and the competition for them is keen. However, college officials retire, which often makes room for aspiring high school officials to advance. Attending camps, as noted earlier, is one way to open the door to advancement.

At advanced levels, games are played with more intensity, the athletes move more swiftly, they are more skilled, and emotional levels frequently are higher. Therefore, you must gear your reactions to the increased speed and skill of the athletes and adjust your personal responses to deal effectively with college athletes and coaches. A lot of experience is necessary for acquiring the judgment skills required to handle college sports. Some officials try to move too quickly, and their advancement is stymied when their abilities don't match their desires.

To officiate at a higher level, you must first know the protocols for entering the collegiate ranks in your geographic region. These protocols vary, but usually you must submit a formal application to the commissioner of officials in your sport. A resume of past experience is usually required, as are recommendations from prominent officials who have either worked directly with you or seen you in action. You may need recommendations from coaches, too.

A fact of life is that sometimes advancement depends more on who you know than what you know. Officials who work the conference or college coaches with whom you are acquainted may aid your entry into collegiate ranks. Most college commissioners, however, rely on their own staff and current officials to recommend those who are ready to make the step to a higher level.

College officiating places extreme demands on an official's time. Officials are required to attend off-season sessions for rules review, training in special tactics, testing, and fitness checks. College games are likely to be far from where you live, requiring you to set aside more time than you would for a high school commitment. You may be required to be at a game site a day in advance, and long hours in an car or a plane may be necessary to reach an out-of-state destination.

Although college officials may enjoy a higher status than high school officials, they often report an added strain on their family lives and marriages. Strong ambition may be a requisite for high-level officiating. High-level officials must be driven to excel, and such a drive sometimes poses problems in primary jobs and family relationships. Upper-level officials admit that an increased paycheck means increased expectations for excellence and less tolerance for error. You can be sure of being evaluated more critically in college than at the high school level. Stress may replace enjoyment for those who do not relish added pressure.

Following are some factors that can inhibit advancement:

- *Overconfidence.* Being overly self-satisfied may hinder your progress. People who select upper-level officials prefer those who are not know-it-alls.

- *Slow reactions.* At higher levels, instant decisiveness is of utmost importance. A desultory or overly casual style of officiating will work against your being considered for high levels.

- *Stubbornness.* You must show a willingness to learn and improve; you cannot be defensive when critiqued.

- *Antagonism.* If you consider coaches as adversaries and treat them in a supercilious way, you are not likely to advance very far. In contrast, talent as a diplomat is likely to earn you quicker advancement than exceptional game techniques. The same goes for how you treat crew members. You have to be a team player to rise.

- *Not staying current.* Currency has so many dimensions. *Referee* magazine, a monthly publication, has regular articles on rules interpretations, new rules, and special officiating techniques in major sports such as baseball and softball, football, basketball, and soccer. It also has feature articles and news stories about officiating issues and personnel. States themselves conduct annual sessions about rule updates and policies, and they provide follow-up information about particular events and selected topics. Local and regional associations are dedicated to the process of keeping officials apprised of new practices. Therefore, you can gain knowledge from many sources.

Staying Fit

As indicated, field sports—and basketball, too—demand a lot of running, not continual, but urgently, in short bursts. You must know territorial responsibilities as well, so you can mesh with your fellow officials. Abrupt action on the field or court will stimulate you to sprint: a pass interception or long kick return in football, a breakaway surge in field hockey or lacrosse, or a steal and fast break in basketball. You must also sense when to cruise, moving intently at a controlled pace. Then there are critical times when merely shuffling to secure a desired angle on play is preferable. A solid mantra for success in officiating is to continually strive to obtain an advantageous angle.

Four of the most popular outdoor sports—football, soccer, field hockey, and lacrosse—require officials to run a great deal. To be an effective official in those sports, you must be prepared to run hard (albeit intermittently) for a full game. This is true also with the vigorous indoor sport, basketball.

Volleyball officials simply stand on an elevated device (stepladder), blow a whistle, and wave their arms. They don't need to concern themselves with conditioning. The same goes for judges in track, swimming, and gymnastics. Baseball and softball umpires must run to cover territory and bases, but those bursts are sporadic. They need to run, but not very much. Umpires on the bases do a lot of standing and taking in the scene.

On the other hand, football officials have to run more, but again, only in spurts, and basketball and soccer officials must run the most of all. It has been calculated that a basketball official may run as many as two or three miles in a college game, with only intermittent stretches of stationary observation.

If the sport you are officiating requires that you run, you should make an effort to be fit (i.e., be able to run on a sustained basis). If you are hobbled in some way, you will likely come up short in serving effectively as a game administrator in a fluid sport in which athletes are exerting a lot of effort and expending much energy. It is a good idea to have a thorough annual physical exam.

There is an irony about officiating basketball: Officials must have a lot of experience to work at high school and college levels successfully; yet they are expected to keep up with young people who are at the peak of their physical prowess, including being able to run at top speed for a full game. This is a large expectation for men who are over 30 years of age. To learn more about staying in shape, refer to Part III, Getting Fit to Officiate.

Some officials use the preseason to train for officiating in which running is required. They may run several miles a week (e.g., a mile a day, every other day, to allow for recuperating), whereas others rely on interval conditioning a few times each week (e.g., running 75- or 100-yard dashes and walking back to the starting point).

Retaining the Enjoyment

The issue of enjoyment can be a delicate matter. Officiating can offer a strong ego boost. When you walk on the field or court, you receive instant respect. People defer to your point of view, because you are automatically in charge. This appeals to many people who take up officiating. You will also have a large measure of control in the game itself. Ego satisfaction is a significant dimension of the role.

Some officials look at every game as a chance to exert their influence. Rather than adopt this attitude, resolve to use your power fairly. People in attendance who are not playing the game are there to see their youngsters and friends in action and to enjoy the game. Therefore, you should not feel that spectators have shown up to see you in action.

If your primary motive is to administer a game with absolute impartiality, you will find that players frequently welcome you with friendly behavior, usually unstated but easily understood by their demeanor. They will offer you automatic acceptance.

These elements contribute to the excitement of officiating. You can be part of a contest and experience its drama. If you observe carefully, you'll notice that participants are often thrilled to take part. Observing this can add to your own vicarious pleasure. You should always be aware that young people, no matter what their age, have devoted long hours trying to be good at playing the game. A game is an opportunity to exhibit the skills they have acquired. This recognition of the players is another element of the contest that you can savor.

Games can be uplifting for everyone present, including those who monitor the action. You can be enthusiastic and still administer a game correctly.

Perhaps the only danger with officiating is overdoing it. No doubt, officiating requires a substantial commitment, often in the evenings and on weekends. You will enter a new world in which camaraderie is a satisfying ingredient, but you must also guard against excessive indulgence. Officiating can offer an emotional high just like any other physical and mental engagement. The secret is to space your assignments so you can build a wholesome life in the times between games.

SUMMARY

Beginning as an official starts like many other professions. Individuals must register, obtain instructional materials and equipment, train, and network to succeed. Before officials may step out onto a field or court, they usually must register with an organization and obtain a license that confirms their qualifications. This is particularly true at the prep level. It's important that officials have the proper equipment for the corresponding athletic events, and this is usually determined by the level worked. Studying the rules and learning to apply them is a crucial skill for all officials. Having an intimate knowledge of a sport's rules and vocabulary is necessary to become an elite official.

The quest for games is most likely the biggest struggle for young officials. Proper networking is a necessity for any official seeking games. It may be as simple as notifying a school or recreation center that you are interested in working games. Learning to become an official can best take place in a training program, and the availability of such programs varies widely according to geographical location. If an outside administrator is in charge of game assignments, which is the case in many scholastic leagues, it's crucial to obtain that person's contact information and inquire about an opportunity. Assigners are often the best resource for training, too. Many times, they will have clinics where young officials can go to learn and potentially work for assignments.

It's evident that officials must strive to keep improving their skills on the field. Whether this means refusing to become self-satisfied, seeking constructive criticism, or attending clinics, it's critical that officials always try to get better. Along those lines, it's important to self-evaluate performances at the end of every contest. Striving to improve abilities is the only way to insure that you keep moving forward and advance to the next level.

Most importantly, it's necessary that officials retain their enjoyment of officiating and continue having fun throughout their careers.

REVIEW QUESTIONS

1. An official's primary role in administering contests is penalizing player transgressions.

   ___ True

   ___ False

2. Combinations of individual sports, such as high jump and dashes in track, can result in team scores when compiled and compared.

   ___ True

   ___ False

3. To officiate properly, an official must have participated in the sport.

   ___ True

   ___ False

4. Sports rules for youngsters under high school age usually have modifications that fit their abilities.

   ___ True

   ___ False

5. Becoming an expert official, such as an umpire in softball, requires only memorizing the rules.

   ___ True

   ___ False

6. Meshing well with fellow officials requires a precise knowledge of territorial responsibilities.

   ___ True

   ___ False

7. Umpires in baseball can start to officiate with a minimum amount of equipment.

   ___ True

   ___ False

8. Officiating associations in various locales ordinarily handle game assignments.

   ___ True

   ___ False

9. In supervising live game action, being too close to a play can be detrimental.

   ___ True

   ___ False

10. People can enter the officiating avocation at almost any age, from teenagers to retirees.

    ___ True

    ___ False

Answers on page 187

Part II

Developing Your Officiating Skills

Chapter 3

Officiating Style

Jerry Grunska

This chapter addresses the following:

- The four styles of officiating, with reasons for their application
- How game context affects officiating style
- How style communicates your purposes to participants
- The personal characteristics and performance principles that lead to success
- The importance of image

In sports officiating, there are preferred ways of operating that tend to lead to success, although there are no guarantees. The ways you choose to operate are revealed in the style you adopt. The four styles described in this chapter are not mutually exclusive, though. You may find yourself justifiably adopting a particular style to fit the occasion. A good official adapts to the age of participants, their skill level, their maturity, their grasp of the game's protocols, the complexity of their strategy, and the overall context of game situations. A preteen, early-season contest may feature participants who are just learning the rudiments of the sport. On the other hand, a late-season game between skilled competitors and a substantial (and partisan) audience poses another set of challenges. Your style should fit the circumstances of the competition. This chapter also contains suggestions for beneficial personal behavior—ways of responding that are shaped by your attitude, performance principles, and the 10 commandments of style. This chapter should help you react positively to game situations.

FOUR STYLES OF OFFICIATING

The officiating styles discussed in this section are somewhat arbitrary, in that no official operates entirely in one mode all the time. In fact, the key to successful officiating is flexibility in adapting your style to the situation. Officiating is very much governed by context, which means that you must adapt your approach to the type of game being played. Styles can change, even during a single game. By knowing how to change your style, you can adapt to fit the circumstances.

Rule Book Style

Some officials say, "You can always hide behind the rule." If a player's action is borderline, you have the option of applying the most stringent interpretation of a rule and thereby have a bona fide excuse for ruling against the player. A stringent interpretation of the rules, however, may not always be the fairest way to judge the action.

Consider the slide in baseball or softball. The rule states that a runner must slide into home plate if a fielder is in position to make a play there. The runner is not permitted to come in standing up, because the catcher is in a stationary, vulnerable position and a collision may result. Therefore, the runner can be called out for failing to slide. Let's say that a runner is trying to score on a hit to the outfield, but the throw toward home plate forces the catcher to move up the third-base line. The ball and the runner arrive in the vicinity of the catcher—who is several feet up the line—at nearly the same time. To avoid the catcher, the runner deftly pirouettes around the fielder and steps on the plate without being tagged. The umpire could call the runner out for not sliding. However, if the runner slides and causes the catcher to topple over, then a player could be hurt. In effect, the runner is in a no-win situation.

A dozen scenarios about collisions or near collisions on plays at home plate could be described. The rules cannot cover all these situations succinctly. They can only describe parameters. If you take those parameters and apply them to the letter, you, in effect, penalize players unfairly. Applied in an overly rigid manner, rules of play can actually be used to sabotage their intent.

Some officials operate in this stringent way. They believe that by applying rules in a punitive manner, they are fulfilling their role

as the game's guardian. But the rules of any sport are subject to wide interpretation simply because there are so many variations in game circumstances.

Rules governing blocking in football also allow considerable latitude in interpretation. Blocking used to be done with the shoulder pads. Players kept using their hands to push, however, and finally the rule makers made pushing legal. But the shoving had to be done within the frame of the body of the player being blocked. What is within the frame? An official who wants to apply the definition precisely can call "illegal use of hands" a lot, even if the contact has no bearing on the result of a play. In other words, a rule-book-style official could interrupt play almost at will, and some officials do just that, believing themselves to be conscientious. Players, coaches, and fans often find their overly strict judgment annoying, even counterproductive.

Some rules, however, do not permit any deviance. The clearest examples are the rules regarding the boundary lines that confine a sport and define its critical areas. When a ball

A starter in track must undergo specific training because protocols require precise timing between steps of instructions to participants.

Bending the Rules

1. Rules say that only captains may be present at the coin toss in football. But in one Vermont community, the Pumpkin Queen, an honorary Miss Cinderella, traditionally bursts from a papier-mâché replica of a pumpkin on Halloween weekend to conduct the coin toss. Because this has been a tradition for many years with no detrimental effect on the game, officials invariably permit this ceremony. The rule was designed to curtail excesses (e.g., having all the seniors march out to call the coin toss), which could be considered an effort to intimidate opponents.

2. Softball umpire Cheryl Perry of Springer, New Mexico, found herself at odds with coaches and administrators when she threatened a coach with ejection for standing in the dugout opening to direct fielders. The dugout itself was restricted because of thick industrial-strength wire, like a cage, and in addition, the mesh was so close to the bench that players were squeezed into stand-up positions to view play. Tradition in the league held that coaches occupy the dugout opening, but Perry was adamant about refusing that privilege, saying that it was dangerous. The league commissioner eventually had to remove her from games, declaring that her stance was "unreasonably belligerent."

3. During an injury time-out in a high school football game, referee Wilbur Pralle of West Salem, Oregon, stopped a coach from talking to his team. "You're here to attend to the injured player only," Pralle said. "But I have to give the substitute directions," the coach protested. "The rules don't permit it," Pralle reiterated, ignoring common sense.

4. A pair of Pentecostal pastors, who happened to be hockey officials from Blanding, Utah, were assigned to a tournament in Moab about 50 miles away. Before going to the match, they called the school athletic director and said they'd be especially watchful for the players taking the Lord's name in vain. When the home coach heard this warning, he said, "How can I deal with that? I've been trying to stop my kids from using obscenities." The officials were given another assignment and told not to call teams with advance warnings of any kind.

possessed by a runner crosses the plane of the goal line in football, it is a touchdown, with no room for equivocation. When a batted ball hits a base in softball or baseball, it is a fair ball. When a basketball bounces on a sideline, it is out of bounds. Accurate judgement (which is not always easy) is the determining factor in these cases.

Another area in which you must follow the letter of rules consistently is in the matter of safety. Certain acts in contact sports can maim an opponent. A body slam in the back, below the waist, in football (clipping) is one example. Furthermore, special protective padding under players' uniforms is stipulated, with exact definitions for some sports (field hockey, ice hockey, wrestling, football), and officials are obliged to carry out a careful inspection to determine compliance before contests.

Although a strict official may be short on discriminating judgment, some coaches like officials who operate by the book, as long as they are evenhanded and equally stringent with both teams. In games that flow rapidly, such as soccer, hockey, and basketball, an official who calls a tight game can hamper teams that play aggressive defense. Consequently, an official who administers hard justice will find a favorable reception in some quarters, particularly with teams having difficulty dealing with a tough defense.

Preventive Style

It is almost always acceptable to talk to players during games. For example, complimenting an athlete on good play can be a positive way to interact, and such a compliment will be even stronger if the player's act was a sporting gesture. Often, the best time to speak to a player may be during a break in the action, such as between innings in softball or baseball.

Sometimes, too, players do not know when a behavior might be close to a foul or violation. The rules forbid a softball pitcher from jumping off the rubber while delivering a pitch for example. An umpire will usually remind the pitcher of that if she is lifting her push-off foot slightly, Also, in football, a quarterback under center and about to receive a snap must keep his head quite still, because a quick jerk of the head can easily draw an opponent into the neutral zone. The quarterback is permitted to bob his head slightly, because it is almost impossible to keep a frozen head when barking signals. Judgments in these types of situations demand refined thinking on the part of officials. Warning players about negative results of their actions is usually a sensible path to take.

Preventive officiating takes two forms. One is helping players avoid technical violations. A basketball official, for instance, will withhold the ball from a player on a throw-in if that player's foot is on the boundary line. A baseball or softball umpire may notify a pitcher who is close to delivering an illegal pitch—say, with improper footwork on the rubber. A football wing official will often put one foot out in an effort to guide a split end, showing the limit of the so-called neutral zone.

The second preventive technique is notifying a player not to commit a foul. Sometimes fouls are the result of inadvertent player behavior. Charging into the snapper on punts is one such action in football. Rules protect the snapper, who is in a vulnerable position after he has put the ball in play. Sometimes a fielder will absentmindedly stand in a base runner's path in softball or baseball, and an umpire can advise against it. A basketball player can be told to avoid excessive hand guarding or to avoid elbowing on rebounds. In this way, officials act to prevent player-to-player contact that could result in fouls.

Any warnings to players about potential violations should be issued during dead ball intervals, although it is sometimes possible to call to players during live action, as when telling football players to stay off a runner whose progress has already been determined.

Laissez-Faire Style

Some officials prefer to let players just play, without interfering very much. This is not an undesirable style as long as games move along smoothly. The difficulty comes when games become heated or when complicated judgments are necessary. The live-and-let-live official may get into trouble by not making calls when they are essential, not attending carefully to the welfare of players, or making a halfhearted decision when a crisp one is called for. Feeble decision making can be the undoing of an official.

The reasons officials operate this way are perhaps just as important as the results. One reason is that the official may not know very much about the game. The rundown in baseball or softball serves to illustrate this. If a runner is caught between bases with fielders trying to make a tag, the runner may throw up her arms and try to hit the ball while it is being tossed between fielders. This is interference, and the runner should be called out. But a clever runner may know that if she can run into a fielder who does not have the ball, the fielder should be called for obstruction and the runner awarded safe passage to a base. An umpire who does not know these restrictions may offer no call at all, and hence the essence of the rule has been ignored. Lack of rule knowledge, particularly of rules that seldom need to be applied, is a prominent shortcoming of many officials. It is one reason for what some call lackadaisical officiating.

Considerable emphasis in recent years has been placed on dead ball officiating—that is, attending with a keen eye to participants after a play has been completed. Some quick examples can illustrate. In baseball and softball, if a sliding runner has been declared out—or even if the runner is safe—an umpire who signals the call may turn away from the play and miss a physical altercation between aggrieved opponents. A hard tag or a hard slide can initiate antagonism.

In basketball, after a foul on a shooter, when the official turns to report the foul, players may bristle and bump chests, and a careless official may miss an opportunity to squelch further animosities.

In football, a prime opportunity for dead ball confrontations can occur anytime a runner is driven backward and dumped on the surface or when two players jostle one another while attempting to catch a forward pass. When these situations arise, an official may abandon focus on the individuals while retrieving the ball. Officials can miss critical opportunities to regulate the game by being overly casual. Sometimes overly casual officials simply fall into lazy patterns of inattentiveness.

In underclass or subvarsity levels of the preceding sports, as well as in hockey, field hockey, and soccer, schools often skimp on the number of officials and assign only one or two people to games that customarily feature more. In these instances, officials may be drawn far away from groups of players and therefore may be unable to monitor the behavior of those who are out of their visual range. If a soccer official, working alone, is on one end of the field, he may be forced to abandon any hope of observing players on the opposite end of the field. These are not personal faults; rather, they are limits imposed by circumstances. However, because the playing surface in these games is so large, an official may give in to ennui when the ball travels some distance and closing in on it is virtually impossible.

Another shortcoming in officials is lack of hustle. An official who is hustling can accurately process the goings-on in a game and anticipate where to be to make calls properly. Many officials don't know when or how to hustle. Hustling demands an intense dedication to being in the right position from which to view a play. Sometimes declining to hustle results in an inability to make a sound call.

Hustle is more than physically dashing to a spot on the court or field. It is also a state of mind. It is an intellectual attribute, one of reading the context of a game, of knowing strategy, and of anticipating outcomes of strategy. An official who knows the intricacies of game strategy can expect certain play action and player behaviors and can move, in a controlled way that may look casual, to cover probable elements of a contest.

When something unusual happens (e.g., unnecessary player aggression), an official should enter the scene by cautioning individuals. In some games players can be notified that their actions have been close to rule transgressions. Players should be warned if they make a hard tag in baseball or softball; if they commit a hard foul in basketball; if they come close to executing an illegal, punishing hold in wrestling; or if they are close to committing a dead ball foul in football, such as jumping on top of the pile after a runner is downed. An official who refrains from warning players about potentially dangerous acts is ignorant of the danger, reluctant to take action, not very knowledgeable, or not very observant. Just wanting to let people play is a poor excuse for not being diligent.

Umpires in baseball and softball believe that at times an emphatic punch-out (a strong

Stop and Go

Officials in all sports must learn the semaphore gestures necessary for administering a game and communicating their decisions. In their training, officials are taught to execute signals in a crisp, emphatic manner. A main function of signals is to declare whether or not play is live or whether the clock should be started or stopped. Every whistle in basketball kills the clock if it is alive. Clock stoppages should be accompanied by a raised arm—an open hand if the ball goes out of bounds, a closed fist if the stoppage is for a foul. Football officials use a scissors of both arms above their heads to stop the clock and a windmill wind of the arm to start it. A clock is not used in baseball, but umpires throw up both arms, stretched overhead, to declare a dead ball (most noticeable on balls hit foul).

Some officials go to games just to act as a decoration. They want to get games over quickly so they can collect their checks and be on their way. They deliberately bypass tough calls to avoid holding up the game. Unlike officials who are ignorant of the rules, these are often hard-bitten veterans who don't really care much about being conscientious. It is disheartening to report that some sports officials are less than dedicated, letting things slide because they just don't want to bother.

Laissez-faire officials are good only when the players themselves take control and run games satisfactorily.

thrust of the arm and a vigorous twist of the body) is necessary for selling a call. Selling calls with vigor and dispatch is necessary at key moments in all sports. An official whose timing is slow, whose signals are lethargic, and who fails to be emphatic at critical times is going to lose the confidence of players and fans. Coaches, too, despair over the official who seems too nonchalant, inattentive, or deficient in courage to make sharp, strong decisions. The official who doesn't want to interfere—or is unsure of how to do so—can be a menace to the welfare of athletes.

An example of using a proper mechanic to stop play as the referee awards a timeout.

Advantage or Disadvantage Style

Naturally, the best officials are those who have a deep sense of what the game is all about, are on top of the rules, and have a healthy respect for the players and the game they are officiating. Their basic intent is to take charge of a game and run it as smartly and efficiently as possible, letting the players play when only minimal intrusion is necessary but intervening in a decisive way when events in the game show that measures of control need to be applied.

Evenhanded could be one way to describe such officiating, but perhaps a better name for it is the advantage or disadvantage style of officiating. Officiating manuals invariably contain a section that advises officials to follow the spirit of the rules and not to act like overzealous enforcers of the letter of the law. One cannot keep a rule's spirit, though, without a keen knowledge of what that spirit is. The key to going with the flow of a game is a thorough grasp of the sport's ideals. What constitutes a good game? How can players be guided (rather than forced) into playing a fair, fervent contest? When does an act that borders on a violation stop short of giving one team a decided advantage? The following examples illustrate situations in which a good official must apply the advantage or disadvantage principle.

• In basketball, a player dribbling down the floor is met by a defender whose arms are outstretched. The dribbler executes a skillful crossover dribble and slides by the defender, although the defender's arm swipes across the body of the ball handler as she moves.

• In soccer, a defender slides feetfirst toward a player dribbling the ball and momentarily causes the dribbler to disengage. But the dribbler hops aside, even though the defender's slide caused a slight imbalance, and moves downfield in possession of the ball.

• In football, a wideout moves into the defensive backfield and cuts in front of a defender on what looks like a pass route. As the wideout moves past the defender, the defender sticks out his arms and gives the potential pass receiver a small shove outside the frame of his body. The play is a draw, however, and no pass is thrown.

In each of the preceding cases, a discriminating official would say that although contact was technically illegal, in the spirit of the game, no advantage accrued. This is not to say that possibly harmful acts should be overlooked. The point is that a genuinely savvy official makes distinctions about play action and penalizes behavior that is clearly illegal while bypassing calls on actions that don't impinge on the spirit of the rules.

It takes a very strong official to function this way and still retain staunch integrity. Such an official must make discrete judgments about a game's intricacies. A considerable amount of experience is necessary before an official can reach this point of making rapid-fire, astute decisions. The judicious no-call is sometimes the best call of all. Officials who approach this point in their development are considered top of the line.

Fast-pitch softball umpire Dee Lyn Jordan of Aurora, Illinois, recently observed a pitcher who was making only an uncertain presentation before winding up. The pitcher was holding the ball beneath her chin but not actually touching it with her mitt. Jordan quietly explained the proper technique to the pitcher between innings (no coach had complained), but when the pitcher repeated the phantom move in the next inning, Jordan stepped sideways behind the catcher, threw up her hands, and called, "No pitch!" Although little advantage could be gained by a pitcher's overlooking the rule book definition of a windup, Dee Lyn chose to enforce the rule in a somewhat dramatic fashion to cement the proper decorum in the player's behavior.

CONTEXT DETERMINES APPROACH

Dr. K. Lee Kuhlke of Englewood, Colorado is a specialist in prosthodontics (i.e., straightening people's bites). As one of the top soccer referees in the state, he also specializes in taking the bite out of aggressive soccer players. But his point of view illustrates the firm control an official must occasionally exercise over a sport competition. At times, an official has to take a stance about the way a game should be handled even before the game begins. Dr. Kuhlke explains that context is key:

> *Depending on the level of play and the intentions of the players, we can assess the situation and either call a "loose" game or else revert to a "tight" style. A lot depends on degrees of player skill and the intensity of rivalries. I had an adult match of players who were of Turkish background against a team composed largely of Greek immigrants. It was fought on American soil, of course, but there was no affection between opponents.*

Though no nationalistic loyalties or animosities are likely to surface in high school competition, schools often have rivalries, and sometimes those rivalries have an underlying basis in the background of the populations they serve. Competing schools may serve youngsters from families of different social or economic backgrounds, religions, races, or points of origin, all of which may play a role in how students view their opponents.

Rivalry could—and often does—arise between schools that are near each other, a community envy of sorts. Proximity sometimes creates long-standing rivals, which brings up another point about context: sometimes lingering anger is the result of an unpleasant incident between schools, which may have happened years ago or only a week before.

How can you know of a history of animosity or rivalry? Often you do not know, and in some ways that is good, because you can approach the contest with pure neutrality. But if you do know of a potentially hostile atmosphere, such knowledge can alert you to be wary, to have your antenna tuned to possible expressions of ill will and acts of retaliation.

At the other end of the emotional scale is a game atmosphere of complete frivolity or a careless attitude on the part of competitors. Perhaps the coaches and players aren't really taking the game seriously. In this type of situation, you may feel left out because whatever you call doesn't matter much to the participants. This situation is rare, however; most people who bother to practice and suit up generally take their roles very seriously.

Another officiating challenge is inept players. Sometimes a school traditionally hasn't had much success in a given sport, the sport is new to the program, or very little training occurs below the high school level. Sometimes only one of the teams lacks skill, making the contest lopsided. At any rate, when play is sloppy, you have to adjust your expectations and operate according to the skill level of players, which may mean overlooking technical violations and making allowances for the lack of ability.

When elementary school youngsters play soccer, an official may bypass a call for an arm contacting the ball. In football, a player wobbling at the line of scrimmage may not be flagged for a false start. Also, an official can overlook double dribbling or traveling in basketball if the youngsters' development has not progressed to the point where they can execute these moves successfully. Surely, a four-foot-tall player should not be whistled for being in the free throw lane too long because she hasn't gained any advantage.

The best kind of competition is an intense game in which players respect one another and are determined to give 100 percent toward the goal of victory, with no quarter given but with an honorable outlook acknowledging that good sporting behavior is just as important as a favorable outcome. This happens a lot at high school events, although newspapers don't trumpet such contests unless a league title is in the balance. Officials can testify that often the most heated battles, fiercely contested but cleanly played, are between schools with poor records. They play that way as a matter of pride, not wanting to be thought of as sore losers and trying to make their followers pleased with their effort. These are exciting games to officiate.

STYLE AND MECHANICS

Signals are fundamental communication devices for all officials. You convince others of your accuracy in judgment by the way you execute signals. Signals are the most visible embodiment of your style. They are an area in which uniqueness stands out.

To rehearse these telling movements, check yourself in a mirror while gesturing to be sure you are projecting the images you want to project. Use professional officials as models. Watch how a Major League Baseball umpire removes his mask, how he observes a pitcher

A Confident Decision

A state play-off football game between East St. Louis and Alton, Illinois, was stopped for an official team time-out. A coach beckoned referee Len Scaduto to the sideline and said that a crisp pass to an end had been trapped on the last play, although no official had declared the pass incomplete. "I'll check it out," said Scaduto. The ref then gathered the crew in the middle of the field and asked what each member had observed, whereupon they verified that it was a good catch.

In reporting the decision to the coach, Scaduto added that he believed that the officials had good angles and that he had complete confidence in their judgment. This judicious pause on the part of Referee Scaduto indicated that he had enough self-confidence to pursue the matter seriously and that he was also convinced that he'd get straight answers from his crew. Scaduto's strong presence of mind was also shown in his willingness to listen to the coach's contrary perception and then secure a satisfactory resolution of the issue.

warming up, the way he brushes the plate, and the propelling motion he uses to cover another crew member's base. Watch how an NBA referee tosses the ball to a free-throw shooter. Notice how NFL officials release their flags, kill the clock, or obtain an out-of-bounds spot. Check the way a soccer official flourishes a yellow card. See how a polished volleyball official notifies a server to put the ball in play. Observe when a wrestling official flops to the mat to check a hold. Many high school officials also exhibit sound habits to copy.

You should master the timing, emphasis, clarity, presentation, and smoothness of signaling that the rule books and manuals illustrate. Move away from clusters of players when you signal. Avoid being loose-jointed, flippant, stiffly mechanical, or exaggeratedly demonstrative. Mechanical is stiff and spasmodic, with muscles taut. Demonstrative is striking a showy pose when only a minimal signal is called for (e.g., in baseball, waving and yelling "Foul!" when a ball is hit into the stands, or in volleyball, using a massive torso twist to denote a simple sideout).

If a basketball player knocks a ball out of bounds, your signal should not reflect the crowd's reaction, regardless of the context. The signal should be clear and measured, but not exuberant. By the same token, touchdown signals or a change-of-possession indicator after a fumble in football should not carry a message that you are happy for the scoring or the recovering team. "I don't care if [the ref] leaps in the air on touchdowns," one coach remarked, "as long as he jumps just as high for us as he does for our opponents." Don't rise off the playing surface when signaling.

On the other hand, firmly planted feet and a solid horizontal swipe are essential when calling a runner safe on a close play in baseball or softball. A strong thrust is also necessary when declaring a charge in basketball. In sum, you must learn when and how to execute the signals required in game administration.

Personal Characteristics

Some personal characteristics are instrumental in helping you become a good official. If you do not have these qualities inherently, you can work to adopt them consciously:

- *Integrity.* Always work to uphold the highest principles.
- *Courage.* Many situations in games will test your ability to be brave and to make decisions that you know in your heart are correct but that may not be popular.
- *Self-confidence.* Start off each game by giving yourself a pep talk about showing everyone that you are completely in charge.
- *Decisiveness.* Some judgments have to be made quickly and emphatically. When you execute such judgments properly, you gain the confidence of those involved in the game.
- *Consistency.* Each situation is unique, to be sure, but strength of purpose is shown in the evenness with which you make decisions, reacting similarly in similar situations.
- *Being even-tempered.* Being even-tempered may be the hardest attribute to achieve, because though it's easy to remain calm

Crisp, authoritative mechanics show that you are in control of the game.

when nothing is happening, it's hard to do so when people react negatively to your decisions.
- *Humility.* Some officials adopt an overly authoritative, defensive posture, but the official who gains the most respect admits that he can be wrong.
- *An understanding of human nature.* Some people whine when they are aggrieved, and they're usually sorry for it later; try to forgive them before they ask for forgiveness.
- *Ability to control situations.* When something odd happens in a game, pause to replay the event mentally; then make a firm decision and resolve to convince others, in a soft but direct way, of the sense behind your decision.
- *Hustle.* There is no substitute for dashing to position for a firm call, and people will appreciate that you're on top of the play, even if they don't say it.

Personal Performance Principles

In addition to the characteristics mentioned in the previous section, there are a number of additional pieces of advice to guide your behavior. The following guidelines, which appeared in *Referee* magazine, will affect your officiating style positively.

- *Be competitive.* The players give maximum effort; so should you—every game. Remind yourself to stay on top of play and to pay attention to peripheral happenings, such as harsh talk among participants, sniping from the sidelines, and overreacting by the crowd. You are hired to make calls that control the game.

- *Have your own head on right.* Your uniform and position in the game do not grant you immunity from criticism. Effective officials know how much to take before responding, and knowing where to draw the line is essential. Be assured that a line of tolerance must be drawn at times in order to prevent intimidation.

- *Avoid a showdown.* If a coach is relentless in negative remarks, stay as far away as possible. This is especially important during breaks in action. Don't invite a blowup. Moving near an irritated party just to show who's in charge will only lead to further acrimony. Some officials adopt a defiant attitude that erodes respect from participants.

- *Get into the game's flow.* Make efforts to understand the game's tempo and to recognize the difference in speedups and slowdowns. At times, officials want to control the rhythm; at other times, they help accommodate or maintain a pace set by the teams. A ragged game demands a different style of officiating than a smooth game.

- *Never bark.* This is a Golden Rule philosophy. No one likes to be yelled at; it sets the recipient on edge and increases tensions. Apply this philosophy when dealing with others. Be firm when necessary, but use a voice with a modulated pitch. Shouting appears to be defensive and indicates a loss of personal control.

The 10 Commandments of Style

Here is a list of style rules to keep in mind at every game:

1. Avoid criticizing other officials; even without your contribution, there will be a sufficient supply of criticism.

2. Avoid second-guessing game strategy; many others feel it is their own right.

3. Strive to avoid the appearance of favoritism; smile, but don't laugh out loud. There should be no such thing as a friendly, neighborhood official.

4. Preface most signals with a distinct pause. Avoid overacting; instead, make signals rhythmic and snappy.

5. Recognize when you've made a controversial call, and permit reasonable disputation. Realize that you are arbitrating a competition. Listen before you respond, but never tolerate a personal attack such as name calling.

6. When in doubt about a ruling, make a firm decision, explain your reasoning, determine the truth later by referring to the rule book, and then reveal your findings accurately and promptly.

7. Never invent calls; be sure of what you observe. Watch the whole play.

8. Don't bluff; if you don't have an answer, admit it. To be positive is to be wrong at the top of your voice.

9. If a judgment call deserves an explanation, provide it.

10. Never be neglectful, cavalier, or nonchalant about your image; people are observing you, and they'll admire a professional demeanor.

- *Show confidence.* Know the line between arrogance and confidence. Your presence should command respect from participants. A sharp appearance, a smooth manner, erect carriage, and a polished voice determine whether or not you'll be readily accepted. Image is indeed important, and body language speaks louder than words.

- *Forget the fans.* The audiences at games tend to exhibit three pronounced characteristics: ignorance of rules, highly emotional partisanship, and delight in berating officials. Accepting that will help you to ignore the crowd and concentrate on the job at hand.

- *Answer reasonable questions.* Courtesy is a vital technique for an official. Treat coaches and players with politeness. Use formal words, never curse, and make listening a strong element in any personal exchange with game participants. Be firm, be gentle, and be relaxed. Weigh each word carefully when answering questions or reacting to challenges. It is impossible to take words back once they have been uttered.

- *Stay cool.* One goal is to establish a calm environment for the game. Edgy officials are easily spotted by fans, coaches, and players. Animatedly chewing gum, fidgeting and pacing nervously, or being over-friendly will make you appear vulnerable to pressure. Indecisiveness can be your downfall. You will be judged the instant you step into the playing area. Therefore, don't greet acquaintances in the stands enthusiastically (your actions may easily be misinterpreted), and avoid throwing your head back in amusement. Your role is not that of an entertainer. Instead, adopt a formal, respectful, businesslike approach with everyone connected to the game. That way, respect is likely to be returned to you.

The Power of Body Image

You can't alter your genetic makeup, but you can control some things about the way you look. You can control your grooming, your manner of speaking, gestures, and body posture. You can also take charge of your personal eating habits and use of tobacco. If your ordinary walk is a shuffle, you can strive to step in a more sprightly fashion. If you have a tendency to slouch, merely by being conscious of the problem you can work toward a cure by throwing your shoulders back. An upright posture—head erect, with toes pointed forward in a brisk and purposeful stride—is characteristic of top-notch officials. Fresh uniforms (not ragged or faded), polished shoes, carefully groomed hair, and a somewhat jaunty manner of moving are also emblematic of superior officials.

Certain less-than-conservative forms of dress and presentation are sweeping the country today. Young people have embraced the grunge look on a wide scale: baggy clothing, a languid walk, body piercing, and tattoos. Major League Baseball players seem to favor five o'clock shadows. Some NBA performers appear to be mobile signboards with their body etchings. But if an official shows up at a game with a nostril ring, people are likely to sneer. An official with a safety pin through the cheek is apt to draw cold stares and a few expressions of disbelief during close calls. Tattoos, although prevalent in society, are best covered up when officiating, if possible, to achieve respect and credulity. In short, some fashions that are acceptable in present culture are not likely to be considered proper for sports officials. Basically, officials are held to more conservative, clean-cut standards. Moreover, if you smoke or chew tobacco, do it somewhere other than near the playing facility.

SUMMARY

Blending may be a key word for this entire chapter, because you will succeed as an official if you combine many facets in your approach to handling athletic contests. For one thing, you must learn to blend various styles according to the type of competition in which you are immersed. Sometimes you can be strict, sometimes you can be lenient, and often these shifts in approach take place within the same game without sacrificing consistency. Officiate the game the way it is being played, which means using the advantage or disadvantage principle wisely.

You must also fortify your personality with characteristics that reflect your strength of purpose, which means blending attributes of self-confidence, tact, assertiveness, and understanding. You can consciously choose these ways of dealing with others, particularly if you think before reacting. Your chief aim as a sports official is to become a sound decision maker in the midst of athletic competition, while maintaining poise and convincing participants of your integrity.

Chapter 4 introduces some of the goals toward which you can reasonably strive. Learning to set and achieve realistic goals can help you plot a course toward improving as a sports official.

REVIEW QUESTIONS

1. Under what circumstances is it best to be strict? What are the guidelines?

2. In what kind of game is a Laissez-Faire Style most appropriate?
   a. when very young unskilled youngsters are playing
   b. in competitions that move along smoothly
   c. when an audience is not challenging any calls
   d. in tense contests between highly skilled players

3. It is best to stop a coach who is shouting at you by
   a. turning and staring at the offender until the shouting stops
   b. shouting back
   c. stopping play, moving toward the perpetrator, and explaining the consequences of such behavior
   d. motioning to an officiating partner to address the problem

4. Exaggerated, flamboyant officiating signals are
   a. often incorrectly executed
   b. ways to establish an officiating presence
   c. attention-getters to convince spectators of your authority
   d. never appropriate

5. Some rules do not permit any variation in officiating styles. Such rules often cover the game's
   a. player freedoms, such as a catcher blocking the plate in softball or baseball or a blocker using his hands in football
   b. player conduct
   c. coaching strategy
   d. designated boundaries

6. One critical ingredient in an official's style is
   a. keeping track of fouls
   b. knowing when and how to issue warnings
   c. learning the psychology of coaches
   d. knowing when to stop play as a result of spectator interference

7. Which of the following is an appropriate response to a potentially harmful player act?
   a. Let it go because what looks like harm to a bystander may be perfectly legal behavior.
   b. Ignore it if the flow of the game is moving harmoniously.
   c. Do not overlook it.
   d. Issue a warning even if the act has not harmed anybody.

8. What is the best way to deal with a coach's objection to a judgment call on a controversial play?
   a. Be sure that it does not affect the score.
   b. Insist that the call was indisputable.
   c. Conduct a conference with partner(s).
   d. Respond only if the objection is stated softly.

9. Which of the following should an official strive for?
   a. Ignore personal attacks and name calling.
   b. Show firmness through sharp retorts to criticism.
   c. Be extracongenial with spectators.
   d. Blend in, and be unobtrusive.

Answers on page 187

Goal Setting

Robert Weinberg

This chapter addresses the following:

- Types of goals
- Why goals work
- Goal-setting principles
- Potential goal-setting problems

GOAL SETTING TO MAINTAIN MOTIVATION

Most officials choose to officiate because they really like the sport they participated in during their playing days and simply want to stay involved. This desire fuels their motivation as they start their careers in officiating or at least start to officiate on a regular basis. However, many officials find it difficult to maintain a high level of motivation game in and game out over the course of their careers. In fact, quitting (which can be related to burnout) often crosses officials' minds as noted by the following quote from a Major League Baseball umpire: "I think every umpire who works in the minor leagues thinks once or twice about quitting."

As an official, you need a strong sense of self and a high level of motivation to overcome the lack of praise and ample criticism you receive. You can't be overly concerned about how others view or evaluate your performance. Rather, you must focus on your own self-perceptions of performance and progress. As long as you see yourself improving and advancing toward meaningful goals, then the chances are extremely high that you will maintain a high level of motivation.

Indeed, goal setting can play an important role in keeping up your level of motivation and commitment to officiate. As Keith Bell (1983) aptly noted in his book *Championship Thinking*, "Floundering in the world of sport without setting goals is like shooting without aiming. You might enjoy the blast and kick of the gun, but you probably won't get the bird. (p. 64)" Most people are fairly familiar with the concept of goal setting, although few actually understand all the principles that make goal setting effective. Setting goals does not assume that the goals will be reached. Rather, they need to be set in a manner that maximizes the principles of effective goal setting. These principles have been developed through hundreds of studies in business, organizational, sport and exercise settings and have been shown to be similar in many situations.

Before addressing these principles, this chapter offers definitions of various types of goals and addresses why they work. A discussion of goal-setting guidelines is followed by some cautionary notes on setting goals.

Goal-Setting Definitions

In most goal-setting studies, the term *goal* refers to attaining a specific level of proficiency on a task, usually within a specified time limit (Locke, Shaw, Saari, and Latham, 1981). In essence, a goal is the aim or purpose of an action. Most of the time, goals are seen as *objective*, with a specific outcome that can be measured. For example, if you want to improve your fitness, you might set a goal to run three miles in under 24 minutes. Or if you want to improve your knowledge of the sport and rule interpretation, you might set a goal of getting 95 percent on a standard written test of rules and knowledge. In essence, these goals focus on achieving a standard of excellence such as getting in better position to make close calls, or being more decisive in making calls in general.

However, besides these more objective goals are what are termed *subjective* goals. These goals can be very important but are usually harder to assess. For example, if you are about to start your second season as a referee, you might want to set a goal to enjoy this season more than the last one, which was very difficult. But how do you measure enjoyment? One way to do this is to think about the things that you do or feel when you are enjoying officiating. For example, you may enjoy (or receive a sense of satisfaction from) making a call that was tough but fair or smoothing over an argument and resuming play in an authoritative but objective manner. You can also rate your enjoyment on a scale of 1 to 10, with 1 indicating a lot less enjoyable than last year and 10 indicating a lot more enjoyable than last year. Although such ratings are subjective, they are still valid.

WHY GOALS WORK

Hundreds of studies attest to the effectiveness of goal setting in enhancing productivity, performance, and positive feelings. Although many people are interested only in the fact that goal setting works, knowing why it works is also important because this information can be used to develop goal-setting interventions. So let's take a closer look at why goals enhance performance.

Goals Focus Your Attention

Research has revealed that the most important reason people set goals is to focus their attention on the task at hand. Remember that many people choose to officiate because it keeps them close to their sport. But this initial impetus will probably be insufficient to maintain your interest for a long period of time. Goals can help keep you focused on the things that make officiating enjoyable (e.g., knowing all the rules of the game) as well as working on things to make you a better official (e.g., staying in good cardiorespiratory condition, especially

if you are officiating a sport such as soccer). Goals can focus your attention on why you got involved in officiating in the first place as well as keep you focused on always improving both your mental and physical skills.

Goals Increase Effort and Persistence

If you set important goals for yourself, you will probably put forth effort to achieve those goals. To use a basketball official example, if your goal is to make sure you are in a good position to make tough calls (e.g., charging versus blocking), you will probably put forth a good deal of effort to get in shape and stay fit so you can move up and down the court easily and quickly. This could involve a daily exercise regimen or a well-rounded diet to help you reach your goal.

Goals Increase Learning

Setting goals also promotes a quest for effective ways to accomplish these goals. In one of my officiating clinics, an official told me that he gets really nervous during critical parts of a competition (e.g., toward the end of the game in a close competition), which negatively affects his performance. He asked what he could do to reduce his anxiety and nervousness. If he set a goal to reduce his nervousness in pressure situations, he could develop a number of strategies such as breath control, progressive relaxation, imagery, or positive self-talk. The point is that setting specific goals can help you increase your use of relevant learning strategies.

GOAL-SETTING PRINCIPLES

Goal setting is not a foolproof process that can be easily implemented without some careful thought and planning. Research has shown that a myriad of personal and task factors influence the effectiveness of any goal-setting program. Although research can illuminate the science of setting goals, the art of setting goals (i.e., when and for whom goals should be set) can only be determined on an individual basis. Specifically, it would be misleading to think that all types of goals are equally effective in achieving particular ends.

Before implementing a goal-setting program, you need to have a firm understanding of the goal-setting process. The key is to structure a program so that it is consistent with the basic principles derived from the organizational and sport psychology literatures as well as from the professional practice knowledge of sport and exercise psychologists working in field settings. However, the effectiveness of any motivational technique depends on the interaction of the individuals and the situations in which the individuals are placed. In essence, you need an understanding of your individual situations (e.g., type of sport, support systems, travel) as well as your personal characteristics (e.g., personality, background, experience) to implement an effective goal-setting program. Following are some recommendations and principles for setting up a goal-setting program.

Identify Your Goals

When first getting started, you must determine exactly what you want to achieve. One way to identify your goals is to ask yourself a series of questions about your skills and attitudes toward officiating. Consider the following questions:

- What are my greatest strengths and weaknesses as an official?
- Am I well versed in the rules and regulations?
- Am I in good physical condition?
- Do I prepare myself mentally for each game?
- What aspects of officiating are most enjoyable to me?
- Do I communicate well with other officials, players, and coaches?
- Are my mechanics and positioning sound?
- Do I keep my confidence up despite being booed by spectators and harassed by coaches?
- Do I stay calm in pressure situations?

You may notice that answering these questions is not necessarily a simple or straightforward process. But just thinking about these things should help clarify what you want to accomplish through your officiating as well as help you target specific areas for improvement.

Set Moderately Difficult and Challenging Goals

One of the most consistent findings from the research literature is that goals should be challenging and difficult, yet attainable (Locke and Latham, 1990). Surveys and interviews have indicated that people prefer moderately difficult goals to very difficult or moderate goals. In essence, effective goals are difficult enough to be challenging, yet realistic enough to be achieved. Setting goals that are too difficult and unrealistic often results in failure. This can lead to frustration, lowered self-confidence and motivation, and decreased performance.

Being an official is a difficult job, and expecting that you will officiate a perfect game is unrealistic, as is expecting a basketball player to make every shot on a given night. Conversely, goals that are too easy do not present a challenge, leading to less than maximum effort and often achieving under your capabilities. This, in turn, might result in being satisfied with a mediocre performance instead of extending yourself to reach your potential. For example, if your goal is simply to be chosen for a particular assignment, then you might be satisfied just to be there instead of focusing on doing a good job as an official. Thus, the secret is to find a balance between setting yourself up for failure and pushing yourself to strive for success. In this middle ground reside challenging, realistic, attainable goals.

Set Specific Goals

One of the most consistent findings from the goal-setting literature is that specific goals produce higher levels of task performance than no goals or general ones. We often hear people tell participants simply, "Go out and do your best." Although this type of instruction can be motivating, it is not as powerful for enhancing motivation and performance as asking participants to go out and achieve specific goals. Furthermore, when giving performers specific goals, it is important that they be measurable and in behavioral terms. For example, having a goal to do your best when refereeing a game between two teams who have a history of a hotly contested rivalry and bad blood would not be as helpful as having a goal to take a deep breath and count to three before speaking

Officials desire to show respect for the game and their country.

to a player or coach who uses bad language or talks to you in a loud, aggressive manner. Following are some examples of vague goals and how to make them more specific:

Vague: I want to become better acquainted with all the rules of the game.

Specific: I will read and understand one section of the rules every night.

Vague: I want to improve my fitness level.

Specific: I will run three times per week for 30 minutes and will ride a stationary bicycle two times per week for 20 minutes.

Vague: I want to improve my self-control.

Specific: When a coach starts to yell and shout at me, I'll count to myself for five seconds before responding, making sure to keep my voice subdued.

Vague: I want to improve my teamwork skills with other officials refereeing the same game.

Specific: I will spend three hours per week observing other officials' styles and their positioning.

Set Both Long- and Short-Term Goals

When you ask people what their goals are, they invariably mention very ambitious long-term goals such as being president of the company, becoming a millionaire, or going to medical school. Officials often tend to set their sights on such grand goals as officiating at the professional level. Although long-term goals provide direction and a final destination, short-term goals are necessary for keeping motivation and performance high over time. In relating short- and long-term goals, think of a staircase with a long-term goal at the top, the present level of ability at the lowest step, and a sequence of progressively linked short-term goals connecting the top and bottom steps. This ties the accomplishment of specific short-term goals to the achievement of a long-term goal.

Based on your progress toward your short-term goals, you may need to reevaluate your long-term goal and set it either higher or lower. In essence, short-term goals are important because they provide feedback concerning progress toward the long-term goal. In addition, short-term goals allow you to focus on smaller increments in improvement that may seem more attainable than an otherwise seemingly impossible long-term goal.

Let's say that you have a long-term goal to become a professional sport official. To monitor your improvement, you might set some short-term goals each game, such as improving your knowledge of the rules, being more decisive, staying calm under pressure, communicating better with coaches and athletes, or becoming more confident (of course these would need to be set in more behavioral and specific terms). This does not mean that you will improve with every game, but short-term goals provide a yardstick by which to evaluate your progress each time you put on your officiating uniform.

Ink It, Don't Think It

The old adage "Out of sight, out of mind" certainly is applicable to the process of setting goals. Several sport psychologists (e.g., Weinberg and Gould, 2011) have emphasized the importance of writing down and recording goals. Doing so will likely increase your commitment to your goals in the form of increased effort and persistence. Charting your progress on paper can help you hang in there during difficult times.

There are several ways to record and monitor your goals, but one way is to record your goal statements and achievements in a notebook. This written feedback can be a powerful motivator and sustain your effort over time. The key thing is not simply to write your goals down; rather, you should make sure they are available and remain salient. Find a highly visible spot to post them so they stay fresh in your mind. Goals written on a card and posted on your bedroom mirror are more effective than an in-depth behavioral contract that you sign and place in a drawer never to be looked at again.

Develop Goal Achievement Strategies

Understanding all goal-setting theories and principles is not going to be very helpful if you do not develop implementation strategies. Along these lines, Locke and Latham (2006) proposed that one of the mechanisms underlying the effectiveness of goals in enhancing performance is the development of relevant learning strategies. Unfortunately, research indicates that many people set goals with no real plan for achieving them; they believe that somehow just by setting a goal, their performance will be miraculously enhanced. In essence, setting goals without developing corresponding goal achievement strategies is like driving a car to a strange city without consulting a map. You must have strategies to accompany the goals you set.

Let's say that one of your goals is to improve your conditioning so you can sustain a high level of performance throughout each officiating assignment. What are you going to do to improve your conditioning? At this point you need to identify a strategy to help you reach your goal. This might involve engaging in aerobic exercise (e.g., running, cycling, stair climbing) for 30 minutes per day for three or four days a week and reducing your caloric intake by 500 calories a day (determined by keeping a food journal). The key is that you must identify learning strategies and incorporate them into your training regimen to actively pursue the goal of improving your fitness level.

Prioritize Various Types of Goals

Many officials have a long-term goal of moving up to the next higher level such as moving from high school to college or from college to the professional leagues, or maybe from Division III to Division I. This would be considered an *outcome goal* because it focuses on the result of your efforts and is mostly out of your control. In essence, even if you do well in all your officiating assignments, you are not guaranteed of moving up to the next level, because someone else decides that.

Although there is nothing wrong with having outcome goals, your focus should be on *process goals*. These are goals that are under your control and can help you reach your outcome goal. For example, if your outcome goal is to officiate at the next higher level, your process goal might be to use imagery to imagine yourself making tough calls at the end of the game with a loud crowd, to practice good listening and communication skills, or to run three miles several days a week to stay in shape. Focus on process rather than outcome goals; if you achieve your process goals, you are likely to achieve your outcome goals. Even if you don't get moved up to the next level of officiating, you are focusing on what you can do as an official, which is all you can do.

Set Positive Goals

You should always word your goals in a positive manner. That is, try to identify the things you would like to do instead of things you don't want to do. Telling yourself not to do something calls attention to the undesired act. If there is a behavior you want to reduce or to eliminate, set a goal to do an alternative, positive behavior.

For example, if you want to reduce the number of times you hesitate before making a call, don't set a goal not to hesitate. Rather, set a goal to improve your decisiveness by practicing making calls immediately after you blow your whistle. In addition, use imagery (see chapter 7) to reinforce your positive goal. Specifically, imagine yourself in situations in which you have been indecisive in the past and imagine yourself blowing your whistle and making a quick, decisive call in an assertive, confident manner. This will help you focus on responding successfully in a situation that has been troublesome in the past. In this way, you are practicing making your decisive response more automatic and just part of what you do as an official.

Provide for Feedback

Once you have set your goals and are committed to achieve them, you need to have a clear way to obtain feedback regarding your movement toward achieving your goals. Feedback sometimes is very evident, such as getting on the scales and seeing that you've lost 6 pounds in a month with your goal being 10 pounds. Other times, progress toward achieving your goal is not as easy to discern (especially if your goal is more subjective).

If you have a goal to control your temper, how would you know that you have achieved or are making progress toward the goal? One way

Officials have to maintain their poise at all times, especially when dealing with unruly crowds.

is to get feedback from an objective observer such as another official or someone else knowledgeable about officiating your sport. Another way would be to objectively define what you mean when you refer to controlling your temper. Does it mean that you hand out fewer technical fouls (in basketball) or that you get into fewer shouting matches with players or coaches over contested calls?

Another way to obtain feedback is to periodically perform a self-assessment regarding your progress toward achieving your goals. Keeping a game-by-game diary of your performance with a particular emphasis on your goals is good way to help determine whether you are on target to achieving your goals. In fact, NFL officials are required to keep a diary every game, which provides them with important feedback regarding their performance. Just as athletes often complete self-assessments regarding their performance, you can also devise a self-assessment, rating yourself along criteria seen as important to reaching your goals or performing well. Following are some questions you might consider as part of a self-assessment:

- How well do I listen to coaches and athletes before responding?
- How well do I understand all the rules of the game?
- How consistently am I in the right position to make the proper call?
- How well do I handle stressful situations?
- How confident am I when I make my calls?
- How well do I maintain my focus of attention throughout a competition?
- How well do I communicate on court with other officials?
- What are the area(s) I need to work on the most?
- How well do I bounce back from making a mistake?

WAS GOAL SETTING SUCCESSFUL?

Interviews of performers in a variety of fields such as business and sports, along with numerous anecdotal reports, reveal that people are often good at getting a goal-setting program started but not very good at seeing it through.

More specifically, one of the most overlooked aspects of setting goals is the evaluation component. In essence, you must ask yourself: Were my goals helpful in making me more successful? As Locke and colleagues (1981) found, evaluative feedback is essential for goals to be effective in enhancing performance. Therefore, it is critical to receive feedback concerning the effectiveness of your goals and to implement goal evaluation strategies continuously throughout the goal-setting process.

Interviews have revealed that most coaches have at least an informal process for goal reevaluation during the season, and at times this occurs on a very regular basis. Officials should do the same thing. Specifically, from time to time, you should review your goals to see whether you are making progress toward achieving them or have achieved them already. You can then reevaluate and adjust your goals upward or downward to provide new motivation and commitment. You need to determine whether goal setting has been successful or what you need to change to become more successful. The sidebar on page 52 provides an example of an official using goal-setting principles.

COMMON PROBLEMS WHEN SETTING GOALS

This chapter thus far has focused on principles to follow when implementing goal setting. Although goals can help improve performance and change behavior, implementing a goal-setting program is not always easy—it requires planning and knowledge about the goal-setting process. People face some common problems when attempting to systematically set goals. Understanding and anticipating these problems can soften their potential negative effects.

Lacking Self-Knowledge

One of the most common errors in any psychological intervention in sport is not recognizing individual characteristics. In the case of coaches, this is about not recognizing the individual qualities of athletes. In the case of officials, this is about not recognizing your own personality makeup, likes and dislikes, attitudes, and values. In essence, it is difficult to achieve goals that are not consistent with your self-concept and self-image. For example,

Using Goal Setting: A Practical Example

Bill was a high school basketball official for 10 years, but he wanted to become a college official. He knew he had to improve in several areas, so he set out to systematically set some goals for himself.

1. The first thing Bill did was assess the areas in which he wanted to improve. These included getting in better shape, making sure his positioning was correct when working with two other officials, communicating more effectively with coaches, keeping his anxiety under control, and making sure he knew any college rules that differed from high school rules.

2. Next, Bill wrote his goals down and put them on his mirror at home so he could see them every day.

3. Bill then made sure that his goals were specific and measurable, and he created an action plan to help him reach them. For example, regarding his communication with coaches, he determined to always take a couple of seconds and a deep breath before responding to negative coach comments. He committed to role-play five minutes each day to get himself accustomed to dealing with this situation. Similarly, regarding getting in better shape, he decided to go to the gym three or four times a week and do cardiorespiratory (aerobic) activity for 30 minutes each time (to improve his speed or distance traveled, which he would check once a month). He scheduled his gym time for 7 a.m. to make sure he would get it done.

4. Bill developed a chart in which he could track the progress he was making toward reaching his goals. If he was not making good progress, he would revisit his goal and determine whether to change it.

5. Bill rewarded himself when he believed he had achieved a goal or made significant progress toward his goal (e.g., buying a piece of clothing he really wanted).

if you believe that you will never be successful as an official (because you are a pessimistic person), then you will probably never achieve a goal of officiating at the next level.

An interesting characteristic of officials (as well as coaches and athletes) is their form of goal orientation (i.e., task versus ego), which makes a significant difference in the specific goals that will be effective. Research indicates that goal effectiveness is maximized when a person's goal orientation and types of goals are matched. *Task-oriented* officials are most motivated by goals focusing on self-improvement, which tend to be in their control (e.g., remaining calmer and taking a deep breath after a coach or athlete argues about a call), whereas *ego-oriented* officials are most motivated by goals that focus on outcome (e.g., whether they move up to a higher competitive level such as high school to college).

Two other important characteristics in the goal-setting area that research has substantiated are preferred goal difficulty and self-efficacy. Specifically, people (including officials) prefer moderately difficult goals, some prefer difficult goals, whereas others prefer moderate goals. You may like to be challenged by very difficult goals because they motivate you to try harder, or you may not want to fail and therefore prefer moderate goals that you are more confident of attaining. Regarding self-efficacy (self-confidence), research has revealed that there is a strong relationship between a person's level of self-efficacy and goal attainment, with high self-efficacy being associated with high goal attainment. Therefore, you must make sure that your confidence stays high, because this is related to goal attainment.

Resisting Goal Setting

Over the years, researchers have found that people in all fields (e.g., athletes, officials, musicians, managers) often need to be convinced to set goals because they have misperceptions about goals and the goal-setting process. Many people believe that goal setting takes too much time. However, goal setting actually results in structuring time much more efficiently. Some people are concerned that if they set goals and don't reach them, they will become a public failure. Because goal failure typically results from setting goals outside of one's control, the focus should be on process goals rather than outcome goals (as noted earlier), which are typically under one's control. Officials often value outcome over process, however, so focusing on process goals requires a concerted effort.

Finally, some people believe that goal setting is too structured and therefore will hamper their spontaneity. However, writing out and working toward specific goals does not mean losing spontaneity or becoming rigid. It simply is a way to focus on accomplishing the things you believe are important.

Failing to Monitor Goal Progress and Readjusting Goals

People are often excited about setting goals and set lots of them at first, and officials are no exception. But as time passes, these goals are often forgotten or at least put on the back burner. Often, situations occur that throw people off course in meeting their goals. With officials it can simply be not prioritizing their officiating goals and thus not finding the time to work at them, getting injured, or simply forgetting their goals. It is therefore critical that you consistently monitor your goals and reevaluate them if necessary.

Let's say that you incurred an injury that kept you from getting into shape and reaching your goal of being able to run three miles in 24 minutes before the start of the soccer season. You know you need to stay in shape to be in the proper position to make the correct calls. Therefore, you may need to adjust your goal to running three miles in 30 minutes and maybe reach your goal of 24 minutes later the soccer season. In essence, instead of losing motivation and possibly letting your goal fall by the wayside, you can establish a new goal based on your current level of fitness and performance. After reevaluating your goals, write them down and post them in a prominent spot so you can see them on a regular basis.

Failing to Set Specific, Measurable Goals

Probably the most frequent problem in setting goals is the failure to set specific and measurable goals. People seem to have a propensity for simply setting general goals such as *improving my fitness, keeping my temper in check, improving my knowledge of the rules,* or simply *doing my best.* These goals are not as effective as more specific goals such as reading one chapter a night of the rule book.

Setting Too Many Goals at the Start

When starting to set goals, many people are very motivated and want to accomplish lots of things. Unfortunately, at the start of many goal-setting programs people often bite off more than they can chew. This is especially the case for those with little experience in goal-setting techniques. It is not the number of goals that causes the problem; rather, it is the fact that monitoring and tracking these goals becomes extremely difficult and time-consuming.

As an official, you can improve in many areas, including knowledge of your sport, communication, proper technique and positioning, and decision making (just to name a few). Monitoring goals in all of these areas can be extremely difficult and create added stress. Therefore, particularly if you have little goal-setting experience, set only a couple of high-priority goals that you can track and measure relatively easily (see earlier examples).

Setting a Goal to Please Someone Else

Although we should set our own goals, at times we are unduly influenced by others and set goals to please them rather than to please ourselves. Children do this when they set a goal they know their parents would want them to achieve, but they may not be committed to the goal. This can also happen to officials as well.

Let's say that your supervisor has been strongly suggesting that you attend an officials' clinic that focuses on knowing all the rules and their interpretations. You don't really want to go, but you set a goal to go to please your supervisor. However, once you get there, you are really bored, don't pay much attention to the speakers, and do not even attend several sessions. Thus, although you set a goal and even achieved it by attending the clinic, you didn't improve yourself, which was the purpose of attending the clinic. The case study in the sidebar on page 54 highlights some of the typical problems officials have when attempting to set goals.

Goal-Setting Problems

Sally had done a little officiating with young athletes but really wanted to get into more structured officiating at the high school level. She knew she had to improve in several areas, so she went about setting some goals. However, she fell into the trap that many people do of not setting goals to maximize her performance.

- First, Sally decided that all she could do was her best, so she set do your best goals in the areas in which she wanted to improve (positioning, confidence, communication with players and coaches, and technique). Unfortunately, research clearly demonstrates that specific, challenging goals produce better performance than do your best goals, because people do not know what really constitutes their best.
- Because Sally knew she needed to improve in several areas to be a high school official, she set several goals. However, research shows that setting goals in too many areas diffuses effort and lessens the likelihood of reaching any of the goals.
- Finally, like many people, Sally had good intentions but never really monitored her progress toward her goals. She really wanted to improve but could never find the time to actually work on achieving her officiating goals.

SUMMARY

Staying motivated as an official can sometimes be difficult because officials seldom receive public praise and certainly the financial remuneration is not high. One effective way to sustain motivation is through the use of goal-setting. When set correctly, goals have been shown to be a very effective tool for both short and long-term motivation as well as improving performance. But to be effective, goal-setting principles need to be followed, such as setting goals that are realistic; have short and long-term rewards; and are written down, measureable, challenging, and positive. It is extremely important to develop specific strategies to implement and accomplish these goals.

In addition, goals should be prioritized with a focus on process (what you need to actually do to be effective). There are potential problems with setting goals, but these road blocks are more in the mind of the person rather than actually being problematic in and of themselves. So get started with your goal-setting program–start slow with the most important goals and then add on different goals as you get more comfortable with the program.

REVIEW QUESTIONS

1. Which of the following is *not* a subjective goal?
   a. Stay relaxed while officiating.
   b. Communicate more effectively with coaches.
   c. Stay confident throughout the game.
   d. Be in the right position 95 percent of the time.
   e. Stay fit so as not to get tired at the end of the game

2. Goals work because they
   a. focus attention
   b. increase persistence
   c. increase the use of relevant learning strategies
   d. all of the above
   e. *a* and *b*

3. Which of the following is/are *not* a specific goal?
   a. I want to improve my fitness level.
   b. I will run three times per week for 30 minutes.
   c. I want to improve my self-control.
   d. When a coach starts to yell and shout at me, I'll count to myself for five seconds before responding.
   e. *a* and *c*

4. Officials' goals should focus on
   a. process
   b. outcome
   c. evaluations by their supervisors
   d. *a* and *b*
   e. *b* and *c*

5. Which of the following is/are *not* a goal-setting principle
   a. Set as many goals as you can—the more the better.
   b. Goals should be fairly easy so the official can experience success.
   c. Goals should be specific.
   d. *a* and *b*
   e. *b* and *c*

6. Which of the following is/are a common problem in goal setting?
   a. Setting too many goals
   b. Failing to readjust goals
   c. Setting goals that are too general
   d. All of the above
   e. *a* and *c*

7. A task-oriented official would be most interested in
   a. being the best official in the conference
   b. improving performance from last year
   c. winning the award for the most technically sound official
   d. *a* and *b*
   e. *b* and *c*

Answers on page 187

Chapter 5

Communication Skills

Kay Rooff-Steffen

This chapter addresses the following:

- How to communicate through listening, speaking, and nonverbal communication
- How to evaluate your current interpersonal skills
- How to improve your skills to heighten your communication experience

DEVELOPING EFFECTIVE COMMUNICATION SKILLS

Three general truths about communication are that (1) it is inevitable, (2) it is irreversible, and (3) it is contextual. A fourth truth—and probably the most obvious yet most important of all—is that communication is more complex than most people think.

There is no way to escape the need to communicate clearly with others, particularly in the field of officiating. Rarely do you have the luxury of leisurely contemplating a concern that takes place on a court or field of play. You often need to assess a situation immediately, take action if necessary, and quickly and clearly explain why you made (or did not make) the calls you did. Of course, after the game you also need to talk to other officials, possibly the coaches, and sometimes others regarding calls, rules, or schedules.

Contrary to what we may have believed as children—that we could take back what we

said and people would erase it from memory—we cannot reverse what we say or how we act toward other people. Five-year-olds typically have thoughts enter their brains and flow right out of their mouths. Adults need to think first and make rational decisions about whether to express their thoughts. If you are reading this text, you probably already know that sports officials deal with more inappropriate and immediate criticism than people in many other professions. If you react as you might want to at any given moment, your career will be short-lived. You are no longer five years old. You cannot take back your message once you have sent it.

Contextual communication is well illustrated in sports. It is perfectly fine for football players to slap each other on their helmets or their seats after good plays. This behavior is acceptable *in that context*. Take those slaps into the boardroom, and they are not appropriate. In a boardroom context, people, would interpret those slaps quite differently. A person from the crowd who asks the official, "What are you looking at? Are you blind, ref?" does not expect a response, nor is the remark really directed at the official; rather, the person is simply reacting to a call that went against his player or team. Officials understand this. However, if that person seeks out the official after the game and asks that question point-blank, the message takes on a very different meaning.

Before we express a message verbally or nonverbally, we need to determine our context first. Is it appropriate for you to wink at your colleague after you express your opinion? Can you be sure that your colleague will read your wink the way you intended it?

Contextual Communication

Communication is contextual, as stated earlier. It takes place in the following six realms:

1. **Physical—in a specific locale**

   This could be a locker room, high school auditorium, or boardroom. Each location hints at the kind of communication that would be expected or acceptable.

2. **Temporal—at a specific time**

   A meeting set up for 3 p.m. could be seen quite differently than one scheduled for 9 p.m. or 7 a.m., and certain behaviors can be expected at different times as well.

3. **Situational—under a given set of circumstances**

   If an officiating team obviously did not work well together, when members are called to a meeting shortly after that game, those officials will probably anticipate what will be discussed.

4. **Psychological—with particular frames of mind, including historical factors (i.e., memory)**

   Coaches will come across one way before a game, another way during a close competition, and yet another way after the outcome is decided.

5. **Relational—how the parties are connected**

   We communicate differently at work than we do at home. We might communicate differently at a game we are watching than at one we are calling.

6. **Cultural—why the parties are present**

   Is this an exhibition game, a regular game, or a play-off game? The attention and reaction to every action, play, or score will depend on the nature of the game.

Communication is not simple. Most communication models don't show just a sender on one end, a receiver on the other, and a message in the middle. There is much more to it than that. The sender must first decide on the message and how to express it clearly to the receiver. This process is called encoding. If you are explaining the rules of baseball to young children, you will need to express yourself in a particular way so they will understand. If you send your message the same way to high school or college athletes, however, they will quickly get bored and tune you out because they will believe that you are talking down to them.

Once the message is encoded correctly and sent off to the listener, the listener then must figure out what the sender means. This is referred to as decoding. Based on your words, your tone of voice, your facial expressions, and perhaps your accompanying gestures, the listener will determine what you meant by your overall verbal and nonverbal message.

But, wait! It's even more complex, because in the middle of this sending and receiving we have distractions that get in the way. These distractions are known as communication noise. It might be external, actual noise (cell phone rings, car horns, crowd noise, whistles) or internal noise, which include concerns, panic, random thoughts, defensiveness. or anything running through the mind of the listener—or the sender—before the message gets across.

The Decoding Process

To visualize this decoding process, try this: Gather six friends and one ball. Person 1 is the sender who initially holds the ball. Person 2 is the receiver. Person 1 tosses the ball to person 2. Simple, huh? Sure. Now bring in the encoder, person 3. Person 1 now must toss the ball to person 3, who decides how to toss or hand the ball to person 2, the receiver. Next? Person 4, the decoder, steps in front of the receiver.

Now try this: person 1 hands the message (ball) to person 3 (the encoder); person 3 delivers it to person 4 (the decoder); and person 4 passes it along to the receiver, person 2. This process is slower, but achievable. Finally, we have person 5, symbolizing external noise (singing, yelling, whistling, and waving arms around the others), and person 6, symbolizing internal noise (quietly wandering in and out and around everyone else, much the way our wandering minds tend to distract us). Clearly, sending a simple message takes more focus and organization than we previously thought.

Communication is not easy, but it is essential and must be effective in the officiating profession. When officials at the upper level of sports are observed in critical situations, they outwardly seem to be communicating in a calm, straightforward manner. This behavior does not come naturally, nor is it always easy in stressful, adrenaline-filled situations. Effective communication skills are learned, and officials work very hard to respond sensibly to game conflicts and verbal attacks. (Effective officials are aware of contextual meanings.) They learn to weigh their words carefully (knowing that communication is irreversible), and they continually hone the listening, verbal, and nonverbal skills that will solve—or at least lessen—conflicts rather than escalate problems. Successful officials understand the imperativeness of successful communication.

LISTENING

People listen for essentially five reasons: to gain information, to empathize, to anticipate responding, to make judgments, and to simply be entertained. As a sport official, you need to hone your listening skills so you can hear about rule changes, additions, or deletions at various levels of the sport you work. You listen for officiating needs during your primary sport season and opportunities to work at the next level. You need to determine whether working certain out-of-town games will pay enough to make it worth your while. You listen to your crew members or counterparts to prepare for an upcoming contest. Sometimes at the end of a long day, you listen to the tales your more experienced colleagues share about how the game or profession has changed from when they started working in sports.

Much of what you will learn about your sport is gained through paying attention to what others impart. Rule books may specify formal practices, but rules change—sometimes frequently. Also, the operating conditions in your area can be unique, or provide special challenges. This information is passed on most effectively by word of mouth. Officials tell each other about many on-field or on-court tactics for handling games. This information might include suggestions for conducting pregame rituals, such as talking to coaches or captains. Sometimes officials share this information just hours or even minutes before the game begins. If you are on the receiving end, you are expected to pay attention and learn quickly.

If you are new to officiating or have been inactive in your sport for a while, after you study the current rules, talk to those who are currently working the sport. In addition to learning about ways to start a game, listening carefully to advice from veteran officials will help you acquire knowledge about anticipating unusual game situations, dealing with controversy, and working with game attendants such as ball persons, scorers, and timers. Listening to learn is one of the most important ways to absorb the data necessary for conducting a fair, professionally run event.

Listening to empathize, or to put yourself in the other person's shoes, is also important. This means being aware of another person's emotions and understanding what their expressions mean—words as well as facial expressions such as grimaces, smiles, frowns, and looks of confusion or anger. Listening carefully, in many instances, means more than just processing sounds. It means listening with the eyes and heart as well as the ears. You may try to remain neutral, but that doesn't preclude you from being receptive to the stress and frustrations of others.

Learning to be a good listener helps develop good working relationships between coaches and officials.

Good listening skills will help you understand why you are being challenged and help you empathize with the person who is challenging you. Remember, empathy does not mean sympathy. Empathy means trying to figure out how a speaker is feeling so you can get on the same wavelength. Experienced officials often say that they must tune their antennae to pick up all the nuances of discord.

Once a coach or player has explained an objection completely, you must weigh the information, keeping a firm grasp of the person's reason for making that objection. Often, the reason may appear obvious: the complainant wants the call reversed. But behind some objections are other factors, such as a coach trying to protect a player, trying to save face after a strategic move goes wrong, or even seeking to obtain an edge on future calls through intimidation. Just as you should try to see the whole play, you must also hear the whole story, and this can only happen through effective, focused listening.

As an official, you could separate the possible motivations of a verbal challenge by taking in the entire context of the message, analyzing the hidden messages, and trusting your instincts (as vague as those may be). Your response, however, usually takes one of two forms: denying the challenge, which takes special skills in verbal diplomacy, or offering a solution to the perceived problem. A solution might include consulting with an officiating partner or explaining a rule in clear, straightforward terms. Regardless, before formulating a solution, you must first hear the problem in its entirety.

Many officiating judgments are based on what is seen, naturally, but sometimes they are also based on what is heard. An obvious example of this in many sports is taunting, which is just as often verbal as nonverbal. Consider a baseball game in which a coach calls out, "That pitcher is throwing at my batters!" The context is perhaps the most important element here. What time of the game is it? What is the score? What are the previous game circumstances that affect the present moment? How have you, the official, reacted to previous events? These central questions should pass through your mind while taking in the message and before arriving at a judgment.

Taking a deep breath before you respond can help you process the entire context and permit you to arrive at a reasonable judgment. Keep in mind that rational reactions require thought. Emotional reactions are impulsive—and often backfire because they are triggered by anger. Pause before you speak, and try adhering to the adage, "Engage brain before opening mouth." To monitor your own listening tendencies, keep track one day of how often you interrupt the speech of others. If you interrupt a lot, it means that you are in the habit of not waiting for the whole story. Mentally focus, then, on biting your tongue and listening before you formulate your response.

Listening for entertainment, or pleasure, is another dimension of the aural sense. And, yes, officials do this too. Although you are not likely to take in the chirping of birds or a particularly well-played riff by the drummer in a marching band while working a game, some of the things you hear can be quite entertaining. Listen to what the players say while in action; sometimes their remarks in the heat of battle are very funny, or even heartwarming, triggering your own memories of when you played sports as a young athlete. Many an official has also been moved by a stirring rendition of the national anthem by a talented student singer.

As an official, you can console players sometimes with a kind word or a pat on the arm. You can smile in amusement if their antics are humorous, without upsetting the continuity of the game. You can also empathize with their celebrations as much as you do with their disappointments. Officiating need not be an entirely impersonal role. People play games for fun or satisfaction. Officials should expect the same payoff once in a while.

Improving Your Active Listening Skills

Of the four major communication skills (reading, writing, speaking, and listening), the one we practice most often on a daily basis is listening (Adler and Elmhorst, 2008). Listening is not to be confused with hearing, which is a physical ability; listening is a conscious effort to decode and interpret messages. Active listening entails putting forth mental effort and emotional restraint to grasp the intended message and respond relevantly.

We've discussed why people listen, but how can we improve our listening skills? First, we need to have good reason to hone our skills. If you have ever seen an overworked high school official miss a few key calls in a girls' basketball game, after working a sophomore boys' game and then a JV game with less than an hour break between them, you can appreciate the constant effort it takes to maintain focus and good listening. Even at the upper levels, officials have often worked a full day elsewhere before stepping onto the field or court. Recognizing barriers to effective listening is key to improving this skill and, as a result, officiating more astutely.

One listening barrier is erroneously anticipating a speaker's response and prematurely preparing responses in your head before any message is spoken (or shown, if nonverbal). Have you ever thought that you knew what a speaker was going to say, only to have the speaker surprise you? To overcome this barrier, you need to carry over your goal of fairness to speakers on and off the athletic field. This involves preparing yourself physically so you become fully aware of the listening context. Plant your feet and lean slightly toward the speaker. Maintain eye contact. This does not necessarily mean continuously staring into the speaker's eyes, though, as this could be interpreted as aggressive behavior, particularly if the message is a heated one. A good rule is to glance into the eyes every few seconds and nod occasionally if you either understand or agree. Moving from the speaker's eyes to something to which they are referring or slightly downward and then back to their eyes shows that you are not only listening, but thinking about the message as well.

Another barrier to effective listening is tuning out, or letting your mind wander. This can be a subconscious result of physical or mental fatigue or of deeming the speaker's message unimportant or incorrect. You could also be distracted by something that occurred more recently. When a coach or player approaches you with an issue, you may be mulling over something that just happened instead of focusing on the new message.

One way to conquer the tendency to let your mind wander is to practice mindfulness. Athletes do this all the time. They often refer to it as getting into the zone, or being focused. Before you can make a sound judgment of an action on the field, you must be aware of what just happened. Before you can verbally react to a concern or complaint fairly, you must

be aware of the intent and meaning of the message. This involves another dimension of listening—empathy.

As mentioned earlier, empathy is putting oneself into another person's shoes. When we listen empathically, we listen not only to the speaker's words, but to her actions, expressions, and feelings as well. Is this coach speaking out of frustration, or is she trying to bully you into changing a call? Is this player aware of the language he is using, or is adrenaline controlling his words? Understanding where someone is coming from helps us listen to what a speaker means, not just to the words spoken.

Imagine that you have been working at your day job for seven hours. Suddenly you get a frantic call from an officiating team leader begging you to cover a game for someone who has to work late. You accept (because you are able to do it and you enjoy the team working that night). You have one more hour of work in your office, and then you need to explain to your spouse or children why you cannot go out to dinner and a movie as previously planned. Now consider the following questions:

1. How much true, focused attention do you give to your last hour of work?
2. What is your reaction when you get home and are rushing to get ready for the game, if your spouse or children complain that you never have time for them?
3. Why do you react this way?
4. Would you react differently if you had already been assigned to this game before your workday began and before you made plans with your family? Why?

Letting our emotions interfere with our listening is another barrier to successful communication. An angry word hurled by an athlete at an opponent or at you can trigger a negative emotional reaction. It is almost impossible to listen dispassionately when you are angry, but how can you avoid it? Be conscious that your emotions are ignited—and that stress can shorten your fuse. Self-talk is extremely helpful in defusing negative emotions. Tell yourself, "I'm getting angry. I refuse to let my anger escalate. It's time for me to take a deep breath, suppress my anger, and shift into my active listening mode."

We have all heard the expression, "Think before speaking," and it is good advice. Ask yourself a few quick questions before responding emotionally to a message:

1. What is the relevant message being sent here? (Sometimes we must cut through the emotional triggers, name-calling, or stray complaints to get to the real question.)

2. Is this an appropriate time, place, and setting for this communication?

3. Do I need to show my emotions here? Is that display relevant to this communication? (Kelly, 2006)

4. Do I want to continue officiating, knowing full well that an official is the target of highly charged comments during athletic competitions?

One other barrier is easy to identify—external noise. What is this? Close your eyes and listen. Everything you hear is external noise. In normal activities, we have conditioned ourselves to filter out irrelevant noise, but sometimes it isn't so easy to do. For officials, like athletes, this is vital for success. The next time you are watching a basketball or volleyball game, see if you can close your eyes and count how many different noises you hear. How many people are shouting advice at athletes? How many spectators are talking loudly, chanting, or cheering? Do you hear coaching going on from the sidelines? Laughter? Buzzers? Music? Cell phones?

As an official, you must learn to filter out extraneous noise and attend to the messages you find important. Shut off all assaults of sound and just concentrate on working the game. You may not eject a parent or fan for shouting, "You missed that call, ref," or "What were you looking at, ump?" Those comments are irrelevant to your role, so realize that those are emotion-driven comments and are not directed at you personally but at how the game is going for that spectator. Filter them out and move on.

VERBAL SKILLS

Although a comparably small part of the three interpersonal communication skills— listening, verbal, and nonverbal—verbal skills are essential in everyday life for securing our preferences, negotiating personal alliances, building and maintaining relationships, and advancing our careers. An official's status

and progress are often determined by her degree of skill in spoken language. Before determining how officials should talk, we need to examine the purpose of communication with the psychological and cultural contexts in mind.

In which contexts must officials communicate verbally? To illustrate this, consider how NFL officials prepare for a typical game. At

---

Choosing Words Carefully

"You make the difference. Be courteous, approachable and confident."

These simple, meaningful words of inspiration come from the University of Idaho's *Intramural Sports Official's Handbook* (Revised 2010). In this handbook for officials-in-training, readers (and soon-to-be officials) are reminded to treat every contest as significant. It states, "To participants, it may be the most important game of their lives (p. 3)." The same should hold true with officials, the authors stress.

Communication needs to be clear and complete. Before the game, the officiating team needs to understand the mechanics and court or field positioning. During the game, players, coaches, and fellow officials might need to be reminded of their roles or the consequences of their actions. After the game, calls might need to be thoroughly explained, regardless of the skill level of the players.

You need to know how to assert yourself without being overbearing. You need to work—and speak—in a way that does not put players on the defensive.

Novice officials are reminded, essentially, to speak to others the way they would want to be spoken to. "Do not bark," says one tip. "If you don't like being shouted at, don't shout at someone else (p. 9)."

Words need to be chosen with care and forethought. "Do not threaten a coach or player," this handbook states. "This will put them on the defensive and you on the spot (p. 10)."

Sports are already emotion-filled enough without the official adding to the drama.

least one crew member must speak clearly and quickly in the following pregame situations:

1. Meeting with security personnel regarding practices for dealing with fans or objects thrown onto the field

2. Talking to the chain crew

3. Making sure everyone operating the clocks understands expectations and procedures

4. Visiting with coaches from both teams and notifying them of any special rules that might go into effect if there are extenuating circumstances

5. If the game is televised, speaking with sound technicians about operating microphones for announcing calls

6. Meeting with the television production crew to confirm the game time

7. Notifying each team of when they have so many minutes to report to the field

The most important thing to keep in mind is this: Meanings are *not* in words; meanings are in people. As an official, you must be aware of the *connotative meanings* of words and phrases. Whereas *denotative meanings* are those you find in the dictionary, connotative meanings are what the words mean in context. An insurance underwriter may use certain professional jargon during his day job, but at night, while he is wearing his striped officiating shirt, he will use a whole new vocabulary. *No smoke, healthy five* and *line feed* are phrases that take on specific meanings to his fellow officials that others outside the field might not understand at all. Part of succeeding in any field is learning to speak correctly and understand the language of the job. Officials use many acronyms (DPL, OPI, ICT) to do their jobs efficiently. These acronyms are a kind of code language among officials (respectively, they mean defensive pass interference, offensive pass interference, and illegal contact) (Stern, 2010).

Proper positioning and adjusting to plays is an important quality for all officials.

Most officials practice pregame introductions with coaches and other game attendants to get acquainted. Introductions often involve small talk about game conditions, the crowd, or the weather. In this role, you should follow regulations by inquiring about the conditions of the game site, the captains' names and numbers, special events connected with the game, and anything else relevant to the environment or time involved. This is not the time to mention anything personal. Avoid intruding on the private thoughts of coaches and game administrators. In preliminary procedures, be direct, formal, and solicitous. You need information, and you need to set the stage for the game. Regardless of whether you happen to know any of the players, their parents, or other coaches, you are not an acquaintance for the duration of this competition. You are the official and must act like the professional you are, regardless of the level of competition.

Once the game starts, any communication between officials and contestants or coaches (e.g., directives to players, answers to questions, warnings, responses to objections, and reactions to game situations) should adhere to the accepted practices for such interchanges. In all communication, including pregame discussions, choose your words carefully so there is no misunderstanding. Poor word choices, even those that may seem so trivial in other, more casual or personal contexts, can greatly affect your professionalism (Rooff-Steffen, 2004). Diplomacy should be the guiding principle all the while you are an acting official.

How would you describe an exciting football play you just watched on television to a good friend? How would you describe the same play to your young children? Would you use the same words? Why or (more likely) why not? How would your word choices differ? In which case might you use swear words casually? Would it be OK if your friend used words similar to yours? How would you feel if your young children used swear words in their conversations with you?

As an official, you need to be constantly aware of the language you use. Regardless of how coaches protest or in what manner disgruntled fans jeer, you must not react with any personal jabs, racial references, or even mild name-calling. This type of language will only trigger further conflict and will probably result in your termination. It is expected that those working in sports officiating not only know how to filter negative criticism, but also can manage their own emotions and adopt relevant responses that are as neutral and formal as possible.

"I've heard enough," or "You've said enough" in a moderate volume and stern tone is about the strongest way you should verbalize the message that the harassment must stop.

Improving Your Verbal Skills

Here are three ways to improve your verbal communication skills:

1. *Address people in respectful terms, even if you are responding to a disrespectful comment.* If a coach or player bellows, "Hey, that was a lousy call!" a soft but firm reply such as, "The pitch was on the outside corner," or "She didn't establish position with both feet on the floor" is just as effective as, or more effective than, an angry response.

2. *Make explanations brief and to the point.* You are not on trial; you were hired because you are expected to know the rules and have more astute skills of observations than the distracted spectators or adrenaline-filled coaches.

3. *Avoid using technical jargon to others on the field.* Only use terms that are readily understood, such as takedown, foot fault, or over the line.

NONVERBAL SKILLS

Just as you need to choose your spoken words carefully, so do you need to choose the language you speak with your face, body, and tone of voice (i.e., nonverbal). Some writers assert that nonverbal communication constitutes more than 70 percent of the message received. As your mother or grandmother may have said, "It's not what you say, but how you say it."

Imagine that you are in your office thinking about which crew members to assign to which team or game. A colleague walks by and sees you staring at your computer screen with your chin in your hands. "What's wrong?" she asks. Your reply is a slight smile in her direction and a quiet "Nothing," with eyebrows raised and a small shrug. A couple of minutes later, another person stops by your desk and asks, "Hey, what's wrong?" You wonder why every-

AP Photo/The (Troy) Messenger, Thomas Graning

Learning to handle conflicts during a game is the foundation for any officiating career.

one thinks something is wrong—and has to weigh in. You square your shoulders, sit up straighter, and look this person squarely in the eye, replying sternly, but still in an even tone, "Nothing." At the end of the word you now raise your eyebrows, but with no smile, as if challenging him to continue. That person mutters an apology and walks away. Too soon after that encounter, a third person wanders by and sees you, now with a frown on your face, still thinking of how to make the most of the officials you have available before making the assignments. "You look a little upset," that person observes, "What's wrong?" Now you have had it with the constant interruptions and slap your hands on your desk, close your eyes, and shout, "Nothing!" Has your word changed? No. But your message indeed has taken on new meaning each time.

Verbal communication involves words. Only words. Nonverbal communication is far more expansive and includes the following types of communication and more: facial expressions, eye contact, gestures, movement, tone of voice,

rate of speech, and volume. Sounds called *nonfluencies* are also included in this category. These include grunts, audible yawning, vocalizations such as *um, er, uh, huh, hmm*—any sounds you make that are not words but still mean something. Your posture also sends a message, as does your touch.

Proximity is important to the message received as well. Proximity means nearness. Is a coach in your face expressing aggression? Is someone purposely waiting until she is across the room before shouting something to you, knowing you will not respond equally loudly, or knowing you will be embarrassed by the comment? Do you wait until you are next to someone before delivering an important or confidential message? Proximity definitely matters.

Officials rely on nonverbal communication extensively. They use hand signals, obviously, and body positioning, but they also understand why some people say things certain ways and can filter out emotion-laden tones to get to the meat of the message.

It is vital to understand nonverbal communication for four main reasons:

1. *Nonverbal communication is more meaningful than verbal communication.* If your words say, "I understand how you feel," but you roll your eyes and shake your head, your message will say, "I think your point is trivial or pointless."

2. *Nonverbal communication is ambiguous.* Officials see acting all the time. Players who get a little nudge fall down on the court in the hope that their opponents will get called for charging or at least a foul. Someone says something and then winks. Is this a meaningful wink, or is there something in her eye? And interestingly, men and women differ markedly in the way they read facial expressions. Studies show that women judge facial expressions more accurately than men do; men don't register the subtle eye or mouth movements easily (Thayer, 2000).

3. *Nonverbal communication is constant.* A universal truth of nonverbal communication is that we cannot not communicate. Even silent responses send messages. A curl of the lip, a tilt of the head, relative pitch and emphasis on each syllable, or certain words and even pauses between words convey meanings. People frown, fidget, smile, sigh, move, blink, and breathe. (Kelly, 2006). Every one of those actions communicates something, depending on the context and previous message received. If you are aware of these nonverbal tells, you can better control how you communicate with others.

4. *Nonverbal communication is learned behavior.* Although we teach children what certain words mean, we don't often educate them about the even more vital language of nonverbal communication. Nonverbal communication is often seen as the most credible part of the message. (Consider the previous example of replying, "Nothing.") Because it is learned behavior, nonverbal communication, like speaking, can be monitored and improved.

Your nonverbal behavior must convey the same message as the words you use, particularly when making decisions or judgment calls. You won't be taken seriously if you smile and say, "Don't let that happen again." You need to be aware of spatial elements such as proximity and posture; vocal elements such as tone, rate, and volume; and visual cues such as eye contact, hand gestures, and facial expressions. Strive for self-awareness to make sure all of your visual and auditory cues underscore their basic intent, which is to competently and clearly make the call.

Improving Your Nonverbal Skills

As with all of the communication skills, monitoring your own behavior is the first step in improvement. It often helps to enlist the help of another person to get objective feedback about how you communicate nonverbally and whether your body or facial language jives with

---

Body Language Drill

Stand facing another person (or a mirror), and try to convey the following messages without words, using only your hands (held about chest high) and facial expressions. Notice that creating gestures does not take much imagination; they come quite naturally.

- A warning that a quarrel should cease.

- A reply to an inquiry, such as a request for an explanation or more information.

- A disclaimer, such as "I am unable to address that issue" or "That is impossible to rectify."

- A denial of validity, such as "Your point is wrong."

- A cessation or closure of communication, such as "This conversation is over; your plea is denied."

Awareness of often subtle factors of nonverbal communication, such as simple hand gestures, can help you immensely. Ask your observer to cite specific, observable improvements you could make to your responses or reactions to improve your communication.

the verbal messages you are sending. Role-play the following scenarios with another person. Ask a third party to observe the exchange and assess the nature of the messages you delivered.

- Before a high school basketball game, the home team coach explains that he wants to put in the team's special needs manager before the end of the first half and asks for your cooperation. You have never dealt with this situation before. What do you need to clarify to prepare for this? After the exchange, take a mental inventory of how you reacted. Did your movements or facial expressions signal a cooperative attitude, or did you appear impatient?

- A player who has been trash-talking for most of the game tells you that an opponent has committed an unfair act. What facial expressions and upper-body motions did you exhibit while hearing the complaint and while responding? Was your response professional and appropriate? Did you tend to believe or sympathize with this player?

- You are working a wrestling meet with a coach you knew years earlier who has been called back to coaching after a long hiatus. The rules have changed in that time, yet during the match, he calls out that you have missed a major violation.

You know that the rule to which he is referring has changed, but he is getting louder. What is your initial reaction? Analyze both your verbal and nonverbal behavior during this exchange.

SUMMARY

Three key skills in effective communication are active listening, verbal communication, and nonverbal communication. You need to be mindful of the present context and listen to both the words and actions to best evaluate a message being sent. You also need to attempt to put yourself in the sender's shoes and listen with empathy. Although the words in a message are not as meaningful as how those words are delivered, you must choose your words purposefully. Remember your role as a professional, and verbally communicate in sync with your purpose. Nonverbal communication constitutes well over half of any message. To deliver a credible message, be aware of your tone, facial expressions, body movements, and more.

The first step in effective communication in any context, not just in the world of officiating, is monitoring how you currently communicate. By asking others to observe how you speak and act in specific contexts, you will realize how others see you and how you can improve.

REVIEW QUESTIONS

1. What is meant by the statement "Communication is inevitable?"

2. Why must officials be aware of communication contexts?

3. Give three examples of internal noise that officials might deal with.

4. What are three reasons people listen?

5. Why is it important for officials to listen with empathy?

6. Which barrier(s) to effective listening do you find yourself challenged with occasionally?

7. What is the difference between denotative and connotative meanings?

8. In which situations must officials speak clearly?

9. Why is it important for officials to practice diplomacy in choosing their words?

10. Why is nonverbal communication even more important than verbal communication?

11. How could you improve your nonverbal communication?

Answers on page 188

Chapter 6

Decision-Making Skills

Jerry Grunska

This chapter addresses the following:

- The eight essential elements that go into making appropriate decisions
- How to apply decision-making skills in game situations
- How to react companionably with others to ensure accurate judgments
- Modern electronic techniques for honing skills

This chapter explores the decision-making skills you need to become an accomplished official. It also presents ways to evaluate those skills along with suggestions for improving them. The emphasis is on mastering the protocols and nuances of sport so you can administer games intelligently. You must absorb a considerable amount of knowledge and then be so steeped in the game's intricacies that the knowledge becomes ingrained and translates into rapid-fire, automatic decision making. When you make a call, you shouldn't have to think consciously about it.

Important decisions must be made throughout every contest, with perhaps the most vital ones being choices to do nothing; that is, allowing events to happen without interfering. You must learn to move with the game, and that includes anticipating plays so you are in the proper position to make calls. You must know which acts are legitimate and which are not. To be perceived as competent, you must understand and promote the game's signature

rhythms, communicate decisions effectively, and be able to work with partners. Games are often officiated by groups of officials who must work together as well-synchronized teams.

Here are the keys for making good decisions during games:

- Know the rules.
- Know the language of the sport.
- Master the signals, and employ them properly.
- Adapt to the game's rhythms and strategies.
- Be in proper position.
- Concentrate and focus on the essential elements.
- Remain calm.
- Work closely with fellow officials.

KNOW THE RULES

Many experienced officials prepare for each season by reading the entire rule book. They refer to it throughout the season as well. However, rule books are best studied piecemeal, one rule at a time or a few pages at a sitting. They really cannot be read like adventure stories; in fact, sometimes it is best to jump into the text at random instead of taking the sequential approach. For a beginner, trying to absorb all of the intricacies of a sport—even learning the rules language—can indeed be a challenge.

Perhaps the best way for a beginner to learn the rules and their implications is to attend a class in which the sport's jargon is introduced and discussed. Going over rules with an acquaintance is also useful, but the best system is to have a knowledgeable person, such as an experienced official, explain the facets of seemingly simple definitions. Local associations also have rules study groups (officials have to pass a yearly exam to remain certified in most states), plus they offer hints about on-field and on-court techniques, which are called mechanics (see chapter 12 for more information about associations for sports officials).

You have to know exactly what is permitted by the rules. Softball or baseball coaches may want to talk to pitchers, for example, and football and basketball coaches frequently call players to the sidelines for instructions. You must know when and how such communications are permissible. After a sideout in volleyball, you must know how much time a server may take before delivering the ball. After a foul strike in baseball, the limitations of a pitcher's motions before offering the next pitch are specified by the rules. When two wrestlers slide off the mat, you must have a clear notion of when to blow the whistle to hold up action and how to position the combatants correctly for renewing action. The average fan is unlikely to know all of these requirements. You, however, had better have them mastered.

The following sections offer suggestions for learning the rules in logical order.

Terms and Definitions

An official must know exactly what constitutes a legal screen in basketball, a legal pitch in softball or baseball, and a legal block in football. The definitions of these actions delineate what is correct and incorrect for proper rulings. Because the actions of players are swift, you must have parameters firmly in mind when viewing such behavior. Definitions are at the heart of the game and must be memorized.

Player Rights and Restrictions

Descriptions of appropriate player behavior are extensions of the game's basic definitions. Football players may sometimes run with the ball after picking it up from the ground, but at other times they may not. A basketball player may retain possession of the ball after falling down in some very specific and carefully described circumstances. A baseball or softball player may run out of a baseline when certain conditions exist. To execute accurate rulings, you must know what players are free to do.

Violations and Penalties

When a player does something that the rules forbid, including exhibiting unsporting behavior, consequences are spelled out in the rules. In soccer, when a kicked ball hits a player's hand, the rules describe how the circumstances govern the ruling. When a volleyball batted across the net strikes an opponent's head, you must know instantly how to react. In football, a foul during a running play is penalized differently from a foul during a passing play, and spiking the ball is forbidden. The rules explain these differentiations, and you must commit them to memory.

Description of the Game, Including Scoring

The rudiments of play may be well known by a person who has played the sport, but some intricacies of scoring may not be so clear. The football official must know how to treat a kick from placement that hits a goalpost. A baseball or softball umpire must know when to award a runner an extra base, just as a basketball official must know what constitutes

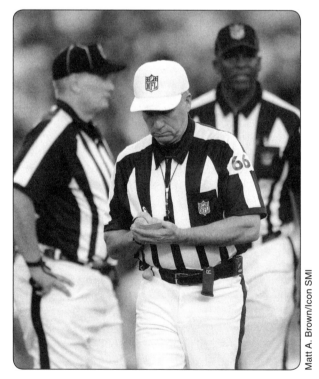

Football officials at all levels must keep track of many things, including writing down scores, timeouts, and penalties.

Matt A. Brown/Icon SMI

a successful free throw. In basketball the rim of the basket and the imaginary cylinder above it have freedoms and restrictions that are carefully delineated by rules. Some invasions of that cylinder by players' hands and arms are forbidden (called goal tending), but other actions inside it (dunking) are permitted. Descriptions of playing and scoring cover the obvious purposes of teams, and they also explain the rare events that may not be clear at first glance.

Dimensions

Although you will probably not be expected to know playing surfaces' measurements or equipment specifications in detail, you must be able to use the rule book as a reference if irregularities are brought to your attention. Some gyms do not meet rule book specifications, and a few baseball and softball diamonds may also be irregular. In these cases special ground rules are usually adopted to deal with the anomalies. Also, in these instances, the safety of the players is the paramount concern.

Peripheral Regulations

In some sports, players' names and uniform numbers have to be recorded correctly in score books. Officials are responsible for approving this. Also, in some sports, playing equipment is very precisely specified, as are requirements for uniforms and protective gear. Players are often forbidden to wear certain items, such as jewelry or derogatory messages on their clothing. As an official, you have to learn what to permit and what to forbid.

In today's sports programming, television watchers and on-site spectators may witness aberrations in player behavior, particularly at the professional level. To some degree, professional play is as much entertainment as sport and often includes boastful or taunting behavior, whereas amateur athletics eschew such behavior. How professionals act is sometimes considered unsporting behavior when teenagers do it. You must know what to accept and what to penalize according to the rules. In many cases this requires making fine distinctions about behavior in games.

Rare Occurrences

An unusual event occasionally takes place during a game: several violations happen almost simultaneously, a ball lodges in an unexpected place, or a player does something peculiar (e.g., a football player comes off the sidelines to tackle a runner). The rules generally account for odd circumstances, and you must know how to make decisions when a rare event takes place.

KNOW THE LANGUAGE OF THE SPORT

Basic to any sport is its formal language, and the essence of this lies in the rule book's definitions of terms. A bunt, an infield fly, and the strike zone, for example, are very carefully defined in baseball and softball rule books. If you can recite the definition of the strike zone in rule book terms, you have a better chance of getting it right consistently, just as recalling the definition of traveling may serve a basketball official. A wrestling official has to have the meanings of *takedown* and *escape* firmly in mind to make effective rulings.

Players' positions in the game have names: forwards, guards, tackles, fullbacks, wideouts, quarterbacks, snappers, shortstops. Their play actions have names too: screening, dribbling, passing, batting, fielding, pitching, relaying, shooting, blocking, guarding. You have to know exactly what these designations mean in the rules to pass judgment on game maneuvers.

You must learn and master the rules lingo until you can both speak the language and think in it. Rote memorization is the only route to a solid grasp of these fundamentals; a diligent reading of the sport's case book will then illustrate the application of these terms—that is, how the definitions operate in various game situations.

MASTER THE MECHANICS OF COMMUNICATING DECISIONS

A basketball official blows a whistle to announce a foul. Immediately after sounding the whistle, the official has several prescribed steps to follow. Step 1 is pointing toward the feet of the accused player while raising the other arm overhead, hand clenched in a fist. Step 2 is remaining poised momentarily to observe any follow-through or retaliatory actions by players. Step 3 is turning to the scoring table and reporting the foul, a customary system of flashing the number of the offending player, the type of foul, and the ultimate result, either a throw-in from out of bounds or a free throw.

Each sport has such designated systems for announcing decisions. Sometimes they are solely visual, using arm and hand semaphores, and sometimes they include vocalization. In baseball and softball, for instance, it is important for an umpire to accompany a gestured call at a base with a vocal notification because the result of a call often furnishes the impetus for subsequent plays at other bases. In football, signals about the nature of fouls can be given silently (they speak for themselves), but many officials accompany their signaling with a verbal explanation to ensure that violations are communicated to the bench area. Verbalizing is also a good way for officials to assure themselves that they are administering the penalty correctly.

Sometimes an official's decision in a game is a no-call. What may look like a foul from an onlooker's viewpoint may actually be a helpful act (e.g., in football, an opponent may hold a punter upright so that he doesn't tip over, or a tackler may vault over a pile of players to avoid illegal contact). There are no designated signals for no-calls, but some officials use an open-hand gesture, like a baseball safe call, to notify spectators and coaches that they witnessed the act and have concluded that it was legal.

Although we can offer some advice, learning how to make game decisions is something you need to explore on your own in your specific sport. Keep in mind the advice in chapter 2 about learning what to call and what not to call.

You must also learn the sport-specific protocols for how and when to talk to players and coaches, as well as when to explain decisions and when to let decisions speak for themselves. You must also learn when to ask for help from other officials during a game and when to offer help yourself, as discussed later in this chapter.

With the advent of instant TV replays in popular team sports, some rules have been modified to include technical scrutiny. This, in turn, has stimulated the practice of crew (or partner) conferences to share opinions and ensure accurate rulings.

ADAPT TO GAME RHYTHMS AND STRATEGIES

If you are a neophyte official and have played the sport or followed it as a fan, you may already have a reasonable grasp of the game's rules and objectives. However, games have rhythms, rituals, and subtleties that former participants may have forgotten or may never have learned. You should become familiar with these ingredients of the sport to be in tune with its sophisticated aspects.

A football official should develop a regular pace in declaring the ball ready for play; a baseball umpire needs to speed things up by urging players to hurry to their positions between innings; a basketball official should put the ball in a player's hands rapidly for a throw-in. Tempo is a factor in many games and is often determined by the players themselves, although to some degree it is controlled by the officials. You must be aware of the game's inherent rhythms and try not to alter them. Also, do not intrude on the game unnecessarily.

Careless or frivolous breaches of the game's tempo may annoy participants, coaches, and spectators. Their impatience may result in complaints, moans of anguish over routine calls, and even outcries of disagreement. Even many experienced officials are unaware of game rhythms; as a result, they may be puzzled at the expressed frustration from participants and spectators who may subconsciously be responding to needless officiating interruptions.

Some games are very intricate, and the official must be aware of the complexities to anticipate strategic moves by either team. A baseball umpire must know when to expect a sacrifice, a double steal, a squeeze play, a tag-up on a fly, or an attempt to nail the lead runner on a hit to the outfield. Basketball officials must sense a potential press, fast break, trap, or strategic deliberate foul by the team that is behind in the score.

A team that is behind in the score in any sport may employ certain techniques to overcome that disadvantage, just as the team in front will strive to keep its lead. A losing volleyball team may increase its attempts to block spikes instead of simply trying for a defensive dig and subsequent set. A losing baseball team may try to pick runners off base or even block base paths while in the field. A winning football team may reduce its passing attempts and rely on ball control to keep the other team from coming back. In soccer or hockey, a losing team may abandon the net by pulling its own goalie and inserting a replacement as an extra attack player in a desperate effort to score. A solid axiom of officiating asserts, "Anticipate the play, not the foul." You will benefit from a knowledge of strategy that allows you to look for special tactics.

Spectators tend to watch the ball, but officials have to see both the movement of the ball and the actions of other players. In baseball, for example, outfielders must be observed retrieving a hit, runners must be observed to make sure they touch bases and do not run past teammates on the bases, and infielders must be observed to see whether they are placing themselves in the runners' paths. Umpires have to watch a lot of almost simultaneous action, and they have to watch the ball, too, because the ball will take them to the spot where a judgment is necessary.

Almost any sport requires that officials view a wide range of simultaneous player actions. Football may be the most problematic of all. At the snap, more than a dozen people at the line collide in an instant. Others are running pass routes, while defenders are backpedaling in pursuit and players in the offensive backfield are setting up to pass or trying to flee with the ball. If you are a football referee, you must develop the habit of seeing a play unfold as a sequence of discrete, miniature actions and watching the potential receiver instead of the ball. This is called off-ball coverage, and you must know your precise assignment, must hustle to be in a position to make the proper judgment, and must know the rights and restrictions of players toward whom the ball is aimed.

BE IN PROPER POSITION

Along with sound judgment, the mechanics of positioning and moving with the action of the game are fundamental to your role as a sport official. As discussed in the previous section, your attention often must be focused on areas that spectators are not watching: potential recipients of the ball, for instance, or players who are moving so as to obstruct illegally. You must learn how to select and react to the behavior of particular key players. Readying to block an attempted spike in volleyball, running pass routes in football, vying for position under the rim in basketball, and relaying outfield throws in baseball are all examples of vital player actions that may go unnoticed by

With play safety being crucial, wrestling officials must get very close to combatants to make precise, accurate judgements.

spectators. You have to discard your spectator cap when working games.

To be at the proper spot to make correct calls, you have to read what teams are trying to do in games. You have to know how a fast break operates in basketball, for instance, and how teams attack a zone press and half-court trap. In football, you should be able to decipher the strengths of formations such as double wideouts, unbalanced lines, and spread attacks. Baseball and softball infielders sometimes position themselves to cut off a key run, or the team at bat may bunt or try to stretch base runners in an attempt to force the defense into a mistake. Knowing how teams react to the score is a big asset. With knowledge of what a team is trying to do, you can anticipate where the next call is likely to take place and what kind of action to expect. Judicious anticipation allows you to move into the most advantageous position.

Each sport has its carefully detailed manual about reacting to the game: how to observe and where to situate yourself to see things clearly. You can also gain knowledge and effective habits from others (mentors, partners, or association members) or in formal classes. Emulating officials in professional sports is another option, even though you may not aspire to join their ranks. In televised games, close-ups of officials often reveal their facial expressions. They give a distinct impression of alertness without obvious signs of tension. Watch them run from one spot to the next. Their bursts of energy show hustle, a determination to be on top of things and to reach the right place at the right time. Notice them stop to observe a play. They seldom are comfortable making critical decisions on the run. See how an NFL official obtains a runner's forward progress spot or an out-of-bounds designation. Persistent intensity when covering action and exceptional judgment elevate officials to prominent positions. Compare the maneuvers of professionals with those of officials you watch at high school games. See whether they convey an impression of complete control—nothing hesitant and nothing frantic. Some officials at higher levels may actually seem to float to address a proper perspective.

One way top-flight officials practice good tactics is to imagine scenarios in their minds, mentally creating game situations, particular phases that pose problems, problems in judgment and execution, and even problems with

difficult people. All effective people—whether managers formulating an address to staff, engineers mulling the design of a structure, attorneys preparing to address a jury, or sports officials preparing for a game—use imaging, or inward rehearsing, to enhance their performance (this is addressed in more depth in chapter 7).

Despite the best preparation, even seasoned officials find themselves occasionally drawn to the wrong spots on the field or floor. Although professional officials are trained to engage all their senses, taking in the whole play and processing it briefly before making a decision, they unfortunately cannot slow a lightning blur of action, see action from various angles, or replay the action as television cameras can. Mistakes in college and professional officiating are often magnified and repeated by the media, and the prolonged criticism places tremendous pressure on officials at that level of broad exposure.

An official who is out of position to make a call has two choices: make the best long-distance call, or rely on partners. Officials often have signals for communicating with partners when necessary, as discussed later in this chapter.

FOCUS

Just as players focus on what they have to do to achieve success in a game, you must do the same. You have to know when game action sets up a critical decision. When the batter hits a ground ball and runners begin to move, you know that a decision is imminent at a base. Even when runners are obviously safe, you have to be on top of the play to make the call. When bodies collide, you must make an instant choice about the legality of the contact. "Ready or not, here I come," is what play action says to officials.

Dead spots occur in every game, at which point the temptation to let the mind wander is strong. Take these opportunities to review the action so far, assess the current game situation, and analyze what is likely to happen next. Try to anticipate what strategy a coach will employ when play resumes. Dead spots should be opportunities for analyzing the game at hand.

Focus means concentration. Like a superior athlete, you must focus on the game and shut out distractions. A wide variety of irrelevant distractions clamor for attention during a game, so you must search for essential events throughout the game by adopting a narrow focus. Fatigue and overriding outside influences, such as sharp and prolonged criticism, may be obstacles to concentration. You must be able to push these aside to be effective.

BE CALM

Game action and people's responses to it can get hectic from time to time. When something unusual happens in a game, players, coaches, and spectators may become wild-eyed and unreasonable. At such times, you must make a conscious effort to remain calm, to view the flurry dispassionately. The more furious play becomes, the more you should adopt a cool, deliberate approach to ensure a clear vision of what is going on. Sometimes a calculated pause will allow you to process events more clearly. Though this seems to contradict the advice to keep a game moving, an outburst of fury or an exceptionally strange occurrence disrupts the tempo anyway. At these times, you do not want to appear excited or emotionally wrought. In the midst of frenzied action, you will have to work to relax. You may well be the only calm person on the scene.

By measuring people's brain waves, psychologists have discovered that it is impossible to maintain a completely focused mental state at all times. The mind operating at maximum speed, such as when all five senses are zeroed in on game action, can lead to sensory overload, which cannot be maintained for long periods. Such bursts of intense focus cause people to experience anxiety and later drift into lethargy during a swing phase of recovery. When officiating, you should try to maintain an alert but not intense state of mind. You can consciously control your rate of brain wave activity by talking to yourself and programming your reactions.

A deliberate slowing of the mental process can produce a level attitude. The term *level attitude* derives from the training of airline pilots: Keeping the wings level with the horizon in emergencies readily counters a force that interferes with flight. Keeping the wings level is a good image to keep in mind when you are officiating.

The best way to approach a game so that you remain alert but at ease is to use positive self-talk. Assure yourself that the experience is going to be enjoyable, that your decisions will be accepted in a spirit of wholesome competition, and that if problems arise, you are the catalyst who will solve them. Tell yourself: "I'm in charge, but I will use a serene kind of game administration—not demonstrative, but quietly competent. I'll deal with every controversy with a level outlook."

WORK WITH FELLOW OFFICIALS

Often, you'll be paired with other officials when working games. There are sensible ways to get along. Fellow officials will usually tell you how they intend to operate, and they will in turn ask how you plan to work. This is not the time to be vague. Exchange honest points of view about positioning and techniques, and be accommodating. "I like to follow a dribbler from about 10 yards away, in a parallel position," a soccer referee may say. If that is different from what you are accustomed to, instead of insisting on a contrary method, try hard to adjust to your partner's preference. Inflexible officials tend to be mediocre, primarily because they are unable to accommodate the preferences of others.

The mechanics manual for each sport outlines the jurisdictions of particular officials at various points in games. In many geographic regions, special practices for dovetailing and sharing responsibilities have been adopted. For example, you need to know when to leave the infield as a base umpire to judge whether a fly ball or line drive has been trapped, muffed, or caught or has cleared a fence. At the same time, you need to feel confident that a partner is covering for you as players run the bases.

Basketball officials have to rotate coverage, sliding across the floor in smooth synchrony. Football officials are assigned certain areas to observe contact, direction of attack, and pass routes. Sometimes jurisdictions overlap, meaning that more than one official can make a call in a given area. Sometimes the jurisdiction is not well defined, so officials have to notify one another during play action about how they are going to cover a specific area or play.

Meshing duties with others is an art. In some cases visual signals are used, but in other cases vocal cues are necessary. A football official can point to an eligible receiver whom he is going to watch at the snap. A softball or baseball umpire can call "I've got the runner" on a long hit with the bases empty so that the base umpire knows to move toward home plate in case of overthrows. Players sometimes get in the way of officials, so other officials have to compensate. Officials must alert one another as necessary to help a crew member whose view may have been obscured or who may have fallen.

Although you should follow recommended guidelines about your jurisdictions, those guidelines cannot be absolute. If you see a play, you should call it, particularly if you are the only official to see it with certainty.

You should learn when to help and when to get assistance from other officials. It is not always polite to volunteer an opinion. Many officials have dug themselves into the proverbial hole by refusing to seek a partner's help,

If You See It, Make the Call

When a plunge toward the goal occurs in football, customary responsibility for declaring a touchdown rests with the two side officials who are pledged to watch the penetration of the plane—that is, the ball being carried over the goal. But often, a quarterback sneak carries the ball into the end zone, and only the umpire observes it. The quarterback can actually be pushed back into the field of play after nudging the ball across the line. Even referees have seen runners twisted and thrust back after scoring a touchdown. In many parts of the country, officials have devised unobtrusive, partly concealed (hidden from cameras) signals to convey information to one another about possible scores: widening the eyes, tilting the chin, looking away, and so on. After the signal, officials should consult with each other to make sure they are in accord on their ruling.

but just as many get themselves in trouble by saying the wrong thing at the wrong time. One practice that has filtered down from the professional level to the high school level is holding a conference to decide what is right when a question arises about a ruling.

Often, one official is responsible for making a call but a partner has had a better view of the play. Did a punt brush a receiver's leg downfield? Was a pass catchable? Was a pass trapped? Was it tipped? Did it travel forward? These are just a few examples of situations in football that can be clarified by consultation among or between officials. A truly prime football example is the foul called intentional grounding. The word *intentional* means that a referee has to get inside the mind of a passer to presume his purpose. For a foul to be called, a receiver must be in the vicinity when the ball landed. Judgments such as these almost require that officials confer to determine a correct ruling. Players move so quickly in basketball that officials frequently have a hard time identifying who committed a foul (particularly in under-the-basket skirmishes). Again, a brief discussion can also lead to an accurate ruling. If you are just learning to officiate, seek advice from veteran officials about when to ask for help.

Working as a team is crucial for officials, and developing good camaraderie helps facilitate teamwork.

Sometimes, also, a conference about an on-field or on-court happening can clarify an officiating judgment, not just a rule application. Hearing from an earnest partner who had a different angle may result in an accurate consensus about a judgment call.

Modern technology has helped to facilitate precision in making judgments about play action in sports. Many schools and other amateur organizations videotape games. Some officials bring blank tapes to games and ask that a copy of the game tape be recorded for their review. In many cases this can be done at once, so that officials head for home with a game video in hand.

Schools and even television outlets (places that air either live or tape-delayed contests) often have multiple cameras at games: in the end zone, on the goal lines, at ground level, and so on. That way, even though the videos are not focused exclusively on officials, a considerable amount of play action can be viewed, sometimes in slow motion and even in replay segments. Officials can learn a lot from these live action shots about how they've made game action judgments.

Some officials engage a cooperating friend, perhaps a fellow official, to record the game from high in the stands to capture them in action.

As a result of electronic recording, the practice of partner affirmation during games has increased. That is, in sports in which masses of players are in states of fluidity, critical action often occurs between officials, with neither official having an exclusive angle on a play (e.g., opponents leaping for a pass in football, a dribbler driving past a defender in soccer or basketball, a batter trying to check a swing in baseball). The custom, in cases of uncertainty, is to approach a partner and ask, "What did you see?"

Officiating groups also employ technology to advantage in conducting clinics. Video clips, PowerPoint presentations about reading keys, and film illustrations of mechanics coverage are widely used for training. All of these electronic devices and the cooperating partnerships they promote are extremely helpful in shaping officials' decision-making abilities.

Team sports that lend themselves to this kind of educational visual display include lacrosse, field and ice hockey, soccer, rugby, football, and basketball.

SUMMARY

Officiating requires complex decisions. These decisions, to be fair and accurate, require a deep knowledge of the sport, both technical knowledge of the rules and a feel for the spirit of the game. To make good calls, you must apply principles of fairness and not let unfair acts slip by. You must understand the rules, logic, terminology, and strategy of the game and know where, when, and how to make calls. You also need to know when to consult with or defer to other officials.

Because sport is competition and your decisions may sometimes be controversial, misunderstandings and disputes can arise. Chapter 8 offers ideas for resolving contentions that happen during a game.

REVIEW QUESTIONS

1. Why are pace and game rhythms important for officials to take into account?

2. What is a good way to absorb the rules of a sport?

3. Identify a player restriction in a sport that you are interested in.

4. Identify a rare occurrence that could take place in a sport of your interest.

5. Why would an official need to be aware of the language of a sport?

6. In a sport involving a ball or other object (e.g., puck), why is it important for an official to look off the ball frequently?

7. What is the principal reason for intricate knowledge of the rules in collision sports?

8. Why is pregame imaging important for an official?

9. Identify one way to accommodate a fellow official.

10. In the sport of your preference, identify a play or a situation in which you would expect or permit a partner to make a decision without your input.

Answers on pages 188-189

Chapter 7

Mental Training Strategies

Robert Weinberg

This chapter addresses the following:

- How to control your self-talk
- How to image your upcoming officiating performance
- How to relax in pressure situations
- The mental qualities of successful officials
- How to stop negative thoughts

Have you ever done any of the following?

- Questioned your confidence in making the correct call
- Lost your concentration for a brief moment during the competition
- Felt nervous and anxious about a big event or a potentially hostile crowd
- Did not feel really motivated for a specific officiating assignment
- Wondered what you would say to an irate coach
- Believed that you could have made better decisions during the competition
- Felt pressure and uneasiness deciding what score to give an athlete
- Kept replaying the game and calls you made (or did not make) in your mind after the game was over

If you have experienced one or more of the preceding as an official, don't worry, because you are not alone. All officials have had these doubts at some point in their officiating careers. Why do officials experience this inner turmoil? Much of it is simply a consequence of their unique roles. Good officiating facilitates the sport, ensuring that the outcome is dependent on the skills of the athletes. Conversely, poor officiating detracts from the competition and decreases the enjoyment of the game for everyone involved. Unfortunately, if officials make mistakes, they become publicized and often appear on SportsCenter. But if officials do a good job and the game runs smoothly, nobody even notices them. So, when you do your job well, you are not noticed; but make a mistake, and everyone knows about it. This is one reason that being an official is mentally tough.

MENTAL AND PHYSICAL DEMANDS OF OFFICIATING

Most certainly, your physical skills are an important part of your success as an official. If you work in a sport such as soccer or basketball, you have to be in excellent cardiorespiratory condition to run up and down the court or field to get in a good position to make the proper call. Of course, you also need to know the rules of the game well, as well as the proper technique and mechanics for making calls. However, being fit and knowing rules and mechanics are not really sufficient for excellent performance. When officials talk about doing a good job, their focus is typically on the mental aspects such as staying cool under pressure, making unpopular calls, not becoming rattled despite a raucous crowd, communicating effectively with coaches and players, and remaining confident despite constant chatter from the coaches. In fact, veteran officials claim that managing mental skills accounts for 50 to 70 percent of their success.

Given the importance of the mental aspects of officiating, it is strange that officiating clinics and camps emphasize physical techniques, rule interpretation, proper attire, and written and practical tests. Interestingly, when evaluating officials, supervisors typically emphasize things such as consistency, calmness, quick and accurate decision making, mental toughness, fairness, and confidence.

Research has generally revealed a constellation of attributes that top officials appear to have in common. Of course, if you gathered 100 officials together and asked them to rate the most important officiating attributes, you would probably get 100 different responses. Therefore, the attributes noted here are not rank-ordered, and you would probably include some attributes that are not on the list. Given this caveat, these are the characteristics shared by most top officials:

- Rapport
- Decisiveness
- Poise
- Integrity
- Judgment
- Confidence
- Enjoyment and motivation

These skills (which are basically mental) all converge to help make officials consistent. Consistency is one of the key attributes of elite athletes as well as top officials. Players and coaches expect decisions to be identical in similar circumstances, and rules should be applied equally to both opponents. Officials themselves recognize the importance of consistency in their work; 75 percent of officials agree with the statement, "I believe consistency in one's officiating is more important than following the rules to the letter" (Snyder & Purdy, 1987).

True consistency is achieved not by attempting to even up calls, but by applying a uniform rule interpretation to each competitive action. Thus, if a certain level of contact is allowed at one end of the floor in basketball, then you have to allow the same amount on the other end. In essence, proper judgment and interpretation are the main sources of consistency and fairness.

Although within-game consistency is important, between-game consistency is equally important. Good officials apply rules correctly and consistently from game to game. Achieving consistency requires two basic capacities: (1) good technique, positioning, and knowledge of the rules, and (2) strong mental and emotional skills. Peaks and valleys in officiating performance are often directly tied to mental states. Therefore, the ability to get into the proper

Officials need to maintain constant focus regardless of the situation.

AP Photo/Tom E. Puskar

frame of mind and maintain it throughout a competition is critical for officiating success.

To maintain a proper frame of mind, you need to learn and practice mental skills such as those listed earlier. For example, establishing a rapport with coaches, players, and fans requires the development of communication skills. Learning to express yourself effectively, being a good listener, and facilitating cooperation are all aspects of good communication. Poise is related to the skill of relaxation. Dealing with upset and irate coaches, players, and fans requires the ability to remain relaxed in the face of their comments and gestures. This can be developed through breath control, self-talk, and progressive relaxation, which will be discussed later in the chapter. Decisiveness requires good concentration skills and proper focus. If you are distracted, even for a moment, you might miss an important call. Staying in the present and using imagery and concentrative cues can help you develop this skill.

In summary, the qualities you need to excel are predominantly mental, and these skills can be learned and practiced. Unfortunately, as noted earlier, most officiating training programs focus on physical techniques. The rest of this chapter focuses on strategies that will help you build some of these critical mental skills—namely, imagery, self-talk, and relaxation.

IMAGERY

The use of imagery by officials is demonstrated by the following quote from a high school basketball and football official:

> *Officials generally do not get to practice their skills the way athletes do. We just can't go out and shoot some baskets, hit some golf balls, or practice our tennis strokes. So how I get ready for a game is to imagine different plays, situations, and circumstances; and then I see myself making the call. If I don't like the decision I made, then I'll replay the same situation again in my mind until I am comfortable with the decision. By doing this I feel confident that I am prepared for the game since I have gone over things in my mind already.*

> Weinberg and
> Richardson, 1990,
> p. 127

Understanding Imagery

Imagery refers to creating or recreating experiences in your mind. Even when you are not officiating a game, imagery enables you to experience it vividly in your mind. You've probably used imagery without even making a systematic effort to do so. For example, have you ever watched professional officials and then tried to imitate their performances in your mind? Or have you ever recalled a particularly good performance and then tried to recreate that feeling or experience in your mind? You can also create or picture new events that have not yet occurred. For instance, the official quoted at the beginning of this section spoke of trying to create a mental picture of the game that he was about to work.

You can also create situations that have given you trouble in the past and see yourself successfully dealing with them in the future (this is called coping imagery). For example, a soccer referee who has been inconsistent in calling fouls might imagine herself correctly and decisively citing players for various violations. Similarly, a hockey official who has had difficulty dealing with certain argumentative players might see himself acting in a calm yet firm manner in these situations.

Although sight is usually the dominant sense, imagery involves much more than simply visualizing yourself performing an activity. In addition to the visual sense, the auditory and kinesthetic senses are especially important in officiating. The auditory sense refers to sound, such as hearing the game-ending buzzer above the roar of the home team crowd. The kinesthetic sense is the feeling or sensation of the body as it moves in different positions, such as the feeling of various arm positions to signal certain calls. The emotions associated with various officiating experiences are also important in the practice of imagery. Recreating emotions such as anxiety, anger, confidence, and joy through imagery can help you control them when you are officiating.

Uses of Imagery

You can use imagery for other things besides helping you improve the physical aspect of your performance. Here are some examples:

- *Controlling emotional responses.* Officials sometimes let their anxiety or anger get the best of them during a game. If coaches, players, or fans are rude or abusive, it is easy to lose your cool and act inappropriately. In your role as an official, however, you must maintain your composure and act professionally. Imagery helps you picture provoking situations and then allows you to see yourself (include other senses as appropriate) keeping under control and dealing with the problem positively.

• *Improving concentration.* You can improve concentration by focusing on an upcoming assignment. Specifically, imagining what you want to do and how you want to react can keep your mind from wandering. In addition, you can imagine yourself in situations in which you sometimes lose your concentration (e.g., hostile crowd situations) and instead see yourself maintaining your composure and refocusing on the action of the performers.

• *Building confidence.* Most officials gain confidence simply by officiating in many competitions and gaining important experience with different situations. However, not all officials have the luxury of officiating many games to build their confidence. Imagery can help you build confidence by allowing you to see yourself performing well in a variety of situations.

Types of Imagery

The two major types of imagery are internal and external. External imagery involves watching yourself as if you were in a movie or on video. For example, if you were picturing yourself making a close call at home plate, you would see not only the runner, the catcher, home plate, and the ball, but also the back of your head, just as a spectator might. Internal imagery refers to imagining the scene through your own eyes. You see what you ordinarily see when performing the particular action. It is as if a camera were on your head taking pictures of everything you would see in the situation. To use the previous example, you would see the ball, the runner, home plate and the catcher, but you would not see your back or the back of your head.

Which type of imagery should you use? The latest research reveals that internal and external imagery are equally effective in enhancing performance. In fact, many athletes report that they switch back and forth between internal and external imagery automatically, without really trying. The important point is to make sure your imagery is clear, controllable, and detailed. Some officials believe they get more

Using imagery can help you learn to handle extremely difficult situations, such as fights.

feeling (muscle involvement) when they use internal imagery, whereas others like to see themselves because it gives them feedback regarding how they look (body movements) when making calls. Choose a combination of internal and external imagery based on what works best for you.

When to Use Imagery

Imagery can be practiced virtually any time but might be most useful and effective only for certain circumstances. Most officials (like athletes) prefer to use imagery prior to a competition as part of a pregame mental preparation. Some officials like to do it immediately before a game, whereas other like to use imagery an hour or more before a game. One option is to use imagery a couple of times before a competition with each time lasting about 10 minutes (but no more than 15) to maximize concentration.

A good time to use imagery is right after a competition. With the competition clearly in mind, you can replay the calls and situations you dealt with effectively as well as replay any calls or reactions you were not satisfied with and then imagine yourself confidently and decisively handling the situation. In essence, using imagery as a form of review and critique of your performance right after a competition is a great way to cement certain positive behaviors and try to change bad habits.

Most sporting events have some extended breaks in the action between periods or quarters or during a half. These break times afford you the chance use imagery and get ready for what might happen when play resumes. Find a quiet spot during these breaks to reflect on what has occurred and imagine handling situations effectively and confidently. You can also use imagery at home (or in another convenient place) for about 10 minutes at a time. The more you practice imagery, the better you will become at it and the more it will help your performance.

Developing and Implementing an Imagery Training Program

Like physical skills, mental skills must be practiced systematically for maximum effectiveness. This practice does not need to be cumbersome or complex but should fit into your daily schedule. 10 to 15 minutes per day should be sufficient. Following are some tips for creating an imagery program:

- *Proper setting.* When getting started, it is a good idea to practice where there are no distractions. You could practice at home before going to sleep, in an empty locker room before a game, or in any other spot that is quiet so you can concentrate.
- *Relaxed concentration.* Research has revealed that relaxing before using imagery enhances its effectiveness. A couple of deep breaths from the diaphragm (belly) while exhaling slowly will get you on your way to a relaxed state. Relaxing helps you temporarily forget daily hassles and worries and focus your attention on officiating an upcoming game.
- *Realistic expectations and sufficient motivation.* Some people believe that imagery is a panacea that will help them become something they are not. The fact is, if you don't know the rules and basic mechanics and positioning of officiating, all the imagery in the world won't help you. Conversely, some people refuse to believe that imagery can help them perform better. They subscribe to the notion that hard physical practice is the only way to achieve success. These people typically don't practice imagery regularly or with much enthusiasm. The truth lies somewhere between these two views. That is, imagery can improve performance if done systematically, but it won't turn an average official into a great official overnight.
- *Vivid images.* As noted earlier, the closer your images are to what you actually do in competition, the more effective they will be at transferring to actual performance. Pay particular attention to environmental details such as the layout of the facilities, playing surface, background, colors, and the positioning of fences and bleachers. Officiating in a place where you have worked before will help you create these detailed, vivid images. In addition, attempt to experience the emotions and thoughts of the officiating situation. Remember, the more vivid your imagery is in terms of using all your senses, the more difficult it is for your body to tell the difference between real and vividly imagined stimuli.
- *Controlled images.* You may assume that what people want to imagine is what

they do imagine. In fact, many people have trouble controlling their images, often to the point of repeating the same mistakes in their minds. For example, some officials have reported that, when using imagery, they sometimes see themselves making the wrong call again and again. Of course, you want to see yourself making the correct decision with confidence. If you are having difficulty controlling your images, start with some very simple everyday tasks such as doing household chores, taking a walk, reading a book, or working on the computer. Practice with these familiar tasks to develop your ability to control images. When you are ready to begin imaging your officiating performance, set up a specific situation and try to devise an appropriate strategy for dealing with it. For example, you might imagine yourself maintaining your composure and handling an unruly coach in a congenial, yet assertive manner without losing your temper.

- *Positive focus.* Generally, you want to focus on successful performances when you practice imagery, such as seeing yourself in a perfect position to make a correct call or communicating effectively with a fellow official. However, all officials make mistakes, and when you do, you need to know how to leave the call behind and refocus your attention on the action. Through imagery, you can occasionally see yourself making a mistake or bad call, but then immediately getting refocused and making excellent calls.

- *Video-recorded performances.* One common problem in trying to improve your officiating skills is that you can't see what you are doing right or wrong. Besides having a colleague provide you with feedback on your officiating performance, you can observe yourself on video to get a better idea of how you perform as an official. Or you can observe a video of an experienced and excellent official and use these images to create your own pictures in your head. The point is that you can use videos of yourself or other competent officials to help build positive images in your own mind of the way you want to officiate.

SELF-TALK

We are not disturbed by things, but rather the view we take of them.

Epictetus

There is nothing either good or bad, but thinking makes it so.

Shakespeare

These two quotes underscore the importance of thinking on our interpretation of events and situations. The way you evaluate and interpret events when you are officiating most certainly can either help or hinder you in a variety of ways, one of which is your focus of attention. Specifically, a critical part of your performance is the ability to stay focused and concentrated on the action from start to finish. A variety of external factors can cause distractions, such as crowd noise, media, coaches' antics, planes flying overhead, and the flashing of cameras. You might not have control over these external factors or events, but you do have control over how you react to them. One of the important internal distractions you do have control of is your self-talk, although it can also be a way to deal with distractions. *Self-talk* refers to anything that you say to yourself either silently or out loud. Self-talk has many potential uses (besides enhancing concentration) including breaking bad habits, sustaining effort, initiating action, and acquiring new skills.

The three types of self-talk are (1) positive, which focuses on motivating yourself to put forth more effort (e.g., *Hang in there*); (2) instructional, which focuses on how to perform the skill (e.g., *Make sure you get the proper angle to make a good call*), and (3) negative, which focuses on putting yourself or your actions down (e.g., *What a stupid mistake*).

Understanding and Identifying Your Self-Talk

Before you can change a behavior, you need to identify when it occurs, how often it occurs, and whether it is beneficial or detrimental. One way to better understand your self-talk is through retrospection (which is really a form of self-monitoring), especially right after a match or practice. Specifically, as soon as possible after a match, make a list of your thoughts and self-statements and the situations in which they occurred. In essence, you are really starting a journal or log of your self-talk during practices and matches, including your thoughts and verbal reactions to a variety of situations. Especially be aware of the circumstances that trigger the type of negative self-talk that can create anxiety, reduce motivation, and undermine performance.

Research has revealed that most officials determine that they employ positive and instructional self-talk in their better performances and negative self-talk in their poorer performances. Some of the typical events noted by officials that typically trigger negative self-talk include (1) blowing a call, (2) losing their temper, (3) losing concentration, (4) listening to the crowd, and (5) forgetting a rule. Once you have identified your self-talk and the situations that trigger it, the next step is to try to change it to enhance your performance.

Changing Negative Self-Talk to Positive

The process of self-talk can be thought of as mediating the relationship between an event and a response. In essence, it plays a key role in reactions to situations, which in turn can affect future behaviors. For example, as an official, it is inevitable that you will make a bad, inappropriate, or controversial call. You might think that this would directly affect your reaction (e.g., frustration), but in reality, your reaction depends in large part on your self-talk. Specifically, after a bad call you can get down on yourself and employ negative self-talk (e.g., *What a stupid mistake*), or you can deal with your mistake in a more effective manner (e.g., *That's OK; nobody's perfect*). Whatever the form of the self-talk is, it is the self-talk itself that directly leads to your response to the situation in the form of frustration or self-forgiveness.

Unfortunately, most people tend to have a lot more negative self-talk than positive self-talk. Negative self-talk is critical and demeaning and gets in the way of performing up to your level of competence. Being negative usually creates anxiety and fosters self-doubt. People who think positively about negative events are usually the most successful.

It would be great if we could eliminate all of our negative self-talk. However, even the most positive-minded people occasionally allow negative thoughts to intrude into their minds. The best way to effectively cope with these negative thoughts is to change them into positive ones. These changes can result in reduced anxiety, focused attention, increased motivation, and enhanced confidence. One of the best ways to change your self-talk is to make a list of the kinds of thoughts that upset you and interfere with your officiating performance, along with the situations that trigger these negative responses. By recognizing this self-defeating self-talk, you can then substitute positive statements for the negative ones. Some examples are shown in table 7.1.

Table 7.1 Changing Negative Self-Talk to Positive

Negative self-talk	Positive self-talk (change to)
I hate when I lose my cool.	Take a deep breath and regain control.
You just don't have any guts.	Just keep your composure and be decisive.
I'll never be a top-notch official.	I can make it if I continue to work hard.
That was a terrible call, you idiot.	That's OK; nobody's perfect.
What will people think if I mess up?	Just go out and do your job.
You choked again.	Just relax and do your job.
How many times are you going to be out of position?	Just focus on the getting into good position.
What if the coach gets irate?	Listen carefully, but then be decisive.

Concentrative Cues

To stay focused on the task at hand, you can use concentrative cues (think these to yourself) such as *deep breath, position, focus,* or *keep low,* to name a few. Such cues can be either emotional or instructive. In either case, the concentrative cue acts as a reminder of what to do in the heat of competition. These cues are similar to self-talk but are more focused on the specific task at hand.

Self-Talk Training

Practicing self-talk will help train you to use appropriate self-talk when it's most important. The first thing you need to do is understand and identify your self-talk. This can be done by monitoring your self-talk under various conditions and situations. Ask yourself the following:

- Do I experience a lot of negative self-talk?

- What situations cause negative or positive self-talk?

- Does officiating with certain coaches cause more negative self-talk?

- Do certain venues produce more negative self-talk?

- Does self-talk occur before I even start to officiate?

Once you have become more aware of your self-talk, you can start practicing the techniques described in this section. For example, you could identify the various types of negative self-talk you have and then change those negative statements to positive ones. In this way, when an event such as being yelled at by a coach produces negative self-talk (e.g., *I hate refereeing when this person coaches*), you could be ready with a positive self-statement (e.g., *Just focus on the game*). Similarly, you could practice thought stopping or using concentrative cues so that when the situation occurs where you are officiating, you will ready for an appropriate response.

Thought Stopping

Another way to cope with negative self-talk is to stop it before it can negatively affect your performance. Thought stopping involves being aware of when negative self-talk occurs. Thus, when you catch yourself being negative, immediately use a cue or trigger to stop the thought and clear your mind. The trigger can be a simple word such as *stop*, or it can be snapping your fingers or hitting your hand against your thigh. The important thing is that you find a cue that is comfortable for you.

Initially, it is best to restrict thought stopping to practice situations. However, as noted earlier, officials don't usually have the luxury of practicing the way athletes do. So, as discussed earlier, imagery could be used instead of physical practice. When using imagery to practice thought stopping, whenever you start thinking a negative thought, just tell yourself to stop (or use whatever cue you have chosen) and then take a deep breath before speaking with an irate coach. If a particular situation causes you a problem, such as not making calls in a deliberate, decisive manner (which results in your berating yourself), you might want to focus on that situation and say "Stop" before you beat yourself up with negative self-talk. Old habits die hard, so practice thought stopping as often as you can.

Ironic Processes

One of the common mistakes that officials and other performers make is using the word *not* as part of the instructions they give themselves. The fact that trying to not perform a specific action can inadvertently trigger its occurrence is known as an ironic process. How many times have you heard tennis players say to themselves "Whatever you do, don't double fault," or a golfer say, "Just don't hit the ball in the water hazard." Of course, what happens is that the tennis player double faults and the golfer hits the ball into the water. So instructions officials give themselves, such as "Don't lose your cool," "Just don't choke," and "Don't talk back to athletes who are complaining," typically produce the unwanted behavior. When formulating self-talk, keep in mind that the body does not hear the word *don't;* instead, it focuses on the words *lose your cool* or *choke*.

Following are six guidelines for developing self-talk cues to enhance skill execution:

- Keep your phrases short and specific.
- Use the first person and the present tense.
- Construct positive phrases.
- Speak kindly to yourself.
- Repeat phrases often.
- Say the phrases with meaning.

RELAXATION

Officiating can most certainly be very emotional and stressful. Various surveys of officials have revealed that approximately 50 percent of them experience their job as either stressful or very stressful. In addition, the officials reporting the most stress also reported more physical symptoms such as headaches, muscle tension, and hypertension. Referees are often targets of unruly fans, belligerent and frustrated athletes, and agitated coaches. Although it may sound far-fetched to equate officiating with performing in battle, officials have been seriously hurt and even killed because of crowd rioting and player aggression. For example, a disputed call at a soccer game in Lima, Peru, in 1964 led to a brawl in which 300 people, including officials, died. In 1969, the World Cup playoff series between Honduras and El Salvador turned into the Soccer War that listed the series officials among the thousands of causalities. More typically, referees are threatened and intimidated by spectators, coaches, and athletes both through physical and verbal aggression. Research has revealed that these threats influence officials' concentration, performance, and motivation, including prematch worries (Folkesson, Nyberg, Archer, and Norlander, 2002). Coping with stress requires fortitude and conviction as pointed out by official Kelly Nutt:

You can bring your whistle and you can bring your flag, but if you don't bring your guts you might as well stay home.

Tunney, 1987 p. 26.

Sources of Stress

Although threats of physical violence definitely exist, the stress that officials feel can come from a variety of places and sources. The few general categories of stressors that influence officials include (1) fear of failure, (2) fear of inadequacy, and (3) loss of control. At the core of most officials' anxiety is the fear of failure. In its most basic form, fear of failure includes worrying about blowing an important call, being out of position, having a bad game, being poorly rated by supervisors and coaches, and not meeting one's own expectations. To further complicate matters, officials know that if they do a good job they will probably go unnoticed, whereas if there is a controversial call, a fight between players, an ejection of a player or coach, or any other unusual happening that requires an official's judgment, the official is usually thrust into the spotlight. Thus, your success goes unappreciated, whereas your failures (or at least controversial calls) become highly scrutinized.

Consider the example of a call in the sixth game of the 1985 World Series between the Kansas City Royals and the St. Louis Cardinals. With the Cardinals leading 4 to 3 (3 to 2 in games) in the ninth inning, a Kansas City batter hit a ground ball that resulted in a close call at first base. The umpire, Don Denkinger, called the runner safe, although instant replay clearly showed that he was out. Vehement arguing by St. Louis was to no avail. Kansas City took advantage of this call and rallied to win the game and then win the seventh game. Many St. Louis players blamed Denkinger for their loss, and he endured much abuse over the call. Thus, despite a longtime successful career in Major League Baseball, including thousands of calls, he is forever linked to this mistake, which he made in a high-visibility game.

You don't have to be officiating a World Series game to feel pressure. Officiating a recreational league or varsity game can be just as stressful, because these games are important to the athletes, and they expect high-quality officiating.

Feelings of stress can also be brought on by feelings of mental or physical inadequacy regarding an upcoming event. Fear of inadequacy is specifically characterized by the attitude that "something is wrong with me," an attitude that reflects self-depreciation and personal dissatisfaction. Some of the typical things officials report feeling inadequate about are their inability to (1) sustain self-confidence, (2) control the game, (3) maintain concentration, (4) control stress, (5) interpret and apply the rules, and (6) be in top physical condition.

Good officials try to prevent feelings of inadequacy by preparing themselves for every assignment. This preparation might include previewing the players and coaches and anticipating any potential problem areas; staying on a solid exercise training regimen; being aware of any uniqueness in the facility site; reviewing specific rules that might apply to this competition; and mentally rehearsing

Officials have to maintain their composure in high-intensity situations and not let stress make them do inappropriate things, such as pointing fingers at athletes.

difficult situations as well as being aware of special circumstances that could lead to a heated game, such as crosstown rivalries or certain players or coaches who are known to be temperamental. Consider the following quote by a soccer official:

> *It is extremely important for officials to project an athletic image. Officials must be able to maintain the physical pace of the game and be free to concentrate, without being concerned about their stamina. If officials don't project such an image, they open themselves up to additional criticism from coaches, players, and fans. An official's job is difficult enough under normal circumstances; any avenue for unnecessary criticism should be avoided.*

> Weinberg and
> Richardson, 1990,
> p. 80.

Another area that can produce stress for officials is lack of control. Being in control of a game is very important, because a perceived loss of control is usually associated with feelings of ineffectiveness. For example, officials have reported that they have lost control when they were baited by coaches, working with incompetent officials, or criticized in the press.

Working a game when a player (John McEnroe) or coach (Bob Knight) is known to give officials a hard time can create feelings of loss of control. These confrontations can be very stressful, but what you need to remember is that, although the actions of players and coaches might be beyond your control, you can control your own actions and behavior. Acting decisively and professionally often defuses the anger or discontent of the player or coach, or of spectators who also can get very unruly, loud, and belligerent. Keeping control over the situation and your emotions takes some experience and practice.

Managing Stress Physically and Psychologically

One way to break down stress management techniques is through mental and physical techniques. Physically oriented techniques focus on lowering your physical reaction to stress, which can include increased heart rate, muscle tension, respiration, sweating, or a number of other autonomic nervous system reactions. Conversely, mental, or cognitively oriented, strategies focus on reducing worry and negative thinking (we already discussed a couple of ways to deal with these cognitive issues through imagery and changing self-talk). In essence, anxiety is manifested at the mental level.

Research has demonstrated that the most effective stress-reduction techniques match the specific kind of anxiety experienced. This is termed the matching hypothesis. For example, if you primarily manifest anxiety physically (e.g., increased heart rate and muscle tension), then a physically oriented technique such as progressive relaxation would be most effective for you. Conversely, if you manifest anxiety cognitively (e.g., worry), then a cognitively oriented technique such as the relaxation response would be most beneficial. Because we discussed mentally oriented techniques in the sections on imagery and self-talk, we now focus on relaxing physically.

Physical Relaxation

There are a variety of physical relaxation techniques, but only a couple will be discussed here. One of the easiest, yet most effective, is breath control.

Breath Control

Breathing is the key to achieving relaxation. Of course, most of us take breathing for granted because we do it many times every minute of the day. But the pressure of officiating (especially in some circumstances) can change the way you breathe, making breathing short, shallow, and irregular instead of smooth, deep, and rhythmical. Thus, you can learn about your mental state just by taking stock of your breathing pattern.

To practice breath control, take a deep, complete breath, and imagine that your lungs are divided into three levels. Focus on filling the lower level of your lungs with air, first by pushing the diaphragm down and forcing the abdomen out. Then fill the middle portion of your lungs by expanding the chest cavity and raising your rib cage. Finally, fill the upper level of your lungs by raising your chest and shoulders slightly. Hold this breath for several seconds and then exhale slowly by pulling your abdomen in and lowering your shoulders and chest. Focusing on the lowering (inhalation) and raising (exhalation) of the diaphragm will give you an increased sense of stability, centeredness, and relaxation. To help enhance the importance and awareness of the exhalation phase, inhale to a count of four and exhale to a count of eight. This 1:2 ratio of inhalation to exhalation helps slow breathing and deepens the relaxation by focusing on the exhalation phase.

The best time to use breath control during competition is during a time-out or break in the action. The slow and deliberate inhalation–exhalation sequence will help you maintain composure and control over your anxiety during particularly stressful times. By focusing on your breathing, you are less likely to be bothered by irrelevant cues or distractions (such as the crowd), and you will relax your shoulder and neck muscles in the process.

Finally, deep breathing provides a short mental break from the pressure of officiating and can renew your energy.

Progressive Relaxation (Muscle Relaxation)

Progressive relaxation was developed by Dr. Edmund Jacobson in the 1930s, and his technique has formed the cornerstone for modern relaxation procedures. It is called progressive relaxation because the procedure progresses from one muscle group to the next until all the major muscle groups are completely relaxed. The technique has been modified considerably over the years so it can be done in a shorter period of time. However, the essence of the procedure remains the same: to help people learn the difference between tension and lack of tension in their muscles Following are some of the basic tenets of progressive relaxation:

- It teaches people to feel the difference between tension and lack of tension in the muscles.
- Tension and relaxation are mutually exclusive. It is not possible for a muscle to be relaxed and tense at the same time.
- Progressive relaxation involves systematically contracting and relaxing each major muscle group in the body.
- Relaxation of the body through decreased muscular tension will, in turn, decrease mental tension. In essence, relaxing physically helps you relax mentally.

Developing a Relaxation Training Program

The tension–relaxation cycles achieved through progressive relaxation helps develop an awareness of the difference between tension and lack of tension. Each cycle involves maximally contracting one specific muscle group and then attempting to totally relax that same muscle group while focusing on the difference between tension and relaxation. People skillful in this technique can detect tension in a specific muscle such as in the neck and then relax that muscle. Most officials use time-outs (or other stoppages in play) to employ this technique during a game.

Before you can relax spontaneously, however, you may need to do the following:

- Find a quiet place.
- Dim the lights.
- Loosen any tight-fitting clothing.
- Lie down in a comfortable position (but not in a sleeping position).

It is beyond the scope of this chapter to provide step-by-step instructions in how to use progressive relaxation. Commercial resources, including texts, are available (e.g., Weinberg & Gould, 2011, pp. 275-276). In general, your first few practice sessions might take about 30 minutes, but after three or four trials, you should be able to achieve relaxation in 5 to 10 minutes. When you can achieve relaxation regularly within 10 minutes, you can drop the tension phase and focus only on the relaxation phase. Remember, the final goal of progressive relaxation is to learn how to completely relax within a short period of time in the midst of stressful officiating situations.

SUMMARY

Officials need to have well-honed mental skills just as athletes do. However, in most cases, officials are taught only the rules, techniques, proper positioning, and mechanics. When asked what really makes an excellent official, both coaches and officials alike talk about mental skills such as dealing with pressure, maintaining focused concentration, staying motivated, and communicating effectively. This chapter focused on some of the critical mental skills needed for achieving these mental skills.

REVIEW QUESTIONS

1. Which of the following is *not* a characteristic that separates top officials from average officials?
   a. decisiveness
   b. poise
   c. integrity
   d. court or field positioning
   e. confidence

2. Imagery is often used by officials to
   a. improve confidence
   b. cope with emotions
   c. enhance concentration
   d. all of the above
   e. *a* and *b*

3. Which statement(s) regarding progressive relaxation is/are *false*?
   a. It works from the physical to the mental.
   b. A muscle cannot be relaxed and tense at the same time.
   c. It involves progressively contracting and relaxing the muscles in the neck and shoulder region because these are the most likely to get tense.
   d. *a* and *c*
   e. *a* and *b*

4. The ratio of inhalation to exhalation for breath control should be
   a. 1:2
   b. 2:1
   c. 4:1
   d. 1:4
   e. 1:1

5. Which of the following is/are sources of anxiety for officials?
   a. fear of failure
   b. fear of inadequacy
   c. loss of control
   d. all of the above
   e. *a* and *b*

6. The fact that trying not to perform a specific action can inadvertently trigger its occurrence is known as
   a. limited channel capacity
   b. ironic process
   c. reversal theory
   d. negative self-talk
   e. none of the above

7. Thought stopping is a technique to help deal with
   a. inappropriate focus
   b. changing negative to positive self-talk
   c. difficult athletes
   d. excess anxiety
   e. lack of motivation

8. Which of the following is/are *not* a basic premise of progressive relaxation?
   a. If you relax the mind, the body will relax.
   b. Learn the difference between a tense and relaxed muscle.
   c. Progressively contract and relax the major muscle groups.
   d. *a* and *b*
   e. *b* and *c*

Answers on page 189

Chapter 8

Conflict Management

Jon Bible

This chapter addresses the following:

- How conflict can result from misperceptions about officials
- The signs of potential conflict from game participants
- The importance of having a conflict management plan
- How to implement a management plan

"Please don't shoot the umpire: He is doing the best he can." A Kansas City baseball park posted that inscription on a sign in 1880 because of the proliferation of abusive baseball fans. We've come a long way since then because we don't talk about shooting game officials (except perhaps in South American soccer venues). But the fact is that officials continue to be regularly subjected to verbal and, at times, physical abuse and blamed when things don't work out the way players, coaches, and fans want. This chapter discusses the kinds of conflicts you will encounter as an official, some of the reasons they occur, and ways to manage them.

CONFLICT IS INEVITABLE

To manage conflict effectively, you must first understand that it is inevitable. Some commonplaces about conflict should be acknowledged right from the start. When two teams compete in a sporting event, conflict is already present. It may be mild, it may be subdued, and

it may even be masked by the appearance of harmony, but the potential for aggrieved feelings is always lurking. An event in the game may trigger an eruption, a series of difficulties may cause frustration to build, and sometimes your decisions or nondecisions will make you the focal point of anger.

As an official, you must approach any contest with the notion that a central part of the job requirement is handling conflict successfully. Although you cannot gauge your success with a scoreboard, when you manage conflict well, you can take a measure of satisfaction in your role.

Today, moreover, the higher up on the officiating ladder you are, the more likely it is that your success in defusing and handling situations and in communicating well with players and coaches will be among the criteria by which your overall effectiveness is judged. In the professional and collegiate ranks, and increasingly in state and local high school officials' organizations, supervisors spend a great deal of time working with officials on these issues. Handling situations is a hot topic in the officiating camps and clinics that have proliferated in recent years. In sum, the old days in which officials took care of business by simply barking at complainers are long gone.

A favorite slogan among officials is, "You've got to love it when they boo," because it is a fact that onlookers sometimes direct catcalls and sarcastic comments to officials. Coaches, players, and game administrators often show politeness, even deference, before a game begins, but once the contest starts, participants' and their followers' behavior can become snide, if not downright ugly.

As an objective participant who must make calls that affect either team, you won't be able to please people consistently. Therefore, your goal should not be to please people. You are there to arbitrate competition, and the most you can hope for is respect. Officiating is not a popularity contest.

The reasons spectators and participants vent their anger at officials are complex and numerous. Exploring this issue reveals that the problem does not always lie with the official. Understanding that may make the anger easier to forgive. We live in a society that insists on placing blame. Often blame is placed on officials unfairly. Keep that in mind as we explore ways to deal with conflicts.

Conflicts With Players' Parents

Officials are sometimes blamed for other people's inadequacies. Parents may want to shift the blame for a player's lack of talent, a coaching strategy that misfires, or players' or coaches' inadequate play. Other factors can be identified, too: perceptions that are clouded by the desire for a favorable judgment in a close play, a general lack of respect for authority figures, and a warped sense of tradition that says it's all right to take frustrations out on the officials.

Consider a Little League father who barks at an umpire. Does he do this to save face with neighbors after his daughter struck out? To diminish the pressure on his daughter? In frustration with perceived inadequacies of the youngster? Out of impatience with his own lack of success in athletics? To displace his anger at a coach for failing to teach the daughter properly, or his own shame because he himself did not teach his daughter properly? Out of fury at the girl's mother, who forced the daughter into the sport? Frustration can be compounded by contextual factors, too, such as whether this was the girl's first at-bat of the season, whether her team was ahead or behind 26 to 0, or whether the game was close with the bases loaded in the last inning. The reasons for parents' frustrations when their children don't succeed are innumerable, and blaming officials is sometimes a convenient outlet.

Conflicts With Players

Players, too, sometimes react to officials negatively. Responsible players play the game and adjust to officials' styles, personalities, and abilities without complaining. They genuinely respect authority. However, some players—even professionals—blame officials (and teammates and coaches) for their own inadequacies. Those who blame others for their own shortcomings have a convenient excuse for failing. It is certainly easier on the psyche to make someone else the scapegoat than it is to accept responsibility for one's own actions.

Some high school players view sports officials the way they view police officers or school authority figures. Rebellion is often a part of a child's growth process, especially in the formative teen years. Rebellious kids like to break rules. Referees enforce rules. Conflict results.

Some players, as well as parents, coaches, fans, and the media, believe that opposing players are getting breaks from officials. The perception that their opponents are not judged according to the same criteria as their own team can make an official an easy target for criticism. Officials are only human, too, and officials' honest mistakes can be perceived as biases.

AP Photo/Anderson Independent-Mail, Mark Crammer

Officials need to know how to handle a variety of situations, including contact with players.

Conflicts With Coaches

Coaches can also be antagonistic. "A coach spends his entire life thinking he's fighting off alligators. A referee is just another alligator," said Jack Pardee, former Houston Oilers football coach (*Referee* magazine, March 1999, p. 28).

Coaches and officials can have an adversarial relationship because of one major factor: Coaches care who wins and officials don't. Because coaches are pulling for their teams, devising offensive and defensive strategies, and keeping a keen eye on their players, they see the game with a built-in bias. They want things to go their way. As a consequence, they are sometimes quick to view officials' decisions as unfair. They may sometimes believe that they have to fight the officials as well as their opponents.

Newer officials in particular also need to understand that officials can catch flak from coaches for reasons having little to do with the call they made (seasoned officials have figured this out). Some coaches, for example, even view their role as a contriver or antagonist in relation to officials. Even if they don't think an official missed a call, they may howl, whine, and plead in an effort to gain a presumed edge from officials. They believe that if they get on the officials about this call, maybe the next one will go in their favor. This attitude can come from assistant coaches who have worked out a system with the head coach in which they are the designated "attack dog" who will accept an unsporting conduct penalty as the price of "working the officials" in the hope of intimidating them to favor the coach's team. In this way, the head coach does not have to get his hands dirty. In addition, when they think

Why Coaches Yell: An Inside Look

A basketball team is flat (playing with no enthusiasm), appears to be taking the other team for granted, or is just playing poorly overall in front of a large home crowd. There is a block-charge call that the official seems clearly to have gotten right, but the coach of the team that the call went against jumps up off the bench, starts yelling and screaming and waving his arms, and eventually throws his clipboard to the ground. At first the official is stunned, because he knows the call wasn't close enough to warrant such a vociferous response, but then he gets angry and assesses the coach a technical foul.

A neophyte official, in particular, might assume that the coach really thought the official missed the call, but veterans know that there may be a myriad of other reasons for the coach's behavior. Many coaches assume that officials, being human, don't want to be yelled at, so they might "work" the officials in the hope that they'll make borderline calls in their favor to keep the crowd off their backs (especially if they are playing in front of a home crowd). They might also react loudly and visibly to a seemingly innocuous call to get their players fired up, even to the point of drawing a technical foul. They figure this is a small price to pay for what may be large dividends. And this technique often works, with players assuming an "us against them" mentality and rallying

around their poor "victimized" coach by taking off their gloves and going after the other team far more aggressively than they were beforehand. Finally, coaches may react this way with younger officials or officials they don't know to see whether they can intimidate them into making future calls their way. An official who takes care of business by calmly and unemotionally assessing a technical foul will earn the coach's respect, but one who doesn't do this will be in for a long night, and possibly a short career.

Although officials sometimes prefer to look the other way and ignore such behavior when they sense that it's part of a plan having nothing to do with the call itself, they can't afford to overlook egregious behavior just because of what they think motivated it. Doing so will cause the game to degenerate and result in a loss of the respect of the participants. But it can help an official to know that in some instances an especially heated response has nothing to do with the call itself.

It must also be stressed that coaches will play close attention to how the opposing coach acts and how the officials respond. If a coach sees the other coach (especially if it's a visiting coach watching the home coach) getting away with complaining about calls in a loud or prolonged manner with no penalty, it is almost a sure bet that the first coach will start behaving the same way.

their teams are too lethargic, some coaches yell at the officials to fire the team up.

Coaches can also get frustrated because they believe (mistakenly, in most instances, as has been discussed) that officials aren't accountable. This is especially true at the subcollegiate levels. A typical lament is, "If I foul up, I could lose my job. If an official goofs, the league says they're sorry, and the official keeps the job. Sanctions and reprimands should result from bad calls." In fact, such penalties are increasingly being imposed, and officials can be dropped from leagues as a result of their shortcomings. Many coaches, however, don't know this, just as they are unaware of the in-depth training programs and assessment processes that are more and more a feature of officiating life these days.

Conflicts With Administrators

Athletic administrators can be dismissive of officials. For years people have looked on umpiring as a job they could get any postman to do. In fact, Joe Cronin (once American League president), in an argument during a meeting with the umpires, told them, "You guys better look at this," and pulled out a list of umpires who had written to him and their applications. He said, "I can get 24 postmen to replace you guys." "That's really the way they sometimes feel about you," said Doug Harvey, retired National League umpire and recent Baseball Hall of Fame inductee (*Referee* magazine, August 1982, p. 8).

Athletic directors may be officials' biggest supporters or worst detractors. Officials need the support of game administrators for securing dressing facilities, handling equipment adjustments at the game, controlling spectators, arranging game assistants (scorekeepers, ball chasers, timers, chain crews), and providing postgame escorts after controversial contests. Administrators may or may not be conscientious and efficient in these duties. They are getting better, largely because they fear the consequences in terms of legal liability if an official is attacked or abused and it turns out that they failed to take any security precautions or that the ones they took were inadequate. But many administrators continue to be deficient, and when they are, officials themselves may have to solve problems that arise. Poor game administrators are recognized by their absence.

Administrators at all levels know that officials are necessary to conduct a contest, but more problems are related to officiating than any other aspect of their job. For example, scheduling officials is time-consuming, finding last-minute replacement officials is troublesome, listening to complaints from coaches and fans about officials' perceived inabilities is tiresome, and justifying expenses for officials is sometimes difficult when dealing with budget-conscious school boards.

PLANNING FOR CONFLICT: USING PREVENTIVE OFFICIATING

Part of being a good official is being a strategist. Just like successful people in any endeavor, good officials have a game plan. Getting ready for a game usually involves a pregame conference with partners. The majority of conferences focus on rules, mechanics, court coverage, and foul-calling philosophy. Rarely discussed but equally important is a conflict management game plan.

The best plans include preventive officiating. In fact, most of your efforts in conflict management should be focused on preventing conflict from escalating. If you can stop a potentially bad situation from developing, you will have less conflict to deal with. Following are some basic techniques that can help prevent conflicts from arising or escalating further.

Clear Your Head

One of your first challenges is to forget temporarily other parts of your life before the game. When you've had a stressful day, it is imperative to shelve your problems while you officiate your game. You have a duty to the game and its participants to be ready to officiate. Many people enjoy officiating because it gives them the chance to forget about everything else for a while.

Know Your Participants

Part of a good conflict management plan is gaining knowledge about participants. There is a fine line between preparation and prejudice. On the surface it would seem that the more information you have, the better prepared you will be. The dangerous flip side is letting the information you've gathered negatively influence the way you handle a situation. The following example shows how information can help; the example in the following section, Stay Objective, shows how information can hurt.

You've been assigned to referee a football game between crosstown rivals. Because you're familiar with the history of the rivalry, you know there's been trouble between the two in the past. The teams and coaches don't like each other. Based on that history, you correctly assume that there's likely to be a lot of emotion in the game, probably more than in a typical game. You've heard through the officiating grapevine that last year when the teams played, a bench-clearing brawl erupted, and threats of payback were often heard.

As an official, you want that type of information. You're less likely to be surprised by unseemly events. You want to be prepared for bad blood between teams in every game you work, and having detailed information helps you and your crew focus on potential situations before they become real problems.

In a situation like the one in this example, you may need to deal with things differently than you would in a less hostile situation. For example, a playful jibe by a player to an opponent in a normal setting might not merit a strong reaction. You might use preventive officiating by talking to the player who made the comment to make sure it doesn't happen again. That same comment in an emotion-filled game might draw a more volatile reaction from an opponent. You need to understand the context and deal with the problem more sternly, using stronger language or even penalizing without warning if necessary to control the situation.

You should also let your supervisor or assigner know if there is an unusual amount of trouble between two teams, or if a team routinely pushes the boundaries in terms of trash-talking, taunting, off-the-ball or dead ball fouls, and the like. Too often we keep quiet about these things because we don't want to upset people. Bringing these sorts of problems to the attention of league officers may result in a correction of the behavior, and at least it allows those officers to alert future crews who work games involving these teams to be on guard for problems. You should also share this information with fellow officials. As has been noted, you should not enter a contest looking for trouble or with preconceived notions about what may or may not occur, but being unaware of the histories of the teams involved in the game can result in your not having your guard up from the start, which can lead to disaster.

Stay Objective

Having good information before a game gives you the proper context to handle things appropriately during that game. However, prior information can sway your opinion if you don't make objectivity your goal. Here's a situation in which information negatively prejudices an official:

A new head coach takes over the baseball program at a high school in a district in which you umpire. You've heard from your umpire buddies who work in the area that the coach came from that he can be a terror—that he seems to dislike umpires in general and constantly whines about calls. When your schedule comes out, you see that you're working a game involving his school in late March. For several days beforehand, you think about how you should deal with this coach, and you decide to put him in his place from the get-go, show him who is boss, and let him know in no uncertain terms that whatever he got away with at his former school won't fly with you.

You're the plate umpire, and in the second inning of the game, the coach, on offense, says from the dugout "That pitch was low." He didn't yell or wave his arms around, but his comment was loud enough for you to hear it. Immediately you spin around, jerk your mask off, point directly at him, and say in a stern voice, "That's enough! I'm not going to listen to you complaining about balls and strikes. If you think you're going to intimidate me, you've got another think coming. One more word out of you and you're gone!" The coach doesn't say anything at the time, but after the game he calls the umpire assigner for that district and tells him what happened. You later discover that he has spread the word among his coaching brethren that you're unapproachable and have a bad attitude.

Did the coach's comment deserve a response? Maybe, maybe not. Some umpires (very likely most) would say no—it was one comment and it was made quietly without inciting the crowd. If he says anything more, a warning is in order, but this one should be ignored. Others would argue that an informal or even formal warning about arguing balls and strikes should have been given. It is beyond dispute, however, that you grossly overreacted, almost certainly because of your knowledge of the coach's reputation and the fact that you thought about the matter for several days. You came into the game loaded for bear, as it were, ready to jump at the first provocation, no matter how minor. Because of your behavior, you've created a situation in which your reputation is likely to suffer, perhaps irreparably.

Processing the knowledge gained about a particular team, player, coach, or game calls for careful judgment. Gain enough information to help you understand why certain things are happening in the game. Be responsible enough to sort through the information, and treat each game as a new one.

Don't Take It Personally

A coach tells you, "Shake your head, your eyes are stuck. You're terrible. If you had one more eye you'd be a cyclops." As an official, you have to deal with such comments but not take them personally. One of the most difficult aspects to understand about officiating is that generally when people yell at you, they're really yelling at your uniform and what it represents. When you're challenged by anyone involved in the game, there's a good chance that the victim could have been any official who happened to be there. That doesn't make it right, but knowing ahead of time that the challenge is not personal will help you deal with it better.

No matter how well you do in officiating, some people will vent their frustrations on you. Coaches, players, and fans have an intensely personal interest in games, which means that their judgment tends to be impaired and their comments unreliable. Understand and accept that participants are going to see things differently than you do. An old officiating saying goes, "Coaches, players, and fans see the game with their hearts. Refs see the game with their eyes." That wisdom should be applied to both negative and positive comments. Winning coaches, simply because they've won, are perhaps more likely than losing coaches to believe that the officials have done a decent job. If you're willing to believe them when they tell you you're good, you're also going to have to believe them when they tell you you're bad.

Decide What Deserves a Response

Part of your management plan must include deciding whether to respond to people. You are going to be challenged in varying degrees. Every question does not need a response; in fact, often the best reply is no reply. Realize that coaches and players are often simply venting their frustrations when challenging you. Always decide whether to respond before you start responding. This is difficult to do in a heated situation, but if you take that moment to think before speaking, you can prevent a conflict from escalating.

If a basketball coach says, "She's camping in the lane," what is more effective: ignoring the statement or saying to the coach, "No way; she's been fine all night"? Most of the time, ignoring a harmless statement or acknowledging it with a simple head nod ends the matter. When you defend your position, the coach instinctively may go on the offensive and continue the debate. Ask yourself, "If I say something, will it do more harm than good?"

Understand Game Context

The intensity of the game, the closeness of the score, and the time left all play a part in how much and what type of conflict you must deal with. With a close score at the end of a game—no matter the sport or level—emotions rise. A foul called in the early stages of the game may draw few complaints from players, coaches, and fans. A similar foul call in the final moments of a tight game will likely elicit a more emotional response from all involved. Consider allowing the participants a bit more leeway in such situations.

That doesn't mean you should let a player or coach get away with extremely poor sporting conduct simply because the score is close at the end of a game. It does mean, however, that the way you handle that end-of-game situation will likely have a great impact on the result, so you should consider the emotional charge of the situation and tolerate a bit more than you normally would in less critical situations.

You must be consistent throughout the game in terms of what you deem to be conduct deserving of an unsporting conduct penalty. If you let behavior that warrants a penalty go unpunished in the early stages, the game can degenerate to the point that bad behavior is rampant and you can never regain control. It's also hard to justify imposing a penalty at the end of the game if you let the same behavior slide at the start.

RECOGNIZING CONFLICT

You can't manage a conflict if you don't recognize clues to volatile emotions. Some conflicts are easy to recognize; others are more subtle. Learning to recognize signs of conflict—whether it is two opponents swinging at each other or clues that a player or coach is about to explode—can help you deal with a conflict before it escalates. When you read the signs correctly, you can prevent major blowups.

Signs From Players

Frustrated players tend to complain or demonstrate nonverbal signs of disgust. Knowing the signs of frustration gives you the context to deal with players appropriately. Here are some tips for recognizing or anticipating player misconduct:

- *Players who play poorly often experience frustration.* If a player is playing well, you're less likely to hear complaining. If a star player is struggling, you'll hear more complaining.
- *Look at players' facial expressions and body language for clues about their feelings.* Staring or glaring at an opponent is an obvious attempt at intimidation. Tense facial muscles, such as a set jaw, may indicate that a player is close to acting aggressively. Players who scold teammates are usually frustrated also.
- *Always watch for contact away from the ball or after a play ends.* Because of the perception that no one is watching in those two situations, players may execute a verbal or physical cheap shot.
- *Be on a constant lookout for paybacks.* For example, after a hard foul, look for the offended player to attempt to get the fouling player back at some point. Some players attempt to retaliate immediately; they are often caught because the officials are still focused on them. Sneakier players try to retaliate later, hoping the referees aren't watching anymore.

Signs From Coaches

When coaches' comments to you are repetitive, it is usually a sign of frustration or an attempt to manipulate you. Listen to how they talk to their own players and assistant coaches, too. If they're haranguing them, you may also become a target at some point. The volume of their comments is also a sign.

Body language is also a crucial sign of a coach's state of mind. Look for stern facial expressions that express anger or a roll of the eyes and a wry smile that suggest sarcasm. A coach who flails his arms or uses officiating signals is playing to the crowd in an attempt to intimidate you.

IMPLEMENTING A CONFLICT MANAGEMENT PLAN

During each game, you must recognize the signs of conflict, prevent it from escalating, and deal with it directly by penalizing when appropriate. How you handle each of these elements will determine whether you are an average official or an exceptional one.

Conflict Management Tools

Former tennis professional Andre Agassi was once in a television advertisement in which he said, "Image is everything." This is so true in officiating. The image you create from the start is especially important when you're unknown to the players, coaches, and fans. Keep in mind that perception can be far more important than reality. If, based on your physical presence, voice control, body language, use of your whistle and flag, and so on, people think you know what you're doing, they'll be more accepting of you, tend to give you the benefit of the doubt when the inevitable close calls occur, and be more likely to react positively to your efforts to maintain control of the game. If, by contrast, you're deficient in these areas, you'll encounter more difficulties.

Your Presence

Marshall McLuhan, known as the father of advertising, suggested that how you do something is sometimes more important than what you do. As an official, you must sell your calls effectively. Presence is a crucial selling tool.

Presence is difficult to define. An official with presence looks athletic and has a confident demeanor that says, "This isn't my first rodeo." An official without presence often looks nervous and anxious. Coaches can sense a lack of confidence and may become aggressive, thinking that they can easily influence that official to gain an advantage. Again, this is particularly true of newer officials who are not yet known quantities or are working in new places. When they first walk on the field or court (if not before), participants form instant impressions of them, and these are likely to endure. Indeed, longtime college baseball coach Tommy Harmon, who was in professional baseball for many years, once told a group of officials that he had pretty well decided whether an umpire could work or not by the time the umpire got to home plate for the pregame conference, and that it took a lot to change the negative—or positive—impression he formed.

If you are a younger official, you should be prepared to deal with more conflict than older officials do. Coaches tend to test rookies because they believe that rookies are more easily influenced than veterans. Although age is a factor that you can't control, if you are young, you can be well prepared by thinking about what you are going to say before you say it.

Good officials look good. They are physically fit and appear athletic. They walk confidently with a strong posture. How does that relate to managing conflict? The more authoritative you look, the more accepting people are. The more accepting people are, the less conflict you'll have to manage. Your physical presence also has to do with where you are in relation to the conflict. Sometimes you can defuse a problematic situation merely by being in the same physical location.

When players end up on the ground as a result of aggressive playing action, such as diving for a loose ball or a collision, you should immediately move into the area. If the first person a player sees is an official, there is less likelihood of verbal or physical retaliation. If you aren't there, a player might try to get away with an intentional elbow or a push to the opponent.

Your Voice

Words can cut deeper and fester longer than sword wounds. Therefore, you must keep in mind, especially in the heat of battle, that the way you talk to a person has a tremendous impact on the response you receive. An inappropriate reply can cause a conflict with a coach or player. As an official, you have to ask yourself the extent to which you are the problem. Never indulge in verbal retaliation. Remember to enhance your professionalism, treat people with dignity and respect, and use the good communication and listening skills discussed in chapter 5.

Be firm and loud enough to be heard, but not challenging. Your voice can be a positive tool that helps you control a game, or it can be a dagger used to hurt a perceived opponent. Remember, the more you say in a situation of conflict, the less it means. In many cases, deciding not to say anything is the best way to use your voice.

There's an old adage that "You can't misquote silence." This is good to remember.

Keep Emotion Out of Your Voice How you say something can be as or more important than what you say. Use your voice to defuse situations, not add emotion to them. What is a person's first reaction to a barked order? During a conflict, she may become defiant, tense her muscles, and yell back. It's a natural defense mechanism. Consequently, when you bark at a player or coach, the person's first instinct is to snap back. Although he may not reply defiantly right away to avoid a penalty, the person may store that anger. It will likely surface later, and you want to avoid that.

Avoid Threats Any ultimatum you deliver can back you into a corner. If you use the phrase, "One more word and you're gone!" do you understand the ramifications? How literally should you interpret that threat? For example, if the coach responds, "You're an overofficious jerk," the coach has clearly gone too far; you have no choice but to penalize. But what if the coach replies, "You're right. I apologize. I'll just coach my team from now on"? Because the coach did say one more word, would you penalize just to keep your word, or accept the apology and back down from your threat? Getting backed into such corners is a problem with using threats. Instead of using threatening words, use phrases such as, "I've heard enough." These are far less provocative and don't carry an ultimatum that may have unintended consequences, yet get your message across.

Officials obviously have the power to command people to do or not do something and to penalize them if they don't comply. As a rule, less experienced officials tend to do this. But the better officials have learned that they don't get others to respect them, which should be the goal, by threatening or instilling fear or anger in them.

Point to a Shared Goal George Thompson, the author of *Verbal Judo*, (HarperCollins, 1993) stresses that a key to getting others to do what we want is to show that we respect and empathize with them, to develop a creative solution, and then to use tools of persuasion to show them that this solution can produce a win–win for both sides without either side losing face. If, for example, you need to address something that a player or coach is doing—before assessing a penalty if you use preventive officiating—keep a common goal in mind. Here's an example: "Coach, we need to work together to ensure the safety of all players. Can you please talk to number 45 about the rough play out here? That will help us protect the players. Thank you." By letting the coach know that you both have a common goal—in this case, protecting the players—you're more likely to get cooperation from the coach.

Avoid Arguments A person who can upset you to the point that both of you are yelling owns you at some level. Stay calm, with your voice modulated, and try to bring the other person down to your decibel level. Simply state, "When we can talk to each other instead of screaming, I'll enter the conversation." Avoid aggressive body language, and talk calmly and slowly to lower the emotion of the conversation. It's not an argument if you don't participate!

Tell the Truth An old school of thought in officiating was "Never admit to making a mistake." That philosophy has gone away. If you blow a call, it's OK to admit it quietly to the coach or player. Many times, they'll respect you more for your honesty than if you try to twist the truth and equivocate. Most coaches understand that you can't change judgment calls, but admitting you messed up often ends the argument. If you do it too often, however, your reputation will suffer.

Don't Trivialize Though you may be tempted, don't utter the phrase, "It's just a game." Few phrases enrage participants more quickly than that one. Remember, they've worked all week,

all season, and all their careers for that game. It is critically important to them, no matter what the sport or level. That phrase is often interpreted by coaches and players as flippant, uncaring, and demeaning. Also, avoid seemingly innocuous throw-away comments because they can be thrown back in your face. Once, in a pregame coach–umpire meeting before a college football game, the umpire, a seasoned veteran, told the coach, who was 0–4 at that time, "Regardless of the score, we know it will be a hard-fought game." Later, when a close call went against that coach, he went on a tirade, yelling that the umpire's comment showed that he assumed the coach's team was going to lose. It took quite a while to get him calmed down.

Your Body Language

When a player or coach challenges you, consider what your body language says to observers. Avoid crossing your arms in front of your chest. That movement appears too aggressive. Also avoid an aggressive hands-on-hips stance with your chest thrust out. When an argument ensues, consider placing your hands behind your back. Stand tall and strong while doing so. That stance does not appear confrontational yet shows you're in control. At all times, avoid pointing at a player or coach. That gesture appears too aggressive and almost always gets a heated response, such as, "Get your finger out of my face!" Make solid eye contact. If your eyes wander or your head moves around, you give the impression that you're intimidated by the coach or not sure of your position. Try hard not to scowl.

From the moment you arrive at the game site, you're on stage. Think about what you would look like if you were on TV and there were no sound. Constantly ask yourself, What does this look like? By doing so, you'll remember to use body language that sends positive signals. As a result, your challenges will decrease.

Here's a situation illustrating how body language alone can escalate a conflict. You call a balk on a pitcher. The head coach starts out of the dugout to ask you what the pitcher did wrong. The coach is not yelling, running, or waving his arms, but is simply walking toward you. When he gets to you and asks why you called the balk, you don't say anything at first, but instead you fold your arms in front of your

Hustling to be in proper position is vital for any official.

Dale Garvey

chest and look at him with a firmly set jaw and facial expression. Then you put up your hand and say, "Just go on back to the dugout. You don't belong out here arguing judgment calls." Upset by your body language, dismissive attitude, and confrontational way of talking, the coach says, "Hey, I'm just asking a question. I don't know if the kid balked or not, but if he did, I don't want him called for it again." You reply by saying, "I'm warning you. If you don't get out of my face and back to the dugout, you're history." The coach yells, "You've got an attitude problem!" You then eject him from the game, and as he's leaving, he says that he'll be calling your state association to talk about this.

Throughout the scenario, you verbally didn't lose control, yet your body language screamed at the coach a variety of negative messages, including disrespect, arrogance, and an unwillingness to listen. Better body language (eye contact, a comfortable stance with hands behind your back, a nod to let the coach know you understood the concern) coupled with a solid verbal explanation would have helped you

address the coach professionally and avoid a heated argument.

Your Whistle or Flag

Your whistle and your flag are also communication tools. Think of them as an extension of your voice. When you blow a weak whistle, you're more likely to be challenged because it sounds as though you're not sure of yourself. Conversely, an overly loud whistle equates to screeching. There are times when you need a loud whistle (e.g., to get a person's attention, in a loud setting, to help sell a call), but constantly blowing your whistle as loudly as you can is like yelling every call. Blow a strong, steady whistle with normal volume in most situations. If the situation requires you to be a bit louder and firmer, blow your whistle a bit harder, but use that tone sparingly. Don't use short, repetitive blasts except to get someone's attention in a loud setting because they draw unnecessary attention to you and can be perceived as overaggressiveness or hostility to the offender.

The same principles apply to use of the flag in football or soccer. In football, throwing a weak flag so that it looks as if it simply fell out of your pocket suggests that you're unsure about your call. On the other hand, slamming an angry flag into the ground equates to screaming; you appear to have lost control and are belittling the offender. Throw the flag on an arc and unaggressively. If the spot of the foul is relevant because the penalty will be enforced from there, toss the flag toward that spot; if need be, you can adjust it to the proper location after the play ends. If the spot doesn't matter, just toss the flag out in front of you. Similarly, if in soccer you raise the flag slowly or at half mast, you will appear unsure of the call. Extend the flag in an even line directly from your shoulder to the tip of the flag.

Team Captains

The team captain is an often underused yet critically important game management tool for officials. A good relationship with a captain gives you another way to handle players and coaches. To use the captain effectively, you must understand what captains are supposed to do and how they usually think.

The captain is a player whose duties include communicating with the officials. Pregame formalities and duties, such as going over ground rules, the coin toss, and so on, are often performed with captains. The captain serves as team spokesperson and acts as a liaison between officials and the team's players and coaches.

Sometimes the person selected as captain is not the real team leader, especially if the appointment rotates. As an official, you want to find and work with the team leader, even if that leader is not the designated captain. Watch the teams during warm-ups and early in the game. Which player has the most influence on the team? Who does the team look to for answers when the coach is not around? If a team has more than one captain, have the team designate one as the lead spokesperson. You don't want three or four captains asking questions throughout the game; one can handle it.

Let the captain have the first chance to address a player who is getting out of line but deserves a warning and not a penalty. During dead time, say something like, "Captain, number 24 is starting to talk a bit to the opponent. Could you please handle that?" A good leader will quiet the offending player immediately. If that happens, thank the captain. Most captains take their roles very seriously. If you communicate with them and give them an opportunity to be leaders, they can help you do your job.

Resolving Conflict

When you are involved in a conflict, your goal as an official is to resolve it. You have to fight the tendency to try to win the argument. The difference between resolving a conflict and winning it is critical to conflict management.

When resolving a conflict, the best outcome is when everyone wins. If there is only one winner, the loser's self-esteem and trust are eroded. To avoid that, strive to have an open dialog and think about the words you choose and the way they affect the situation. An old officiating saying summarizes this philosophy: "As officials, we always have the last word. However, we don't always have to say it."

In a *Referee* magazine feature story titled "Count to Ten," psychologist Bruce Baldwin (January 1992, p. 44) detailed a plan to help resolve conflict:

1. *Permit the other person to talk without interrupting.* Have the courtesy to listen before you say anything. The other person is then more likely to extend you the same courtesy. When both sides have been adequately heard, problem solving begins. Retired National League umpire and Hall of Fame member Doug Harvey applied his "10-second rule." He gave a manager who argued with him 10 seconds to vent before responding. His theory was that the comments from the arguer were so emotional that his breath couldn't last for more than 10 seconds. When he stopped to take a breath, Harvey could calmly begin his explanation.

2. *Limit discussion to the immediate issue that is adversely affecting your relationship.* One of the fastest ways to get off to a bad start in solving a problem is to rehash the past or bring other impertinent issues into the discussion, as a few coaches like to do. You must "keep them in the box," that is, focused on the play or situation at hand. Coaches may try to talk about things that happened earlier in the game. When they do that, say something like, "Let's focus on this play and get it resolved. Now, how did you see this play?"

3. *Choose an optimal time to bring up and discuss problems.* Many problems that compromise positive conflict resolution can be avoided by carefully choosing the time to discuss a particular issue. To find that time, approach the other person when you are both calm and free to talk. Dead-ball time, such as a time-out or between periods, is a great time for officials to talk to people. Keep the conversations focused and brief.

4. *Judiciously avoid the other person's vulnerabilities or emotional sensitivities.* A deliberate strike at a personal vulnerability is irrelevant as well as hurtful. It also invites a counterattack that focuses on your areas of sensitivity. No one will trust you with emotionally sensitive information if you use it as a weapon whenever there is a problem. In other words, it is inappropriate for the official to counterattack. A testy softball umpire once shouted to a coach who had questioned a call, "I see that white hair under your cap. You probably think your huge experience entitles you to second guess." Sarcasm is never a good instrument for promoting conflict resolution. Probably the biggest temptation to avoid is using a team's record or game score as a weapon. When a team is losing by a large margin and a coach or player is complaining about a call, it is tempting to fire back with, "You've won only three games this year, and you're way behind today. Maybe you should start focusing on playing instead of officiating." Even if this is true, saying it is using a team's vulnerability to your advantage, which is a conflict management taboo.

5. *Regularly touch base with the other person.* It is customary not to take the time to talk when things seem to be going well. If you don't talk when things are going well, then angry interactions may be the only times when you have contact with coaches and players. Make it a point to comment periodically on the progress of the game, even if those remarks are trivial. Ongoing dialog is one of the best possible ways to avoid problems, but this can be difficult for officials because they can't have a constant running dialog with participants. Conversation should be limited to a few words at appropriate times, such as during a dead-ball interval. You should send the message that you are willing to communicate, not that you are commenting on all facets of play.

Tricks of the Trade

Preventive officiating is an important step in managing conflict. You can use of the following tips and tricks to get your point across to players and coaches before penalizing them.

Use Your Lineup Card In baseball or softball, if you need to talk to a coach about a problem, pull out your lineup card before approaching the coach. Suppose, for example, you're the plate umpire and the third base coach has chirped on a couple of strike calls—not enough to issue a formal warning (warnings are covered later) but enough not to ignore. You could take out your card, motion for him to approach you, and when you meet, say "Coach, I don't want to hear anything more on balls and strikes. I'd like to avoid warnings, but anything more and you're going to leave me no choice." Everyone else in the ballpark thinks you're talking about something involving the lineup. You've accomplished what you wanted without embarrassing or challenging the coach in front of players or other observers.

Wipe the Ball Anytime players sweat, they give you a conflict management tool. When a participant is causing problems in the game, use the "wipe the ball" technique to start a discreet discussion. During a dead ball (e.g., when a basketball goes out of bounds) ask the nearest bench assistant for a towel to wipe the ball. While wiping off the ball, approach the problem participants and give your warning. Baseball umpires can accomplish the same thing by wiping off the plate. You can send the message unobtrusively while most people think you're simply doing routine cleaning.

Talk to Your Partner Talk to your partner so players can hear. For example, during a dead ball, in a normal, nonthreatening tone, tell your partner in front of the players, "Joe, number 4 for blue and 5 for white are starting to talk a bit too much to each other. Let's keep an eye on them." You've sent the message without directly confronting the players, which is a good preventive technique in the early stages of the problem.

Make a Deal One of the more consistent complaints from football linemen is that the opponent is holding. When you've decided the complaint needs to be addressed, make a deal with the complainant, for example, "OK, number 76. I've heard you. I'm going to watch you exclusively for the next three plays. If he doesn't hold you in the next three plays, the complaining stops." The player will almost always accept the conditions. If the complaint is true, call it. If not, gently tell the complaining player so: "He looked clean on those plays." More often than not, the player will return to playing and stop complaining.

Preventing Fights

When a fight erupts in a game, the officials may be held accountable—which can be damaging to their reputations and sometimes can result in legal action. It's hard for even the most competent and respected officials to bounce back from being labeled as someone who can't control a tough game. The best way to handle a fight is to prevent it from starting.

Know the Background

As previously discussed, information about the participants and possible rivalries can help prevent conflicts. To learn participants' history, talk to other officials. Share with other officials how and why fights that you've had to deal with took place.

In extreme situations, caution players and coaches before the game as a reminder that you are aware of potential problems. It's OK to let them think that you're going to call the game more tightly or be tougher on them but then call in your normal style. When addressing players or coaches before the game, end with a positive thought. Assure them that if they play the game the way it's meant to be played, there won't be any problems and that you will do everything you can to protect them and prevent conflicts from escalating.

Read the Signs

To prevent a fight, you must pick up on the little signs that a bigger problem is imminent. The most obvious signs are verbal—trash-talking or any type of intimidating or threatening words designed to embarrass or incite the opponent. Remember to watch participants' body language as discussed earlier for signs of anger or frustration.

Be Prepared

Prepare for the worst. That doesn't mean overreacting; it means knowing what you will do if certain things happen. Talk with your part-ners about the teams' history and chemistry before every game. Map out your preventive plan of action. Discuss what you will do if a fight breaks out. By talking about potential problems with partners, you will be better prepared and more confident in handling even the worst situations.

Learn From It

If a fight does break out, learn from it. Think about what led up to the fight, which may reveal what you might have done to prevent it. Few fights explode out of nowhere. You may have missed some signs at the time. By taking the time to review, you won't miss them again. Don't blame yourself. Coaches, administrators, and players must accept responsibility, too.

When to Penalize

Preventive officiating means using informal warnings when possible and appropriate before a problem requires more severe action. The rules of many sports stipulate when formal warnings or penalties should be issued for specific infractions. You must know these rules thoroughly and also know how much leeway to grant participants.

When to Forfeit

A forfeit (in soccer sometimes called a termination) is the most serious call you can make. You forfeit a game when you've determined that the game can no longer be played under the current conditions and that no amount of preventive officiating and penalizing can maintain

---

Put the Ball in Play

One of the most effective tricks for avoiding conflict really isn't a trick at all. When someone starts to complain, get the ball back in play as soon as possible. There is generally more complaining during dead ball time than when the game is going on. Players have to play when the ball is live, and they won't have time to argue. Coaches also tend to get back to coaching when the ball is in play. Don't rush to the point of looking hurried, but get the ball back in play as soon as possible after a dead ball. Your conflicts will decrease.

control of the game. Most sports have specific procedures to follow before ruling a forfeit. Be sure to understand those rules thoroughly to ensure that you handle tough situations appropriately. Ruling a forfeit should always be a last resort. You will likely have few in your career.

What to Tolerate From Whom

As an official, you may feel as though you get abuse from just about everyone present at a game, from spectators to players. You should tolerate different levels of abuse from different participants in the game. Though each official draws individual boundaries, the following sections offer guidelines for how much or little you should tolerate from particular groups. Remember, no extremely unsporting conduct should be tolerated from anyone.

Fans

Be more tolerant of fans than any other group. They've often paid money to root for their teams, and some believe that includes the right to boo the officials. Never talk back to fans. Doing so only increases their abuse. At higher levels of play, tolerate more from fans than you would at lower levels of play. For example, a fan using profanity at a youth game shouldn't be tolerated, but fans using profanity at professional games should be ignored. If a fan is using profanity or offensive terms at a youth game, have the fan removed from the premises immediately. Following is the proper method for doing this:

- Do not say anything to the fan.
- Stop the game, approach the game administrator (or the home head coach if an administrator is not present), and explain that a particular fan is to be ejected for using improper language.
- Let the game administrator handle the ejection. It's not your job to escort fans from the premises.
- Delay the game until the problem is rectified. It might be appropriate to send players to their benches during the interruption.

At higher levels of play, it has become trendy for fans to throw coins and small objects onto the floor or field. You should have game administrators warn or remove fans who throw objects. Fans who throw objects directly at an official or a player should be ejected immediately by the game administrator. If the offender can't be found in the crowd, suggest that the game administrator remove the fans from the section from which objects were thrown. Although you usually should be most tolerant with fans, you should have no tolerance for threats to players' or officials' safety.

Head Coaches

Because of the nature of the job, some head coaches create problems for officials. Use preventive officiating whenever you can, and tolerate a bit more from them than you would from players or assistant coaches.

As discussed earlier, coaches sometimes engage in manipulative behavior or grandstanding to gain a psychological advantage. One school of thought says that if you know a coach is deliberately trying to get a penalty or ejection, you should ignore the antics and avoid being taken advantage of, but that rarely works. If a basketball coach whose team is down by 30 points wants to get the crowd fired up by running onto the court and blaming you, there's not much you can do but penalize the offender. If you don't penalize, the coach will likely do something more severe until she is satisfied.

It's not easy to handle a manipulative coach. Here are some practical tips:

- *Game context dictates when a coach is most likely to use an official for motivational purposes.* The time of the game, the score, and the setting are all factors. When a team is playing poorly at home, a coach is more likely to use an official to draw the crowd and the team into the game. Conversely, some coaches playing in a hostile environment may buy a penalty (such as a technical foul in basketball or unsportsmanlike conduct penalty in football) to turn the crowd against that coach's team and reinforce a feeling of "us against the world" in the players. Be aware of the situation, but don't let it dictate how you work the game.

- *Take care of business while maintaining an even keel.* Rewarding a coach with a technical foul or ejection can test your emotional maturity. Good officials administer penalties without losing their cool and continue concentrating on the game.

- *Avoid engaging in a war of wills with a coach who's looking to manipulate you, the crowd, or the team.* It may be tempting to be stubborn ("You can't make me throw you out. If I have to suffer through this, you do too"), but that attitude can backfire. If you let a coach get away with unsporting behavior, the coach of the other team will likely follow suit.

Starting Players

Starting players should get a bit more leeway than reserves, because that's who the fans come to see. Although that doesn't mean that you should give starting players free rein to abuse you, it does mean that you should use preventive officiating as much as possible to keep them in the game. If preventive officiating fails, penalize.

Assistant Coaches

Assistant coaches should get some leeway when they are complaining, but not much. It is your job to hear complaints from a head coach, not to deal with complaints from assistants.

Conflicts with assistants tend to heat up faster than conflicts with head coaches for a number of reasons. Officials expect complaints from head coaches. Dealing with a head coach's complaints one on one is less stressful than when two or three assistants chime in, which can make you feel outnumbered. Many assistants are young; sometimes it's their first coaching job. Assistants may get less respect from older officials simply because they haven't been coaching long. Younger and less experienced coaches tend to be more emotional. And, as has been noted, assistant coaches may complain as part of a plan whereby the assistant works the officials and is prepared to take a flag or technical foul for doing so, while the head coach can stay above the fray. Knowing that this is what might be going on at the time can help you decide how to respond.

Here is how to handle assistant coaches:

- *Don't stereotype.* It's not fair to assume that all assistant coaches are trouble.
- *Don't treat assistants as inferiors.* Today's assistant may be tomorrow's head coach.
- *Use an assistant to help manage the game.* For example, the NFL and college football leagues have instituted an informal get-back coach, an assistant who is in charge of helping keep players in the team box and off the field.

- *Address problems with assistant coaches by talking to the head coach.* In most cases, the head coach will squelch the assistant. The last thing a head coach wants is a penalty because of an assistant.

Bench Personnel

Other people on the bench (e.g., reserve players, trainers, team managers) should receive minimal tolerance. They each have a job to do that does not include commenting on the officiating. Address problems with bench personnel directly with the head coach. Often, the coach will support you to avoid a penalty caused by bench personnel.

Game Attendants

Often, scorers and timers are from the home school. Some can get caught up in being fans and create problems for officials. Remind attendants before the game that they are an important part of the officiating team and that neutrality is important. Most of the time you won't have problems. However, when a game attendant makes unnecessary comments or improper gestures, take care of it immediately. You can deal with the offender directly, or preferably, ask the game administrator to handle the problem. If you deal with it on your own, remind the offender that she is a part of the officiating team and that being a fan while in that role is inappropriate. If improper conduct continues, have the game administrator remove the offender immediately.

Cheerleaders and Mascots

Cheerleaders and mascots should get close to zero tolerance. If you see a cheerleader incite the crowd against the officials or the opponents, deal with it immediately. Cheerleaders are not fans and should not be given as much leeway. They are representing their school or university in a formal manner and should act accordingly. A fan yelling, "Ref, you're horrible!" probably isn't worth bothering with; a cheerleader yelling the same thing is unacceptable.

At more competitive games, cheerleaders may be more vocal, but their job of firing up the crowd should not include berating officials. Notify the game administrator, consider giving one warning, but have them removed for the second offense.

Consider this scenario: You're officiating a basketball game. The opening jump ball is a good one, and you're off and running toward the baseline as the lead official. You round the corner near the baseline, eyes focused on the players, to settle into position for the first half-court action of the game. Suddenly, you're in a collision. Because you're looking where you're supposed to, you don't see the cheerleaders standing on the baseline, and you crash into them. Later, you make a strong block call underneath the basket. You hear someone behind you scream, "That's brutal!" Your head snaps around to find the culprit only to see that there are no fans behind you, just a cheerleader looking innocent.

Here are some things you can do to avoid any problems with cheerleaders on the court or field:

- *Understand the role of cheerleaders and mascots.* Remember that they have worked long hours in preparation for the game, just as the players have. Although cheerleaders are not essential to the game, being dismissive of them only invites conflict.

- *Work with cheerleaders before the game.* Because you are required to be present before the game starts, you will likely have ample time to talk to the cheerleaders and their coach or adviser before the game. Cheerleaders tend to position themselves on the baseline at basketball games, which can leave little room on the baseline for the officials. Ask them to move before the game begins so that the game can proceed smoothly.

- *Encourage safety first.* If the cheerleaders are hesitant to cooperate, explain to their coach or adviser that their positioning is a safety issue. Communicate that you're asking them to move to protect them, the players, and the officials from injury. When in doubt, err on the side of safety, as you would in any other potentially dangerous situation.

- *If all else fails, call on the game administrator to help you take care of the situation.* Once the administrator understands that you're trying to protect the participants—and protect the school from legal liability—the administrator should be cooperative. If problems with the cheerleaders are continual, contact your supervisor or assigner and let that person deal with the school's governing body.

Using Warnings and Penalties

You can use informal warnings in situations that are bad enough to warrant attention but not bad enough to penalize. Most of the time, your voice will be effective. Sometimes no amount of preventive officiating resolves a conflict. That's when it's time to use formal warnings or penalties.

Informal Warnings

Many sports have rules that have specific formal warnings for specific infractions that are issued before a penalty. Before you get to that point, you should use informal warnings when possible and appropriate. The three types of effective informal warnings are the quiet word, the louder word, and the visual warning.

- *The quiet word.* Use the quiet word when you notice something that could develop into a larger problem; for example, "Captain, number 24 needs to get back to playing and let us officiate. Can you help us out?" The conversation should include only those directly involved: the offender and maybe his coach or manager. As you've learned in this chapter, use positive statements and point to a common goal. If you use the quiet word well, you'll likely use it many times throughout the game.

- *The louder word.* When the quiet word doesn't work, sometimes a louder word does. Be firm and strong, but don't ever yell or curse. Consider using the louder word to the offending player in front of other players. Saying, "Number 24, I've heard enough" will alert teammates to keep the offender in check.

- *The visual warning.* When the quiet word and the louder word don't work, use a visual warning. Use a stop gesture—fingers upward and palm extended to the offender—to show all around that you've heard enough and have issued an informal warning. A visual warning, though informal, is considered the last step before issuing a penalty. A smart player or coach will see a stop sign and back off quickly, knowing a penalty is about to be assessed.

Although all three types of informal warnings are great first steps in game management, repeated warnings become ineffective. If you cry wolf by continuing to warn without penalizing, eventually the offenders will realize that you're not going to penalize and will ignore your warnings, especially if you repeat the visual warning.

Formal Warnings, Penalties, and Ejections

The rules of some sports require formal warnings for specific infractions. Often, the second offense (by the same player or by anyone on the team) results in a penalty. Be sure to study your rule book and understand formal warnings to properly deal with each situation.

One of the most difficult things to sort out as a new official is when to penalize. Each case is unique, and officials have varying levels of tolerance. Nevertheless, a few behaviors should be penalized automatically every time, without issuing an informal or formal warning. For example, a curse word yelled by a player out of personal frustration is often given an automatic penalty at the grade school level. Most of the time, you carefully judge behavior based on such things as game context, severity, and reactions from others.

Remember, in many sports, officials can issue penalties before ejecting an offender. Not all offenses require immediate ejection. Here are some behaviors that require a penalty:

• *A curse word clearly audible to others.* Occasionally, frustrated players curse to themselves after botching a play. That usually can be handled with a quiet word of caution. However, at rare times a player's curse words require a penalty. Generally, if it's loud enough for a distant crowd of people to hear, it's worthy of a penalty, even if it was not directed toward an official or opponent. For example, if a high school basketball player misses a three-point shot and mutters an expletive out of frustration, a quiet word to the player is sufficient. However, if the player turns toward the crowd and screams an expletive that other players, coaches, and fans clearly hear, a technical foul penalty is appropriate.

• *Trash talk to an opponent.* Officials play a vital role in encouraging good sporting behavior. Part of that role includes penalizing unsporting behavior. When a player or coach says something derogatory to an opponent, penalize it immediately and without warning.

• *A coach on the court or field arguing with an official.* In almost all sports, a coach is supposed to be in a specific area. If a coach walks onto the court or field to argue with you, penalize the coach. Players' and officials' safety can be jeopardized when a coach is on the court or field during play because a dangerous collision could ensue. Also, a coach who chooses to argue on the field or court draws unnecessary attention to the argument and draws other coaches, players, or fans into it. A notable exception is baseball, where tradition dictates that, within limits, a coach may go onto the field to argue with an umpire.

• *Showing up an official.* If a player or coach is excessively demonstrative while complaining (flailing arms, stomping feet, throwing objects), penalize the offender, especially coaches who throw clipboards or players who throw the game ball. Be sure to watch your partner's back. Sometimes a coach or player waits until the official turns her back before visually demonstrating displeasure with overexuberant gestures. If you see such behavior, protect your partner and penalize it, even though the offender wasn't arguing with you.

• *Anything derogatory that starts with* you. Do not take personal attacks too lightly. Generally, a coach or player who says, "That's a terrible call!" does not deserve to be penalized. However, if a coach or player says, "You're terrible!" penalize the offender.

• *Physical contact with an official.* If you are bumped or pushed, eject the offender immediately. There should be no second chance.

As you gain experience and learn from others, you'll develop your own limits for what behavior is allowable and what isn't. You don't want a reputation as a quick trigger (i.e., an official who looks for trouble and often penalizes borderline offenses without addressing the problem first). Neither do you want to be labeled as someone who won't take care of business (i.e., an official who lacks the courage to penalize actions that clearly warrant a penalty). You must find the middle ground between the two extremes. Use preventive officiating when appropriate, and penalize when necessary.

Here is a simple yet effective guideline: If your concentration is broken by a complaint, it is worth addressing because your most important job is to administer the game. After you've spoken to the offender once, if your concentration is broken again by the same offender, penalize.

Some officials seek reasons to eject players or coaches. Don't look for trouble; there will be plenty for you to handle without having to look for it. If an ejection is necessary, handle it swiftly and professionally.

When penalizing someone, don't get emotional. That's much easier said than done, but think of it as any other call. If you get wrapped up in emotion, you convey the message that you're out of control, and you're more likely to do something that you'll regret later. Therefore, call a technical foul in basketball by unemotionally forming a subtle T with your hands as you walk calmly toward the scorer's table; eject a coach from a baseball game without the big, over-the-top throwing motion; and calmly throw a flag for unsporting conduct in a football game in front of you instead of launching it so high that it threatens to bring rain.

Don't let additional administrative penalties affect your judgment when deciding whether to eject a participant. Many leagues at all levels have adopted automatic suspension rules designed to deter poor behavior. Most of these rules say that when a player or coach is ejected for unsporting conduct, the offender must sit out the next game. Don't worry that if you eject the offender, she will miss another game. The players and coaches are well aware that if they get out of line, they run the risk of missing the next game. If they are not concerned about the additional penalties, you should not be either.

Responding to Violence

In rare instances, game situations turn violent. In the worst cases, fans brawl with other fans, players go into the stands to confront opposing fans, or a fight breaks out on the court and spills into the stands. When a situation involving brawling fans or players escalates to the point at which the game officials and the game administrator can't control it, have the game administrator call the police to restore order. In high-profile sports such as basketball and football at the high school varsity level and above, uniformed police officers often are already assigned to the game site. Know where the police are located so you can find them if you need them.

What to Do if You're Attacked

If you are physically attacked in connection with your officiating, you should know what to do and what not to do. In an interview for *Referee* magazine, the late Mel Narol, an attorney who was an authority on legal issues involving officials, gave the following advice on the proper procedures for handling the legal aspects of an assault (Narol, 1986, p. 32):

1. Don't strike back to attack the player, coach, or fan who assaulted you. If your attacker is injured by your retaliation, you could be subject to criminal liability or a reduction of a potential monetary award. By fighting back physically, you may be placing yourself in a no-win situation.

2. As soon as possible, obtain the names, addresses, and phone numbers of witnesses. The information they supply may be critical to you and your attorney.

3. Immediately write down the complete history of what occurred and how you were injured. Be sure to include the names, addresses, and phone numbers of everyone who was present, including your attackers, if known, coaches and managers, other officials, and game attendants.

4. Determine whether a video of the game and incident were made; if so, obtain a copy. Visual evidence can be of great value to you and your attorney.

5. Don't discuss the incident with anyone; simply gather information. Often what you say is misunderstood or misinterpreted, which may return to haunt you during litigation.

6. Obtain competent legal counsel. Discuss whether you have a civil or criminal complaint to make against your attackers. If you are assaulted during or after a game that you've worked, you have the right to pursue both civil and criminal actions. Those options should be discussed with legal counsel.

Assaults against sports officials are drawing unprecedented attention. Many states have passed legislation designed specifically to protect sports officials. Contact the police if you or a partner has been assaulted. File appropriate police reports, and follow through with charges as appropriate. One way to help deter violence against officials is to fight it in the proper way—in the judicial system. You do a disservice to the profession if you're involved in a physical altercation and decide to look the other way to avoid trouble.

Handling Conflict After the Game

Most games end without serious conflict. However, conflict management does not stop when the game ends. The following sections discuss things you should think about after the game.

Immediately After the Game

Get off the court or field as soon as your officiating duties are over. In most sports, the official's job ends soon after the game ends, but some sports (such as hockey) require officials to watch the teams' postgame handshakes.

Hanging around the court or field after a game can invite trouble, even if the game went well in your mind. Remember, sports are competitive, and sometimes competition brings out hostile emotions against officials. Avoid possible postgame conflicts by getting to the locker room or away from participants as soon as the game is over. Always leave with your partners; make sure they are right behind you if you're in the lead to ensure their safety.

Off the Field or Court

Once you're in your locker room, you can begin to unwind mentally. Keep in mind, however, that participants (usually coaches) are sometimes so unhappy that they'll want to enter your locker room to confront you. Ideally, only officials and possibly a game administrator should be allowed into the officials' locker room. Don't let anyone else in to discuss your officiating or the game, not even the home coach if possible.

Because of space limitations, many times your locker room is the home coach's office. In this case, before the game, ask the game administrator to have the coach wait until after the officials have left the premises to get into the office after the game. If a coach does enter your locker room, as frequently happens in shared space at grade school or high school levels, avoid conversation. Be polite if any response is necessary. If the coach begins an inappropriate discussion about the game or your officiating, ask the coach to leave the locker room until the officials have left. If the problem escalates, contact the governing body (e.g., league administrator, assigner, or state association) to report the incident.

When you head for the parking lot, go with your partners or an escort if possible. In rare cases, upset people linger in the parking lot after a game to confront officials. Having other people around will help control the situation, and they can serve as witnesses in the event of a confrontation. In cold weather, make sure all your partners' cars start properly before leaving the premises.

Reporting Conflicts

Writing reports is becoming commonplace in officiating today. More frequently than in the past, officials are required to submit misconduct reports to schools, league offices, or governing bodies, such as state high school associations. Some organizations require officials to submit a game report after every game, even if there is no misconduct to report.

Why so many reports? The reports are usually used to protect officials, school personnel, and other responsible entities from legal liability. Thirty years ago, it was rare for a game incident to end up in court. Today, it's more commonplace. If you're involved in a court case, you probably will be asked to reconstruct the incident—possibly months or years after it happened. That's a difficult, if not impossible, task without a report written just after the incident.

If you've had an unsporting incident during a game, call the league administrator or assigner first, before sending a written report. Most administrators want to hear about incidents from officials first, before an angry coach calls, so they can deal with the angry coach appropriately. Don't let your assigner be surprised by a coach's phone call if you have time to give the assigner advance warning about the situation.

Be brutally honest in writing reports. Don't sugarcoat what the other party did to try to protect your ability to get future game assignments. If you said or did something to exacerbate the situation, own up to it. Very little angers supervisors or assigners more than going to bat for officials who were involved in some incident only to find out that the officials did not accurately report their role. If profanity was used against (or by) you, report it verbatim. For appropriate action to be taken, the powers-that-be must know precisely what occurred and was said by everyone involved. If you were physically contacted, make that clear.

Misconduct Reports

Send misconduct reports or incident reports to the proper authorities, even if reports are not required. Report any ejection, flagrant foul, unsporting conduct, or unruly fan behavior. Reporting such incidents accomplishes two important things: it ensures that the incident is reported accurately, and it protects your own interests.

Some officials look at writing reports as a laborious chore, but you risk forgetting key information if you are required to reconstruct an incident much later and you have not written a report. Equally important, not writing a report does an injustice to other officials. If you don't identify an offender in a misconduct report, the proper authorities and other officials may not know about the problem and cannot track patterns of poor behavior.

In the very rare situation in which there is the potential for litigation and you are asked to give a deposition, keep in mind how that legal "discovery" tool can be used. It is designed to allow each side to ascertain the facts about the situation so they can decide whether, and how, to proceed. But it can also be a trap for the unwary. If there is a trial, it will occur several months later. The deponent may be put on the witness stand and asked the same questions he was asked in the deposition. If the answers are or appear to be different, the judge or jury may infer that the witness is uncertain or being evasive or dishonest. Therefore, in the deposition, think before you speak, be honest, be as concise as possible, and never guess. If you're not 100 percent certain about the answer, say, "I don't know" or "I can't recall."

Game Reports

Game reports are different from misconduct reports but are equally important. In some conferences or leagues, game reports are required from officials after every contest. Game reports are not always negative. They identify patterns of problem behavior and player injuries but also note positive experiences and good sporting behavior.

Writing Your Report

There's no need to report every cross word you have with a coach or player, but when in doubt, file an incident report. These are some details that should appear in each report:

1. Date and time of the incident
2. Game site
3. Names of all the officials involved, the teams, and if possible, the head coaches
4. Weather conditions (if played outdoors)
5. Field or court conditions
6. Light conditions, especially if the light was a factor (e.g., a softball game finishing at dusk)
7. Game situation at the time of the incident (e.g., the inning or time left in the period)
8. Detailed description of the incident or injury, including whether and by whom medical attention was given
9. If possible, the names or numbers of players involved
10. Additional notes or diagrams if necessary and events that led to the incident if relevant

The tone you set in your report is very important. It reflects on your credibility. Stick to the facts. Don't exaggerate, make false statements, or arrive at unfounded conclusions (e.g., "He approached the player with anger in his eyes and punched him"). Avoid vague or subjective statements such as, "The coach lost total control of himself." Relate only what you observed. Don't bring up hearsay or past experiences unless they're directly related to the incident at hand. Don't speculate, as in, "The players' actions are a direct result of the coach's lack of control." Report the events in the order they took place, but don't add unprovable opinions about cause and effect.

Avoid recommending a course of action, such as, "The coach should be suspended for his actions." Your job is to relate the facts, not pass judgment. Let the appropriate authorities handle the punishment. Also, don't threaten (e.g., "If someone doesn't stop this team from acting as they do, I'm not going to work any more of their games. I'll spread the word at my local officials' association, and soon no one will work for this team"). Threats diminish your credibility. Keep in mind that what you're reporting is likely not typical behavior.

Jot down pertinent information as soon as possible after the game while the incident is fresh in your mind; the longer you wait, the more you'll forget. Compare your thoughts with those of your partners. Bring a notepad and pen to each game so you're ready if you need them. Audio recorders are also handy tools.

After you've written the report, let it sit for a while and think about something else. Consider having another respected official read it to provide input. Reread the report as if you were the person receiving it. Does it clearly convey what happened? Is it credible? Does it have the proper tone? If so, you're ready to send it. If not, fix what's necessary. Keep a copy of your report. You may be asked later to clarify your statements or reconstruct the incident. Also, follow up with the governing body. You have a right to know what action was taken following an incident.

Postseason Management

During the course of the season, keep a journal. Write down strange plays, your feelings about your performance, notes about your partners, things you did well, and things you can improve. A journal is a great way to look back during and after the season to see whether you have patterns of behavior that need adjusting. If the same problems keep appearing in your journal, you know those things need to be addressed. Reviewing the journal is also a great way to start thinking about officiating and your conflict management plan before your next season. See the sample entry in table 8.1.

Postgame Evaluation

After any game involving an ejection or other unsporting conduct, ask yourself these important questions:

- Did I do anything to lead to the ejection?
- Did I challenge the player or coach?
- Did I lose self-control?
- Did my body language show that I was the aggressor?
- Did I let the coach or player have a chance to get his or her emotions in check?
- Will I do anything differently the next time something similar occurs?

Take a hard look at yourself to see what you could have done better. Ask your partners for their views, or review the incident with respected veterans to gain further insight. Some bad situations can't be prevented, but many can.

After your self-analysis, your next challenge is preparing mentally for your next game. You must learn from the incident, but you also must clear your head to officiate the next game. The biggest challenge is the next time that you must work with the offender. You'll find that often the incident has been forgotten by the offender; you need to forget it, too. Even if the offender's bad feelings have festered, you must remain professional and implement your

Table 8.1 Sample Journal Entry

Time	Action	Comments
Third inning	I called time when the pitcher started delivery.	The coach was correct in objecting that I may have been too late.
Fifth inning	I didn't go out far enough on a line drive.	It may have been trapped; I should have ignored the coach's complaint instead of defending my action.
Seventh inning	The catcher spoke sarcastically to the batter.	I should have warned him and reminded the coach between innings to speak to his catcher.

conflict management plan. It's unfair to the participants to allow your bad feelings to carry over from one game to the next.

SUMMARY

Knowing the rules of the sport and the mechanics of officiating isn't enough; how you handle people indicates your competence as an official. The best officials are not just good at calling fouls, violations, safes, and outs. They can defuse hostility and keep players and coaches in games, but they have the courage to penalize when necessary.

Plan how you will handle conflict. It helps to understand why people treat officials as they do. Implement your plan, and use preventive officiating whenever possible. Deal with people dispassionately and professionally at all times. Learn from each situation.

Conflict management is an important psychological skill for officiating. To become a complete official, you need to prepare both psychologically and physically. The next part of the book discusses physical fitness and why it is important for officials.

REVIEW QUESTIONS

1. Which of the following is *not* among the techniques to use in dealing with youth game fans who are using profanity?

    a. Stop the game, confront the fan, and ask him to behave more civilly.

    b. Ask game management to eject the fan from the premises.

    c. Report the incident to your supervisor or assigner.

    d. All are good techniques to use.

2. Which of the following is *not* true if you are physically attacked by a player, coach, or fan?

    a. You are within your rights to hit the person back.

    b. You should record the details of the incident as soon as you get home.

    c. As soon as possible, you should get the names, addresses, and phone numbers of witnesses.

    d. Both *b* and *c* are true.

3. Which of the following is *not* an appropriate method of issuing an informal warning to a player who is engaging in borderline behavior?

    a. Issue a quiet warning (e.g., "Number 24, you're getting close to holding; work your hands inside the frame of your body").

    b. Issue a louder warning (e.g., "Number 24, I've heard enough").

    c. Issue a visual warning (e.g., turning to a dugout where players are complaining about ball and strike calls and putting your hand up to indicate stop).

    d. All are appropriate methods of issuing an informal warning.

4. Penalizing without a prior warning is appropriate when the person

    a. uses a profanity clearly audible to others

    b. trash-talks an opponent

    c. shows up an official

    d. does any of the above

5. After a game ends, officials should

    a. get off the field or court as quickly as possible

    b. go individually from the dressing room to their cars so as not to attract undue attention from fans

    c. in writing ejection and other game reports, clean up the language reported so as not to offend people who might read the report

    d. do all of the above

    e. do none of the above

6. What are some reasons coaches might complain about an official's call that have nothing to do with the call itself?

7. What are some methods of informal warning that officials can use when players are beginning to get out of line but, in your judgment, do not yet deserve a formal warning?

8. Name some instances in which it is appropriate to issue formal warnings to a player, and perhaps even resort to ejection or a technical foul, with no prior informal warning.

9. Should officials deal in the same manner with complaints from coaches, assistant coaches, players, and bench personnel (e.g., trainers and managers)?

10. What are some nonverbal issues that can cause officials to be negatively perceived by coaches, players, and other observers?

Answers on page 189

Part III

Getting Fit to Officiate

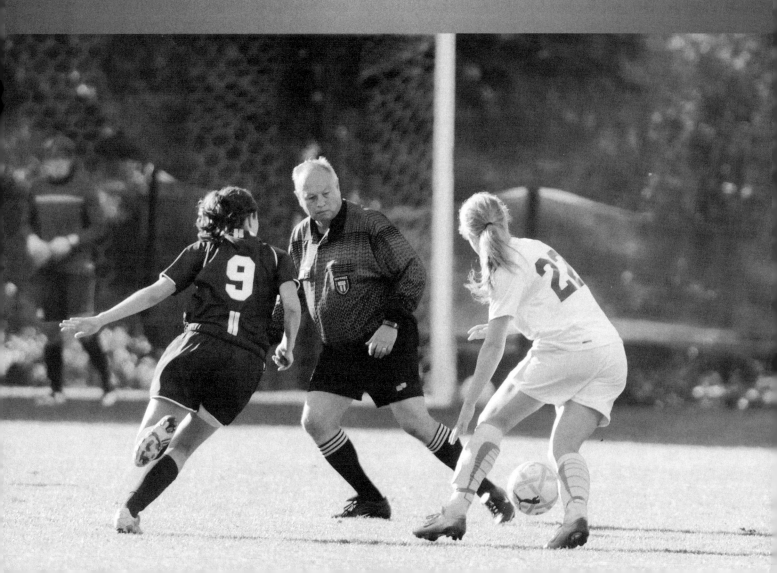

Chapter 9

Fitness Principles for Officials

Jon Poole and Kathleen Poole

This chapter addresses the following:

- The four components of health-related physical fitness
- The importance of staying injury free
- How healthy nutrition can improve your officiating performance
- How physical fitness and health are affected by aging

HEALTH-RELATED PHYSICAL FITNESS

In 2008, the U.S. Department of Health and Human Services released the Physical Activity Guidelines for Americans, recommending physical activity to improve both aerobic fitness and muscle-strengthening fitness. Daily physical activity is positively linked with increased overall health, whereas premature death and illness are associated with sedentary lifestyles.

The 2008 Physical Activity Guidelines for Americans state that all adults need at to accumulate least 150 minutes (2 1/2 hours) of moderate-intensity aerobic activity such as brisk walking per week and workout at least two days a week with muscle-strengthening activities such as weight lifting, push-ups, and resistance bands for improved health. An even greater health benefit (most notably for adults who must perform physical tasks such as officiating) is derived from an increase in aerobic activity up to 300 minutes (5 hours) per week and more than 2 days of muscle-strengthening activities. This recommendation suggests a need for both moderate-intensity activities that raise your heart rate and cause you to break a sweat (such as brisk walking, bicycling on level ground, playing doubles tennis, even gardening and yard work) and more vigorous-intensity activities that raise your heart rate, produce sweat, and increase your breathing rate to the point that you cannot say more than a few words without pausing to catch your breath.

An easy way to remember the difference between moderate-intensity and vigorous-intensity activities is commonly known as the talk test. That is, if you can carry on a conversation while exercising, then the activity is probably moderate. Exercising at a vigorous intensity would make saying more than a couple of words at a time impossible. Activities such as running or jogging, swimming, bicycling fast or over hills, and playing singles tennis are examples of more vigorous-intensity activities. As a rule of thumb, one minute of vigorous-intensity activity is about the same as two minutes of moderate-intensity activity.

It is unrealistic to abuse your body with poor eating and sedentary living during the off-season and then expect it to respond to a month or two of vigorous conditioning and dieting as the preseason nears. Instead, a combination of moderate-intensity and vigorous-intensity aerobic activities along with muscle-strengthening activities needs to become a daily and weekly habit. A commitment to healthy eating and specific exercises that improve flexibility will give you the conditioning you need to begin a season.

The following four health-related fitness components make up what many people think of as physical fitness:

- *Aerobic fitness.* The ability of the body to perform prolonged large-muscle-mass activities at moderate to vigorous intensity.
- *Muscle fitness.* The ability of the muscles to perform forcefully (muscular strength) and repeatedly over time (muscular endurance).
- *Flexibility.* The ability of the joints to move through a full range of motion.
- *Body composition.* The percentage of lean body mass (bone, water, muscle, connective tissue, organ tissues, and teeth) to total body fat.

Aerobic Fitness

The ability to maintain prolonged physical activity means that your body is efficient in performing daily tasks and able to handle physical challenges. The benefits of aerobic exercise (i.e., large-muscle activities performed for a prolonged period) include improved blood circulation, decreased blood pressure, improved metabolism, decreased body fat, better adaptation to stress and anxiety, and better performance in sport-related activities (including officiating).

The tragic on-field death of 328-pound umpire John McSherry from a massive heart attack on opening day of the 1996 Major League Baseball season clearly signaled the need for every official, indeed every adult, to consider the costs of excessive weight and poor aerobic fitness. Poor aerobic fitness is especially harmful for officials who work in extremely hot and humid conditions or those who officiate sports that require a great deal of running (such as lacrosse, soccer, and basketball) or sports that last a long time (such as football and even baseball).

In addition, just as you might expect more penalties from players who experience fatigue in the latter stages of a contest (e.g., the defensive lineman who jumps offsides in the fourth quarter or the basketball player who reaches in to steal the ball rather than move his feet to gain a better defensive position), you can also expect that you will make mistakes when you are fatigued. Thus, aerobic fitness is critical for officiating success.

Improving and Maintaining Aerobic Fitness

If you are starting a new conditioning program, follow your family physician's advice and first seek approval following a general physical exam. Using the 2008 Physical Activity Guidelines for Americans mentioned previously, simply start by walking five days a week (frequency) at a brisk pace (intensity) for 30 minutes (time) (U.S. Department of Health and Human Services, 2008).

Cross-training with bicycling and swimming will keep the wear and tear off your legs, and jumping rope and running or jogging will add intensity and help you gain a higher level of fitness. A general rule of thumb for runners is to increase weekly mileage by only 10 to 15 percent. Thus, adding an extra five minutes a day after a couple of weeks of base training is a reasonable goal. The 2008 Physical Activity Guidelines suggest that you eventually increase aerobic fitness activities to around five days a week (frequency) at both a moderate and vigorous intensity effort for upwards of 60 minutes at a time. These 300 minutes of weekly exercise should be paired with a few days of muscle fitness workouts and flexibility exercises.

Table 9.1 is taken from research conducted over 10 preseason and regular season games during the 2003-2004 NFL season. Please note that the average distance covered for all officiating positions was over six miles. Further, close to 40 percent of the activity was at a moderate pace with several bouts of sprinting at a vigorous pace. This research is based on actual on-field data and should serve as a goal

Table 9.1 Comparison Data by Position

Position	Distance (miles)	Caloric expenditure (calories)	Average heart rate (beats per minute)	Percent maximum heart rate (%)	Maximum heart rate (beats per minute)	Weight change (pounds)	Percentage of game at light intensity (%)	Percentage of game at moderate intensity (%)
Referee	6.6	698	123	74	158	-2.0	58	42
Umpire	6.0	959	126	75	158	-2.0	53	47
Head linesman	4.5	542	123	73	160	-2.9	80	20
Line judge	4.6	536	122	74	162	-2.0	77	23
Field judge	6.5	699	119	70	165	-1.0	60	40
Side judge	6.5	678	131	77	173	-2.0	57	43
Back judge	7.3	799	120	72	159	-3.0	51	49
Average	6.1	709	123	73	162	-2.1	61	39

Reprinted, by permission, from K.P. Poole, J.A. Leiferman, J. Poole, and S.E. Selmon, 2004, "Examination of the physiological demands of National Football League officiating." *Medicine & Science in Sports & Exercise* 36(5 Suppl): S248.

Results by position are provided. Distance covered per game varied by position (e.g., 7.3 miles for back judges, 6.6 miles for referees). Differences in caloric expenditure were also found among positions (e.g., 959 kcal for umpires, 536 kcal for line judges).

for preseason conditioning. Clearly, covering over six miles in various weather conditions with the pressure and stress of game situations is physically demanding.

Muscle Fitness

The ability to exert forceful and prolonged muscle contractions means that your body will not tire easily and will be able to handle the routine tasks and physical challenges of officiating. The benefits of muscle fitness exercises include improved oxygen delivery to working muscles, improved metabolism, decreased body fat, lower risk of injury, and better performance in sport-related activities, including officiating.

Improving and Maintaining Muscle Fitness

Recommendations suggest that adults should perform muscle fitness exercises two to three times per week to improve their overall health. Suggested exercises include push-ups, pull-ups, horizontal bar dips, single-leg lunges, and abdominal crunches. To truly enhance muscle fitness, you need to commit to a greater variety of exercises that include reliance on strength-training equipment, such as barbells and dumbbells, exercise tubes, and home gyms. Specific training guidelines to improve muscle fitness are discussed in chapter 10.

Flexibility

Flexibility is probably most important for overall joint health and the prevention of injuries. Certain sport activities, such as gymnastics and diving, depend highly on flexibility for high-quality performance. For officiating, flexibility is probably less important for performance than for injury prevention. Light stretching exercises included in an overall fitness plan also reduce stress and postexercise muscle soreness.

Improving and Maintaining Flexibility

Recommendations suggest that adults should perform at least 15 minutes of flexibility exercises in conjunction with their five-times-per-week aerobic and muscle fitness workouts. Traditionally, stretching exercises were performed before a warm-up or were considered the actual warm-up. Recent evidence supports first warming the body up with walking, jogging, easy rope jumping, or a similar activity to prepare for being physically active. Only after a warm-up should you attempt stretching exercises. Stretching cold muscles before a warm-up can lead to a greater chance of injury. Most officials depend primarily on their lower bodies to run up and down a court or field, so pre- and postgame stretching routines should specifically address the legs. Specific flexibility exercises are presented in chapter 10.

AP Photo/Willis Glassgow

Officiating has inherent risks, as shown by this umpire falling after taking a vicious foul ball to the mask.

Body Composition

Body composition is important to your ability to move efficiently and feel good about yourself. Unfortunately, our society has been led to believe that body weight (and not body composition) is related to health and success. Height and weight charts are, at best, arbitrary estimates of what males and females should weigh according to height and estimated frame size. Because body weight does not account for the amount of lean body mass, highly muscled people might be unfairly classified as overweight, because muscle weighs more than fat. Conversely, unfit people may be classified as having a healthy body weight when in reality their body composition may be overfat. Another consideration, perhaps unfair, is the negative public perception of officials who are overweight. Officials are part of the sport spectacle (especially at a collegiate or professional level), and an official who appears overweight is not seen in the same positive light as an official who appears fit and trim.

Improving and Maintaining a Healthy Body Composition

Recommendations suggest that females should strive to keep their body fat under 32 percent; a more desirable range is between 15 and 25 percent. Males should strive to keep their body fat under 25 percent; a more desirable range for males is between 10 and 20 percent. Highly fit people may have under 10 percent body fat, but it is considered a threat to health and well-being if body fat drops below 5 percent for men or 12 percent for women.

Body composition is best altered through a combination of healthy eating and a physically active lifestyle. A deficit of just 500 calories a day, which is roughly equivalent to many fast-food sandwiches or running for 30 to 45 minutes, can result in a weight loss of approximately one pound per week (four pounds per month). A goal of 500 calories deficit per day is based on the 3,500-calorie deficit needed for losing one pound of weight. Thus, 500 calories per day over seven days provides a healthy and safe method of eating a little more appropriately and exercising a little more every day helping to make physical fitness a habit and the resultant weight loss healthier than crash diets. A more ambitious, but still reasonable, goal would be a 1,000-calorie deficit per day, which would result in a weight loss of approximately two pounds per week. This is much more preferable than an unreasonable diet or exercise plan that does not fit into your normal lifestyle.

The human body adapts well to the demands placed upon it. The greater the demand, the greater the adaptation. From a physical fitness perspective, small demands every day can translate into measureable improvement over time. Too often, injuries are the result of a lack of patience when people begin working out too hard, too soon. When preparing to improve your physical fitness, you should consider several principles of physical training, including specificity, progressive overload, and reversibility.

Specificity

Specificity simply means that your workouts must use the specific fitness component that you wish to improve. Weight training is wonderful for muscle fitness, for example, but not the best choice for aerobic fitness. Similarly, running is wonderful for aerobic fitness but not the best for flexibility. Along this same line, as an official (and depending on your sport), you may need to be able to run at a moderate pace for the long length of a game but also be able to add several very vigorous, almost sprinting, runs during certain plays in the game. Your conditioning should mirror the demands of your sport. A basketball court, for example, is much smaller than a football field, but basketball officials must also typically sprint shorter distances while rapidly changing directions.

Progressive Overload

Progressive overload means that to continually improve your fitness, you must progressively increase the exercise load as your body adapts to each of the demands you place on it. The amount of overload is critical. Too much exercise can result in injury, and too little results in limited fitness gains. To determine the proper amount of exercise, consider the FITT principle: frequency, intensity, time, and type (AAHPERD, 1999). Frequency refers to how often during the week you exercise, intensity refers to how hard you exercise, time refers to how long you exercise at any given session, and type refers to the type of actual exercise you are doing.

Reversibility

Reversibility is the opposite of adapting to increased physical stress. That is, as you become more sedentary, your body quickly loses, or reverses, your previous fitness gains. More than 50 percent of the improvement from a fitness program can be lost within eight weeks of ending a program. This is why it is so important that physical activity become a lifestyle habit and not just something you do to get ready for a season of officiating. Choose physical activities that you find enjoyable and that suit your lifestyle, geographic area, and financial budget.

Of course, physical fitness training affects different people in different ways. All of us know people who seem to be able to lose or gain weight easily and others who appear to look the same no matter how little or how much they exercise. It is important to set your own unique goals and focus on adopting healthy lifestyle behaviors rather than focusing on comparing yourself to others.

Staying Injury Free

Injury prevention is important to all officials but becomes even more important as we age. As we age, even minor mishaps can result in severe injuries. A seemingly minor injury can bring an officiating career to an end.

Injuries can be caused by muscle imbalance, poor muscle fitness, poor flexibility, poor aerobic fitness, improper equipment, inadequate rehabilitation following a prior injury, and even bad luck. The most important way to stay injury free is to maintain a healthy lifestyle that includes a regular fitness program. You should perform specific exercises that mirror the officiating moves found in your sport (e.g., short, quick, sliding movements for basketball officials). If you are not fit, it is unreasonable to expect your body to perform at the level needed to officiate and still stay injury free. Poor fitness can lead to both acute and chronic injuries. Even if you manage to avoid acute injuries, the repetitive motions of officiating can still lead to a chronic injury.

You should pay additional attention to eyewear and footwear. Eyewear should be unbreakable and include straps to hold it in place. Good footwear should provide proper support, cushioning, and traction. You may need orthotics in shoes to maintain correct foot and lower-extremity alignment during activity. Heel lifts can prevent Achilles tendon and calf injuries. As shoes become worn, they lose cushioning properties and offer poor support and traction. Worn shoes can lead to chronic injuries, such as tendinitis and stress fractures, as well as acute injuries caused by loss of support and poor traction.

Pay close attention to signals from your body. Aches and pains before, during, and after exercise, especially those involving tendons and joints, should be evaluated to determine their cause and corrected before serious injury occurs. Some common injuries of officials and treatments for their care are discussed in chapter 10.

HEALTHY EATING

Nutrition is an essential component of wellness. The foods that we eat affect our energy levels, thereby influencing physical performance, well-being, and overall health. Our diet can also place us at greater risk for major chronic diseases such as cancer, cardiovascular disease, and diabetes, as well as a host of other health problems. The good news is that a well-planned diet combined with regular physical activity can help prevent these diseases and even reverse some of them.

Six Classes of Essential Nutrients

Our bodies require many substances to function properly. We require nutrients, which are substances that the body needs for health

Insights on Vision

"Are ya blind, ump?" "Where were you looking?" "How couldn't you see that when everybody else in the world saw it?" As these commonly shouted phrases indicate, vision care is an important part of your health as an official. Dr. Bradley Rounds, behavioral optometrist, has worked with professional golfers, trap shooters, and members of the U.S. Olympic ski team. He has this to say about officiating and vision: (Poole, Poole, & Toole, 1999, p. 92).

Vision can be a relative thing. Depending on which side of the ball you're on, which side of the field you're on, or who your relatives are, people will see things differently. The problem is, *you* have to see it correctly. You don't have the benefit of reverse angles or ultra slow motion; you must make the split-second decision and get it right. The only tools you have are your intellect, your experience, and your vision.

Twenty-twenty is not perfect vision. Your "eyesight" is pretty much a given thing, be it 20/20 or 20/400. The good thing is, it can be corrected with spectacles, contact lenses, or even with surgery. But, eyesight is just one part of vision. *Vision* incorporates eyesight, focusing, eye-movement, spatial orientation, and visual perception. Focusing and eye-movements require fine motor movements. Like occupational therapy and physi-

cal therapy, vision therapy works to re-teach or enhance these fine motor skills for the utmost precision and efficiency. All components of vision, with the exception of eyesight, are learned through trial and error throughout life. Since vision is learned, it can be relearned, or enhanced through therapy. Visual perception and spatial orientation can be enhanced by improving these visual skills and through use of special training aides. Many professional and collegiate athletes have improved their performance with vision therapy (orthoptics). As an official, your vision is just as important as an athlete's, and therefore must be treated with the same seriousness.

To have your vision tested, see an optometrist specializing in sports vision. These doctors are trained to see the patient as a whole being, not just two eyeballs. They will check ocular health, prescribe corrective devices, or design a plan for vision enhancement training. The American Optometric Association recommends a yearly vision and ocular health examination. It is also recommended that proper eye protection be worn at all time when engaged in sports or sport officiating. Contact the AOA's Sports Vision Section or the International Academy of Sports Vision to find an optometrist near you. Ask your optometrist to prescribe exercises specific to your vision needs as an official.

maintenance, growth, and tissue repair. Nutrients can be classified into the following six categories:

- Carbohydrate
- Fat
- Protein
- Vitamins
- Minerals
- Water

Three of these classes of nutrients actually provide energy: carbohydrate, protein, and fat. Fat supplies the most energy—nine calories per gram—whereas carbohydrate and protein each supply four calories per gram. High-fat diets (more than 30 percent of calories from fat) are not recommended because they place us at greater risk for a variety of diseases, such as cancer, heart disease, stroke, and diabetes. Because high-fat diets supply more calories, they are associated with an increased prevalence of obesity. Health experts recommend that fat intake be less than 30 percent of total daily calories, with no more than 10 percent of these fat calories from saturated fat. Saturated fat comes predominantly from animal sources and is usually solid at room temperature. Plant sources of saturated fat include palm oil, palm kernel oil, coconut oil, and cocoa butter. A diet high in saturated fat is associated with an increased risk of cardiovascular disease.

Protein is an essential component of cell membranes, muscle, bone, blood, enzymes, and some hormones. A well-balanced diet should get about 10 to 15 percent of its calories from protein. Many Americans consume much more than that every day. Excess protein is synthesized into fat to be used as energy or stored in the body. Extra protein is usually not harmful for most Americans; however, many foods high in protein are also high in fat. The protein requirement for adults is generally met by consuming 0.8 grams of protein per kilogram of body weight. The American Dietetic Association (ADA) recommends that a person who is training intensely consume 1.0 to 1.5 grams of protein per kilogram of body weight. Additional protein should be obtained through food choices, not through supplements. According to the ADA's position paper on nutrition and sport performance, "protein or amino acid supplementation has not been shown to positively influence athletic performance" (American Dietetic Association, 2009, p. 515).

The primary function of carbohydrate is to supply energy to the cells of the body. During high-intensity exercise, our muscles get most of their energy from carbohydrate. Fruits, vegetables, and grains are excellent sources of carbohydrate. A well-balanced diet should get about 55 to 60 percent of calories from carbohydrate. No more than 10 percent of carbohydrate calories should come from simple sugars such as those found in candy and sodas. Complex carbohydrates are more nutritionally dense than simple carbohydrates. That is, complex carbohydrates contain more essential nutrients. Another benefit of eating more complex carbohydrates is that they are typically an excellent source of dietary fiber. Fiber helps prevent cancers of the digestive system, hemorrhoids, constipation, and diverticular diseases because it helps food move more easily and quickly through the digestive system. The recommended daily intake of fiber is 25 grams per day for women and 38 grams per day for men. Sources include whole grains, vegetables, fruits, and legumes.

Vitamins are organic compounds that are essential for good health. Because they cannot be synthesized by the human body in sufficient quantities, they must be obtained through your diet. There are currently 14 known essential vitamins that perform a variety of important physiological functions in our bodies. Some vitamins act as coenzymes to help regulate metabolic processes, whereas others are antioxidants that help to protect cell membranes. One vitamin (vitamin D) is classified as a hormone.

Minerals are inorganic elements found in nature. To date, 15 minerals have been discovered, and each has a specific physiological function. For example, iron transports oxygen to the muscles, sodium helps control water balance in the body, and calcium helps build strong bones and teeth.

By eating a well-balanced diet consisting of fruits, vegetables, lean meats, whole grains, and low-fat dairy products, you can consume the right balance of vitamins and minerals necessary for optimal health and performance. Vitamins and minerals are not a source of calories; therefore, they do not provide energy. Do you need a multivitamin and mineral supplement? If you have a well-balanced diet, you probably don't. However, if you are not sure whether you should take a supplement, you may want to consider consulting with a registered dietitian to have your diet evaluated. To find a registered dietitian, go to www.eatright.org.

Water plays an essential role in the normal functioning of the body. The human body is about 60 percent water. Water is necessary for regulating temperature and transport substances throughout the body. It is recommended that people should consume about two liters, or eight cups, of water per day. This need is higher for those who exercise intensely.

Dietary Guidelines for Americans

The new Dietary Guidelines for Americans were developed in 2011 by the USDA and U.S. Department of Health and Human Services. The guidelines do not focus on a specific diet or diet program, but instead on (1) balancing calories to manage weight, (2) increasing certain foods and nutrients, and (3) reducing certain foods and food components.

Balancing Calories to Manage Weight

- Enjoy your food, but eat less to prevent or reduce overweight or obesity.
- Increase physical activity and reduce time spent being physically inactive.
- Avoid oversized portions.

Increasing Certain Foods and Nutrients

- Increase fruits and vegetable consumption by making half your plate fruits and vegetables.

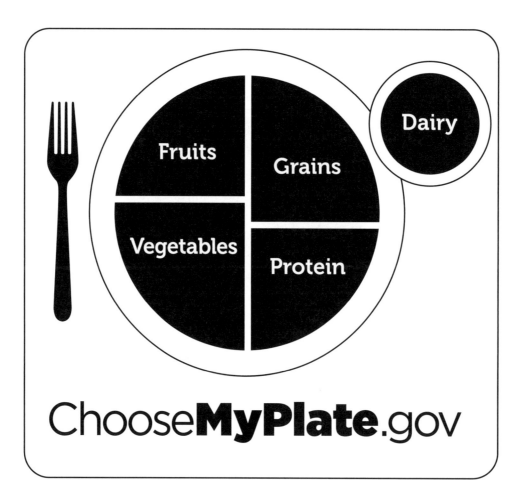

The USDA's revised food plate suggests the proper proportion of nutrients from the major food groups to help keep you at an optimal weight.

- Eat a variety of vegetables especially dark green vegetables such as spinach and broccoli, red vegetables such as peppers, and orange vegetables such as carrots and sweet potatoes.
- Increase whole-grain intake by replacing refined grains with whole grains.
- Increase your intake of fat-free or low-fat milk and milk products.
- Choose a variety of protein foods including seafood, lean meat and poultry, eggs, beans, peas, soy products, and unsalted nuts and seeds.
- Use oils to replace solid fats where possible.

Reducing Certain Foods and Food Components

- Reduce daily sodium intake to less than 2,300 milligrams or 1,500 milligrams for people 51 and older or those of any age who are African American or have hypertension, diabetes, or chronic kidney disease.
- Consume less than 10 percent of calories from saturated fat.
- Consume less than 300 milligrams per day of dietary cholesterol.
- Keep trans fatty acid consumption as low as possible by limiting foods containing partially hydrogenated oils.
- Reduce the intake of calories from solid fat and added sugar.
- Drink water instead of sugary drinks.

Sport Drinks Versus Water

Proper hydration is particularly important for officials. Sweating is the body's primary method for heat dissipation during exercise. The amount of sweat lost during exercise depends on the heat and humidity level, type and intensity of activity, and other factors that vary from individual to individual. Dehydration decreases the body's ability to sweat and can result in impaired performance by reducing coordination, strength, and endurance. Further, dehydration increases a person's risk of heat stroke, heat exhaustion, and heat cramps. The American College of Sports Medicine (ACSM) and the ADA recommend drinking two cups of water two hours before exercising and two more cups within 15 minutes of beginning

an endurance exercise session. During exercise, you should consume about 150 milliliters (about six ounces) of water every 15 minutes, particularly in hot and humid weather. Water should be cold (45 to 55 degrees Fahrenheit).

In general, water is the fluid-replacement drink of choice for euhdraytion (or normal hydration). According to the ACSM,

After exercise, the goal is to fully replace any fluid and electrolyte deficit. The aggressiveness to be taken depends on the speed that rehydration must be accomplished and the magnitude of the fluid-electrolyte deficit. If recovery time and opportunities permit, consumption of normal meals and snacks with a sufficient volume of plain water will restore euhydration, provided the food contains sufficient sodium to replace sweat loss (p. 386).

Unless the exercise bout lasts more than 60 minutes, there is little need to supplement carbohydrate. For continuous, vigorous activity lasting 60 minutes or more, the American College of Sports Medicine recommends consuming a solution containing 4 to 8 percent carbohydrate (glucose, sucrose, or starch). The solution should be ingested in small to moderate quantities (6 to 12 ounces) every 15 to 20 minutes during vigorous activity. For each pound of body weight lost during exercise, 16-24 ounces of fluid should be consumed.

STAYING PHYSICALLY FIT AS YOU AGE

Remaining physically active actually delays the onset of the aging process. Equally important, the benefits of physical activity—such as fewer illnesses, fewer posture problems, greater joint mobility, and less chance of osteoporosis—can help an older person feel younger.

As you move through life, you can expect some loss in your functional capability as an official—for example, your ability to move as quickly as when you were younger, remain injury free, and maintain peak physical conditioning. All four components of health-related physical fitness are negatively affected by the aging process. Joints begin to stiffen and lose mobility, muscles lose strength, and metabolism slows down, making it harder to control weight. Luckily for you, however, this loss in functional capability is not completely

Just like players, it's important to start officiating at a young age and stay physically fit through your career.

age dependent, but is often lifestyle dependent. Remaining active and continuing to eat healthy foods will delay most of the negative effects of aging. Further, with experience on the field or court, you will learn how to move more efficiently to position yourself to make appropriate calls.

Many veteran officials continue to dominate play-off and championship games, not because they are in better physical condition than their younger colleagues, but because they have continued to learn to be better officials. Officials who maintain a high level of physical fitness assure themselves of long and, with luck, injury-free careers. Following the personal fitness plan you develop in chapter 10 will go a long way in helping you to maintain the physically active and healthy lifestyle needed for succeeding in officiating and to ensure a high-quality life.

SUMMARY

As proven by studies, daily physical activity is positively linked with increased overall health, whereas premature death and illness are associated with sedentary lifestyles. Aerobic fitness, muscle fitness, flexibility, and body composition are the four components commonly thought to constitute physical fitness. This chapter discussed the key benefits of strengthening and maintaining these components and improving the quality of your life—thus, making your officiating career longer and better. In addition, proper physical fitness will help keep you injury free and on the field. Also, it's clear that proper nutrition is critical to a healthy lifestyle, and officials should make it a priority to observe proper eating habits.

REVIEW QUESTIONS

1. If all adults are recommended to engage in at least 150 minutes of moderate-intensity aerobic activity every week, would an official need more?

2. What is the difference between moderate-intensity and vigorous-intensity aerobic activity, and what is an easy way to remember the difference?

3. How can you use color to guide your selection of vegetables?

4. The physical training principle that describes the adaptation (i.e., improvement) of the human body to physical stress is known as

   a. aerobic conditioning

   b. progressive overload

   c. reversibility

   d. specificity

5. A healthy and safe goal for losing weight is roughly one or two pounds per week or the equivalent of a daily caloric deficit (by both reducing food intake and increasing physical activity) of

   a. 3,500 to 7,000 calories

   b. 1,500 to 2,500 calories

   c. 500 to 1,000 calories

   d. 100 to 250 calories

Answers on page 190

Chapter 10

Officiating Personal Fitness Plan

Jon Poole and Kathleen Poole

This chapter addresses the following:

- How to design your own personal fitness plan
- The four components of your physical workout
- Stretching exercises to improve your flexibility
- Strength exercises to improve your muscle fitness
- Treatments for injuries common among sports officials

Designing your personal fitness plan involves three basic steps: (1) self-assessment, (2) goal setting, and (3) selection of physical activities. Self-assessment helps you determine your readiness to begin an exercise program and your current fitness levels. Next, you decide what you hope to accomplish with your fitness plan and the components of fitness that you would like to improve. Finally, you select the physical activities that will best help you meet your goals.

SELF-ASSESSMENT

To ensure that your fitness program is appropriate for you, it is wise to assess your current level of fitness. The following sections provide self-assessment tools (Heyward, 2006) that you can use to determine your readiness to begin an exercise program (after seeking approval from your family physician) and your fitness levels in each of the four areas of health-related physical fitness described in chapter 9.

General Readiness Self-Assessment

To determine whether exercise is safe for you, see if you have any of the conditions in the sidebar, Are You Ready for Physical Activity? If you do have any of the conditions on the list or are over 65 and are not accustomed to vigorous exercise, postpone vigorous exercise or exercise testing until after you have consulted your family physician. In addition to the questions in the sidebar, the American College of Sports Medicine (ACSM), in concert with the Canadian Society for Exercise Physiology, has developed pre-exercise recommendations, which are available on the ACSM website: www.myexerciseplan.com/assessment.

Aerobic Fitness Self-Assessment

There are many aerobic fitness tests available today (you may remember some from your days in physical education class). The simplest is probably the one-mile walk test. This test requires you to walk a measured mile on a track or a relatively flat course. You will need a stopwatch and a heart rate monitor, if possible, and you must know your body weight.

Are You Ready for Physical Activity?

If you answer yes to any of the following statements, please talk with your physician or other appropriate health care provider before engaging in exercise.

- I have a heart condition and my health care professional recommends only medically supervised physical activity.
- During or right after exercise, I often have pains or pressure in my neck, left shoulder, or arm.
- I have developed chest pain within the last month.
- I tend to lose consciousness or fall over due to dizziness.
- I feel extremely breathless after mild exertion.
- My health care provider recommended that I take medicine for high blood pressure or a heart condition.
- I have bone or joint problems that limit my ability to do moderate-intensity physical activity.
- I have a medical condition or other physical reason not mentioned here that might need special attention in an exercise program.
- I am pregnant and my health care professional hasn't given me the OK to be physically active.
- I am over 50, haven't been physically active, and am planning a vigorous exercise program.

One-Mile Walk Test

Follow these steps to perform the one-mile walk test:

1. Warm up briefly before taking this test with some easy walking or light jogging, followed by a few stretching exercises specifically for the lower body.
2. Walk the one-mile distance as quickly as possible, at a pace that is brisk yet comfortable and raises your heart rate over 120 beats per minute.
3. As soon as you complete the distance, note your time, and take your pulse for 15 seconds. Continue to cool down with slow walking for several minutes.
4. Record your walking time: minutes _____ seconds _____
5. Record your heart rate: _____ beats per minute (multiply 15-second pulse count by 4)
6. Convert your time from minutes and seconds to minutes as a decimal figure. For example, a time of 13 minutes and 26 seconds is 13 + (26/60), or 13.43 minutes.
7. Determine your maximal oxygen consumption ($\dot{V}O_2$max) by inserting your age (A), sex (S; male = 1, female = 0), weight in pounds (W), walking time (T), and exercise heart rate (H) into the following equation:

$$\dot{V}O_2\text{max} = 132.853 - (0.0769 \times W) - (0.3877 \times A) + (6.315 \times S) - (3.2649 \times T) - (0.1565 \times H)$$

For example, for a 35-year-old male official weighing 190 pounds and completing the mile walk in 12 minutes and 38 seconds with a heart rate response of 142 beats per minute, the equation would look like this:

$$132.85 - (0.0769 \times 190) - (0.3877 \times 35) + (6.315 \times 1) - (3.2649 \times 12.63) - (0.1565 \times 142) = 47.5 \text{ ml/kg/min.}$$

A score of 47.5 ml/kg/min for a 35-year-old male would be in the good range and almost into excellent if we round 47.5 up to 48. See tables 10.1 and 10.2 for cardiorespiratory fitness norms.

Muscle Fitness Self-Assessment

A true assessment of muscle strength would require determining a 1-repetition maximum (1RM) for exercises such as the bench press and squat. Because there is great potential for injury when attempting a 1RM, we do not advocate using this assessment. Instead, we focus on muscular endurance, which can be assessed safely without any special equipment.

Table 10.1 Cardiorespiratory Fitness Norms: Men

Age	Very poor	Poor	Fair	Good	Excellent	Superior
20-29	≤37.9	38.0-41.6	41.7-45.5	45.6-51.0	51.1-55.4	≥55.5
30-39	≤36.6	36.7-40.6	40.7-44.0	44.1-48.2	48.3-54.0	≥54.1
40-49	≤34.7	34.8-38.3	38.4-42.3	42.4-46.3	46.4-52.4	≥52.5
50-59	≤31.9	32.0-35.4	35.5-38.9	39.0-43.2	43.3-48.9	≥49.0
60-69	≤28.6	28.7-32.2	32.3-35.5	35.6-39.5	39.6-45.6	≥45.7
70-79	≤25.6	25.7-29.3	29.4-32.3	32.4-36.6	36.7-43.8	≥43.9

Adapted, by permission, from American College of Sports Medicine, 2011, *ACSM's complete guide to fitness & health* (Champaign, IL: Human Kinetics), 30. Data reprinted with permission from The Cooper Institute, Dallas, Texas, from *Physical Fitness Assessments and Norms for Adults and Law Enforcement.* Available online at www.cooperinstitute.org.

Table 10.2 Cardiorespiratory Fitness Norms: Women

Age	Very poor	Poor	Fair	Good	Excellent	Superior
20-29	≤32.2	32.3-36.0	36.1-39.4	39.5-43.8	43.9-49.5	≥49.6
30-39	≤30.8	30.9-34.1	34.2-37.6	37.7-42.3	42.4-47.3	≥47.4
40-49	≤29.3	29.4-32.7	32.8-35.8	35.9-39.5	39.6-45.2	≥45.3
50-59	≤26.7	26.8-29.8	29.9-32.5	32.6-36.6	36.7-40.9	≥41
60-69	≤24.5	24.6-27.2	27.3-29.6	29.7-32.6	32.7-37.7	≥37.8
70-79	≤23.4	23.5-25.8	25.9-28	28.1-30.5	30.6-37.1	≥37.2

Adapted, by permission, from American College of Sports Medicine, 2011, *ACSM's complete guide to fitness & health* (Champaign, IL: Human Kinetics), 30. Data reprinted with permission from The Cooper Institute, Dallas, Texas, from *Physical Fitness Assessments and Norms for Adults and Law Enforcement.* Available online at www.cooperinstitute.org.

Push-Up Test

Follow these steps to complete the push-up test:

1. On a carpeted floor or exercise mat, perform the maximum number of push-ups that you possibly can.

2. From the starting position, with hands roughly shoulder-width apart and fingers pointing forward, lower your chest to the floor, keeping your back straight. Then return to the starting position. Women may wish to use a modified version which uses the knees as a fulcrum.

3. Perform as many push-ups as possible without stopping.

4. Record your maximum number of push-ups: _____

Let's say, for example, that our 35-year-old male official performs 28 push-ups during this test. His score would place him in the very good range. See tables 10.3 and 10.4 on page 134 for push-up test norms.

Push-Up Test: Men

Modified Push-Up Test: Women

Table 10.3 Push-Up Test Norms: Men

Age	Needs Improvement	Fair	Good	Very Good	Excellent
20-29	≤16	17-21	22-28	29-35	≥36
30-39	≤11	12-16	17-21	22-29	≥30
40-49	≤9	10-12	13-16	17-24	≥25
50-59	≤6	7-9	10-12	13-20	≥21
60 and over	≤4	5-7	8-10	11-17	≥18

Adapted, by permission, from American College of Sports Medicine, 2011, *ACSM's complete guide to fitness & health* (Champaign, IL: Human Kinetics), 36. Source: *Canadian Physical Activity, Fitness & Lifestyle Approach: CSEP-Health & Fitness Program's Health-Related Appraisal and Counselling Strategy,* 3rd edition, © 2003. Reprinted with permission from the Canadian Society for Exercise Physiology.

Table 10.4 Push-Up Test Norms: Women

Age	Needs improvement	Fair	Good	Very Good	Excellent
20-29	≤9	10-14	15-20	21-29	≥30
30-39	≤7	8-12	13-19	20-26	≥27
40-49	≤4	5-10	11-14	15-23	≥24
50-59	≤1 or none	2-6	7-10	11-20	≥21
60 and over	≤1 or none	2-4	5-11	12-16	≥17

Adapted, by permission, from American College of Sports Medicine, 2011, *ACSM's complete guide to fitness & health* (Champaign, IL: Human Kinetics), 36. Source: *Canadian Physical Activity, Fitness & Lifestyle Approach: CSEP-Health & Fitness Program's Health-Related Appraisal and Counselling Strategy,* 3rd edition, © 2003. Reprinted with permission from the Canadian Society for Exercise Physiology.

Flexibility Self-Assessment

Your flexibility varies across different joints, but the generally accepted test for flexibility is the sit-and-reach test of lower-back and hamstring flexibility. This test is best done with the assistance of a partner.

Sit-and-Reach Test

Follow these steps to complete the sit-and-reach test.

1. Remove your shoes, and sit on a carpeted floor or exercise mat with your legs stretched in front of you about 10 to 12 inches apart. Position a yardstick between your feet with the zero mark toward you so that the soles of your feet are even with the 15-inch mark.

2. From the starting position, with your knees straight, hands one on top of the other, and palms down, reach forward as far as possible, and hold this maximum reach for one to two seconds. Keep your knees locked throughout the test.

3. Record the farthest point reached with the fingertips of both your hands. See tables 10.5 and 10.6 for analyzing your results.

Table 10.5 Sit-and-Reach Test Norms: Men

Age	Well below average	Below average	Average	Above average	Well above average
18-25	≤13	14-16	17-18	19-21	≥ 22
26-35	≤12	13-14	15-17	17-20	≥21
36-45	≤12	13-14	15-16	17-20	≥21
46-55	≤9	10-12	13-14	15-18	≥19
56-65	≤8	9-10	11-13	13-16	≥17
66 and older	≤7	8-9	10-12	13-16	≥17

Adapted, by permission, from American College of Sports Medicine, 2011, *ACSM's complete guide to fitness & health* (Champaign, IL: Human Kinetics), 40. Data reprinted with permission from *YMCA Fitness Testing and Assessment Manual,* 4th ed. © 2000 by YMCA of the USA, Chicago. All rights reserved.

Table 10.6 Sit-and-Reach Test Norms: Women

Age	Well below average	Below average	Average	Above average	Well above average
18-25	≤16	17-18	19-20	21-23	≥24
26-35	≤15	16-18	19-20	20-22	≥23
36-45	≤14	15-16	17-18	19-21	≥22
46-55	≤13	14-15	16-17	18-20	≥21
56-65	≤12	13-14	15-16	17-19	≥20
66 and older	≤12	13-14	15-17	17-19	≥20

Adapted, by permission, from American College of Sports Medicine, 2011, *ACSM's complete guide to fitness & health* (Champaign, IL: Human Kinetics), 40. Data reprinted with permission from *YMCA Fitness Testing and Assessment Manual,* 4th ed. © 2000 by YMCA of the USA, Chicago. All rights reserved.

Body Composition Self-Assessment

The most common and accurate measures of body composition in university research labs and health and fitness clubs include underwater weighing, bone mineral density scans (more commonly called DXA for dual-energy X-ray absorptiometry), skinfold calipers, and the Bod Pod. All of these methods, though fairly accurate, are also extremely difficult for self-assessment, expensive, and not readily available to the general public. We advocate measuring body mass index (BMI) and waist circumference for self-assessment, because they do not require sophisticated equipment.

Body Mass Index

Body mass index (BMI) is a measurement that indicates your weight-related level of risk for developing heart disease, high blood pressure, or diabetes. Although the use of BMI is widespread, there are some limitations. Most notably, BMI is a measurement that does not take into account the amount of body fat and lean muscle mass. Thus, highly muscular people are negatively affected by BMI especially if they are short because the BMI formula uses height as it denominator, and thus, for two people of the same weight, the shorter person will have a higher BMI. That being said, most people are not overly muscle bound, so this limitation must really be weighed against the group of people being assessed.

Following are the steps for determining your BMI:

1. Measure your height in inches and weight in pounds, and record those results.

   Height: _____
   Weight: _____

2. Multiply your weight in pounds (W) by 705. Divide the result by your height in inches (H); then divide that result by your height in inches (H) again.

$$BMI = W \times 705 / H / H$$

Using the example we used earlier, let's say our 35-year-old male official weighing 190 pounds is 6 feet 2 inches (or 74 inches) tall. His BMI would calculate as $190 \times 705 / 74 / 74 = 24.5$. This classifies him as normal, but close to overweight.

Underweight < 18.5

Normal weight 18.5-24.9

Overweight 25.0-29.9

Obese ≥ 30

A BMI of 25 or less is considered very low to low risk. A BMI of 25 to 30 is low to moderate risk. A BMI of 30 or more is moderate to very high risk. As noted previously, because BMI does not tell us body composition, a bit more self-assessment will help.

Waist Circumference

Waist circumference is a measurement for determining your fat distribution and therefore your level of risk for developing heart disease, high blood pressure, or diabetes. For most men, the waist circumference measurement area is visually just above the belt line where you might see additional weight being carried. It is very important to note that waist circumference measurements are *not* the waist sizes you use to buy pants. In males, most often, pant size is smaller than the waist circumference measure. One reason for assessing waist circumference is to better determine fat distribution. That is, even someone who is highly muscle bound would still not want to have a large waist.

Excess body fat stored around the abdominal region is also known as android (apple-shaped) obesity and is a risk factor for coronary artery disease, stroke, hypertension, high cholesterol and triglycerides, and type 2 diabetes. Males are particularly prone to android obesity because they tend to store excess fat at their waists, whereas females tend to be more pear-shaped (gynoid obesity), storing excess fat around the hips and thigh region.

To determine your waist measurement, measure the area just above your iliac crest or at the top of your hip bones, and record those results.

Waist: _____

For men, a waist measure of more than 40 inches and for women a waist measure of more than 35 inches is associated with developing heart disease, high blood pressure, or diabetes.

If we continue with our example, if our 35-year-old, 6-foot, 2-inch, 190-pound official has a waist circumference of 36.5 inches, then we would not be too worried about his BMI approaching overweight. On the other hand, if he has a waist measurement of 38 or 39 inches, he is carrying too much weight around his midsection and we would be more concerned about his health.

FITNESS GOAL SETTING

The goal of any personal fitness plan is to improve overall health, but you may have other, more specific goals as well. The long-range goal for your own personal fitness plan might be to improve your officiating performance as a result of your improved ability to move efficiently and with greater endurance. Given the results of your personal self-assessment, what are your goals for each of the four components of health-related physical fitness? To achieve these goals, set short-term targets for the specific areas of fitness that you want to improve. Reward yourself for adopting healthy lifestyle behaviors with small incentives that motivate you to keep working toward your long-term goals.

Reevaluate your goals as your fitness improves. Keep track of your progress by periodically retaking the self-assessment tests. When you have achieved a short-term goal, set another reasonable, short-term goal, and reward yourself as you work to accomplish it.

A physically fit official commands respect.

YOUR PHYSICAL WORKOUT

Your selection of physical activities directly affects your chance for success. A physically active lifestyle offers incredible health benefits if participation is regular, preferably daily. Making physical activity and healthy eating a daily habit is the key to true health and wellness. As you plan your physical workout, keep in mind that you will be much more likely to work out regularly if you select activities that you enjoy and that are convenient for you.

These are the four components of your physical workout:

1. *Warm-up and stretching exercises.* These exercises raise your body's temperature to prepare it for physical activity. After your body's temperature is raised, a series of stretching exercises further help to prepare it for activity and reduce the chance of injury.

2. *Aerobic endurance activities.* Aerobic (long-duration and lower-intensity) activities raise your heart rate for a prolonged period and force your body to become more efficient at transporting oxygen to the working muscles.

3. *Muscle fitness activities.* Anaerobic (short-duration and explosive, or vigorous-intensity) activities enhance your body's ability to respond powerfully through the adaptation of the muscular system to some weight-bearing stress.

4. *Cool-down and stretching exercises.* In contrast to the warm-up, the cool-down gently lowers your body temperature.

Warm-Up and Stretching Activities

Begin your warm-up by walking for five to seven minutes, gradually increasing your pace until you begin a slow jog. You can also jump rope, bicycle, or do another total-body activity, starting at a low intensity and gradually increasing to a moderate intensity for a total of five to seven minutes. After warming up, complete some or all of the 14 stretching exercises listed, holding each position about 15 seconds and repeating each stretch three to five times.

STRETCHING EXERCISES

1. **Butterfly:** Holding the soles of your feet together, gently lean forward and hold.

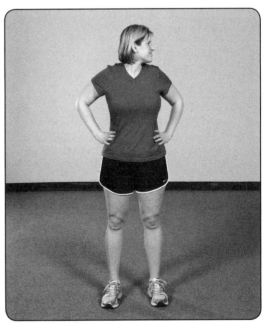

2. **Head turn:** Turn your head slowly to look over one shoulder, and then the other.

(continued)

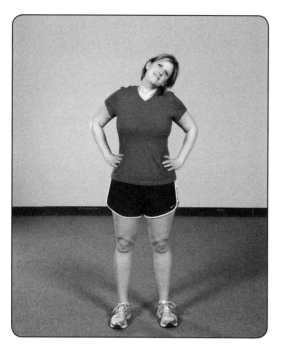

3. **Head lean:** Keeping your shoulders relaxed, lean your head toward one shoulder, and then the other.

4. **Shoulder roll:** With your hands on your hips, gently rotate both shoulders at once.

5. **Shoulder stretch:** Use your left arm to gently pull your right elbow across your chest; then do the same on the opposite side.

6. **Shoulder turn:** With your hands on your knees, slowly turn your upper body right, then left.

(continued)

7. **Triceps stretch:** *(a)* Place your left hand between your shoulder blades, as shown. *(b)* Use your right arm to gently push up and back at your left elbow. Switch sides and repeat.

8. **Side reach:** Reach up, not over, with one arm at a time.

9. **Arm circles:** Slowly circle both arms at once, rotating gently at the shoulder.

10. **Knee to chest:** Place your hands on the back of one knee, or on the thigh close to the knee, and pull your knee toward your chest. Repeat with the other leg.

(continued)

139

Stretching Exercises *(continued)*

11. **Wall lean:** Keeping your back heel on the ground, turn your foot slightly inward. Repeat on the opposite side.

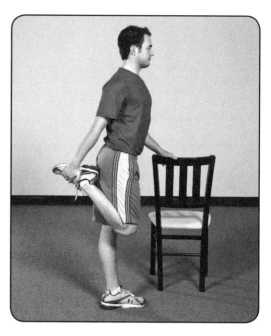

12. **Quadriceps stretch:** Use your right hand to raise your right foot toward your bottom. Repeat on the opposite side.

13. **Lunge:** With hands on hips or at sides, stretch forward on one leg, as shown. Your front knee should be approximately over your front toe. Repeat with the opposite leg.

14. **Hamstring stretch:** Keeping both knees bent slightly, lean over your front toe. Perform on both sides.

Aerobic Endurance Activities

Once your body has warmed up and you have completed your flexibility exercises, you can begin the aerobic endurance portion of your workout. If you are just beginning an exercise program or resuming exercise after a long layoff, start your first week by walking briskly 12 to 15 minutes per day. A good rule of thumb suggests that you should add no more than 10 to 15 percent to the duration of your activity each week. Thus, within a few weeks of beginning a new program, you can increase your time up to 20 or 30 minutes, but you will have gradually accomplished that goal rather than attempting to meet it within a few days.

If you have stayed reasonably active in your off-season, a 15-minute walk may seem a waste of time. We caution you, however, to resist the urge believe that you can run five to eight miles over your lunch hour with ease and still have time to get a sandwich or two. Allow your body to adjust gradually to your more physically active lifestyle, and it will reward you with fewer injuries and more officiating enjoyment.

Depending on the sport you officiate, you should consider adding sport-specific movements as the season draws nearer. If you are physically active and in good condition, now you can reflect on the key movements that you perform in your officiating duties and find ways to mirror those movements in your workout. You might, for example, practice sliding sideways and changing directions quickly to simulate the change of possession in football, basketball, lacrosse, or soccer. Although physical agility depends less on aerobic endurance and more on balance, strength, and power, your overall physical conditioning will help you perform these officiating movements easily through the entire game.

To give your lower body a break during the season, cross-training with swimming, a stationary bike, or even bicycling outside if the weather permits will help you maintain your aerobic fitness without overstressing your legs. The bulk of your conditioning work, though, should be completed prior to the season to lessen your chance of injury.

Because sports such as soccer, football, and lacrosse are played outside on large fields, you should exercise in weather conditions expected during the season. Although you may not enjoy running during the heat of the day or in the rain, you need to be prepared for working in these conditions.

Muscle Fitness Activities

After completing some endurance activity, you should complete a series of muscle fitness activities to enhance your overall physical conditioning. Complete 10 to 12 repetitions of muscle fitness activities such as push-ups or bench presses, sit-ups or crunches, bicep curls, tricep extensions, lateral raises, squats or wall sits, and toe raises.

MUSCLE FITNESS ACTIVITIES

1. **Abdominal crunch:** ([*a*] straight-arm; [*b*] crossed-arm) Lift shoulders off the floor until you feel a mild tension in your abdominals. Hold for a few seconds, then return to original position and repeat.

(continued)

2. **Biceps curls:** *(a)* Bending at the elbow, lift weights toward your shoulders, *(b)* then lower back to your side.

3. **Triceps extension:** *(a)* From the start position, *(b)* raise the weight to the full extension of your arm, then return and repeat.

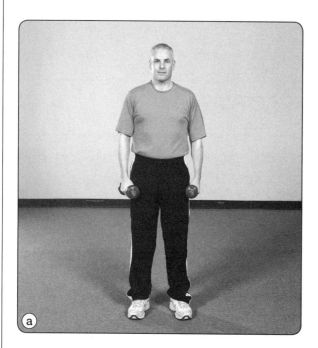

4. **Lateral raises:** *(a)* Keeping your elbows slightly bent, *(b)* lift weights out to either side, then slowly drop arms back to original position.

(continued)

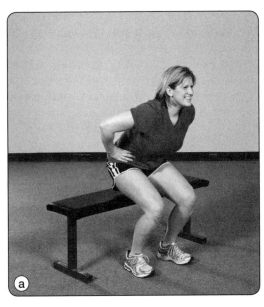 

5. **Half squat:** *(a)* Sit at the edge of a bench with heels approximately under it, *(b)* and with knees slightly bent, stand without trying to lean forward.

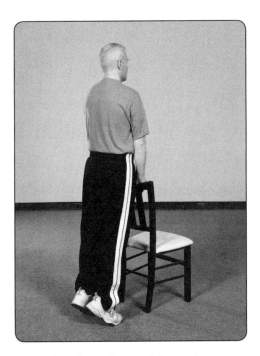

6. **Toe raises:** Using the back of a chair for stability, rise up on your toes, then slowly lower your heels back to the floor.

Cool-Down and Stretching Activities

Following the muscle fitness phase of your workout, it is time to cool down by relaxing and completing the same flexibility exercises you performed during your warm-up and stretching period. Cooling down allows your heart rate and breathing to resume normal rates. Stretching at the end of a workout helps to ease delayed muscle soreness.

TREATING INJURIES

Weakness, poor flexibility, imbalance among muscle groups, and lack of endurance can lead to acute or chronic injuries. Injuries are best avoided by being involved in a well-planned, year-round fitness program. The easiest way to prevent injury is to prepare your body for physical activity.

To prevent injuries, listen to the signals your body gives. Do not ignore these signals. Symptoms such as pain, tightness, swelling, and spasm are often precursors to serious injury. Knowing when these symptoms begin and end during activity is important in identifying the type and severity of injury. Do they begin while warming up, during activity, or after activity? Do you notice a change when you run harder? Do you notice any difference in symptoms when officiating at night or in a colder environment?

Injuries are classified as acute (sudden-onset) or chronic (overuse). Acute injuries occur suddenly and include sprains, strains, dislocations, fractures, contusions, abrasions, and lacerations. Chronic injuries are often caused by muscle imbalance, poor muscle fitness, poor flexibility, poor aerobic fitness, improper equipment, or inadequate rehabilitation following an injury. Another classic cause of chronic injuries is increasing training intensity too much or too quickly. Chronic injuries include tendinitis and stress fractures. To avoid these and others, progress slowly and steadily.

An acute injury requires immediate care to control pain, internal and external bleeding, and swelling, and to reduce the severity of the injury and prevent complications. Immediate care includes the RICE method of treatment: rest, ice, compression, and elevation. Place ice directly over the injured site, apply compression over the ice, and elevate the injured part above the heart. RICE treatment should be carried out for 24 to 72 hours. The injury should be evaluated and diagnosed as early as possible to determine the type and severity and to begin treatment quickly.

Acute injuries most common to officials include sprains, strains, and contusions. A sprain is an injury to a ligament (ligaments connect bone to bone), a strain is an injury to the muscle fibers or tendon (tendons connect muscles to bone), and a contusion (most often thought of as a bruise) is the injury of tissue below the skin when it is struck with enough force to crush it.

Sprains

The management of sprains depends on the severity of the injury. Sprains are graded as follows: grade I, the ligament is stretched but not torn; grade II, the ligament is partially torn with increased laxity of the joint; grade III, the ligament is completely torn with instability of the joint. The most common sprains among officials involve the ligaments of the ankle and knee.

Grade I sprains are treated with rest, ice, compression, and elevation. Grade II sprains are treated with rest, ice, compression, elevation, and immobilization of the joint. Grade III sprains are treated with rest, ice, compression, elevation, prolonged immobilization of the joint, and sometimes surgery. Immobilization of the joint should be controlled by medical professionals and may be only partial to allow some joint movement. Return to activity is determined using the criteria outlined at the end of the chapter.

Strains

Strains are also managed according to the severity of the injury. Muscle strains are classified as mild, moderate, or severe. Mild and moderate strains are differentiated by the amount of pain, weakness, and spasm involved with the injury. Severe strains can involve an actual defect in the muscle, including complete rupture of tendons such as the Achilles and patellar (kneecap) tendons. Common strains in officiating involve the hamstrings, quadriceps, hip adductors (muscles that draw the legs together), and calf muscles.

Mild strains are treated with rest, ice, compression, and elevation. Moderate strains are treated with rest, ice, compression, elevation, and sometimes immobilization. Severe strains are treated with rest, ice, compression, elevation, immobilization, and sometimes surgery. Return to activity is determined as outlined at the end of the chapter.

Contusions

Contusions usually occur when an official collides with a participant or falls onto the playing surface. Contusions may be superficial and involve only tissues near the skin, or they may involve deeper muscle tissue, with increased internal bleeding that causes a hematoma (a swelling that contains blood).

Specific Common Injuries

The following sections address the treatment and management of some injuries common to officials. Before you undertake any treatment, you should have a qualified medical professional evaluate the injury.

Ankle Sprains

The highest percentage of ankle injuries involve the outside ankle ligaments. Treatment of ankle injuries can be separated into three phases: Phase I begins immediately following the injury, phase II begins when the person is able to bear weight without increasing pain or swelling, and phase III begins when the person can perform functional exercises.

Phase I consists of treatment with ice, compression, and elevation (refer to page 144). A brace or taping is used for protection. Weight bearing is encouraged if it can be tolerated, using crutches as needed. Gentle ankle dorsiflexion (flexing the foot upward) and plantar flexion (flexing the foot downward) and isometric exercises are started as soon as possible. These exercises include ankle circles, ankle pumping, and alphabet writing with the big toe. Contrast baths, alternating ice and warm water, can be started 48 to 72 hours after the injury to help decrease swelling.

Phase II begins when the person can bear weight without increased pain or swelling. Exercises to increase strength and increase the range of motion of the ankle are started in this phase, including dorsiflexion, plantar flexion, eversion (turning the foot outward), inversion (turning the foot inward), and Achilles tendon–stretching exercises.

Phase III includes functional exercises to increase conditioning, agility, proprioception (sensing internal stimuli), and endurance. A proprioceptive exercise is standing on the injured foot with the eyes closed. Running exercises in this phase include running straight forward, backward, and in increasingly smaller figure eights.

The three-phase treatment program takes from 10 days to two weeks for minor sprains and up to eight weeks for severe sprains. The use of ankle taping or a brace to protect the injured ankle should be considered when initially returning to regular activities.

Calf Strains

Calf strains usually involve the inside head of the gastrocnemius (calf) muscle. The initial evaluation determines the severity of the injury to rule out the possibility of injury to the Achilles tendon.

Initial treatment of calf strains includes ice, compression, and elevation to control bleeding and swelling. The injured person may need crutches to reduce pain while walking. Elevating the heel by using a heel lift in the shoe relieves stretching of the muscle while walking and during stretching and strengthening exercises of the gastrocnemius muscle. Exercises include towel stretches, gastrocnemius stretches with the knee straight and bent, plantar flexion exercises using surgical tubing, and later, toe raises with weight as tolerated. The injured person should be able to tolerate functional exercises, including running forward, backward, and in figure eights, before returning to normal activity.

Achilles Tendon Strain

Injury to the Achilles tendon can include partial to full rupture of the tendon. It is important to differentiate between an Achilles tendon strain and a gastrocnemius (calf) strain. If pain or tenderness begins in the Achilles tendon (tendinitis), it is important to begin treatment early to prevent progression to partial or full tendon rupture. See a doctor to determine which strain you are experiencing. Exercise and management are similar to what you would undergo for calf strains.

Plantar Fasciitis

Plantar fasciitis is pain in the sole of the foot near the heel where the plantar fascia (a sheet of connective tissue that covers the sole of the foot) attaches to the heel bone. Treatment includes the use of an orthotic for support of the arch of the foot and a heel pad. Stretching the plantar fascia and the Achilles tendon is important. Ice and contrast baths can also be used to relieve symptoms. Normal activities can generally be resumed within six to eight weeks.

Shin Splints

Shin splints is a term used to describe several conditions that cause chronic lower-leg pain. The pain can be caused by excessive running on hard or uneven surfaces, increasing exercise intensity too quickly, stress fractures, and poor running mechanics including overpronation (the inward roll of the foot following heel strike). A medical professional must make a correct diagnosis so that correct treatment can begin as soon as possible.

Stress Fractures

The most common stress fractures for officials are those in the tibia and fibula, the two bones of the lower leg. Stress fractures occur when repeated stress on a bone causes a disruption, or fracture, of the bone. Stress fractures are often so thin that X-rays may not reveal them initially; other tests may be required to determine whether a stress fracture is present. Weight bearing causes pain, which usually increases with running and jumping activities. Treatment includes reduction of activity. Officiating activities should be avoided for four to six weeks. Crutches are necessary only when walking causes pain.

Posterior Tibial Syndrome

Posterior tibial syndrome is caused by repetitive motions or a mechanical misalignment of the foot. Pain is usually felt along the inside edge of the shinbone just below the knee. A medical professional should evaluate the injury to determine whether orthotics are necessary for correcting the alignment of the foot. Treatment includes reducing activities, wearing soft-soled shoes, and performing stretching and strengthening exercises of the gastrocnemius and posterior tibial muscles of the calf. Ice and contrast baths are also used to relieve symptoms.

Anterior Compartment Syndrome

Compartment syndrome is pain that occurs when the muscles in an enclosed compartment of the body enlarge as a result of the increased circulation that occurs with activity. The anterior (front) muscle compartment of the lower leg includes the tibialis anterior, extensor hallucis longus, and extensor muscles of the toes, which are enclosed by the bones of the lower leg and a sheet of connective tissue. Because muscle and nerve damage can occur if this syndrome is not treated, a correct diagnosis and prompt treatment are very important. Treatment should include close observation by medical professionals and may include surgery to relieve symptoms.

Low Back Strains and Sprains

Low back strains are injuries that involve the muscles of the low back; low back sprains are injuries that involve the ligaments of the low back. Pain in the low back area can radiate into the buttocks. Pain usually increases with activity, so see a medical professional before you work another game if you are experiencing low back pain. A doctor should diagnose the injury to rule out a herniated disk or other nerve damage. Treatment includes the use of heat or cold to relieve pain and spasm along with exercises to increase range of motion and strength in the low back.

When to Come Back

When should you return to activity following an injury? This decision should be made only after knowing how the injury occurred and how severe it is. Medical professionals trained in treating sport-related injuries can be of great assistance when making the decision. The following five criteria can help you determine whether you are ready to return to activity:

1. There is no significant pain in the body part that was injured.
2. There is normal range of motion.
3. There is no significant swelling.
4. The injured part has at least 90 percent of the strength of the uninjured part.
5. Activities related to officiating can be performed without pain or limping.

SUMMARY

The three steps in designing a personal fitness plan are self-assessment, goal setting, and selection of physical activities. Self-assessment helps you determine your current fitness levels and set realistic fitness goals. You can then select activities to help you achieve your goals.

Your physical fitness plan should include four key components: a warm-up and stretching period, aerobic endurance activity, muscle fitness activity, and a cool-down and stretching period. The final step in maintaining your health and fitness is learning to avoid, recognize, and get appropriate medical treatment for injuries.

REVIEW QUESTIONS

1. Why is it important to warm-up *before* stretching?

2. How does assessing waist circumference help to interpret BMI?

3. What are the four components of the RICE treatment method?

4. An injury to the muscle fibers or tendons (connecting muscles to bones) is called a
   a. contusion
   b. laceration
   c. sprain
   d. strain

5. A good rule of thumb for increasing the weekly duration of aerobic activity workouts is to add no more than what percentage from the previous week?
   a. 5 to 10 percent
   b. 10 to 15 percent
   c. 25 to 50 percent
   d. greater than 50 percent

Answers on page 190

Part IV

Managing Professional Responsibilities

Chapter 11

Legal Responsibilities

Paul Anderson

This chapter addresses the following:

- How the judicial system reviews officials' game calls
- Officials as independent contractors and not employees
- Potential liability that officials may face for player injuries
- Specific duties officials must uphold when they officiate sport contests

Sometimes legal issues regarding either officials' rulings or the rights of people engaged in athletics affect sports officiating. As rule enforcers, officials are sometimes challenged, often severely, and on occasion courts have been asked to overrule their decisions. Thankfully, courts have seldom overturned the judgment calls that officials make during athletic events.

As an official, you must be conscious of players' rights as well. Specifically, you must take precautions to ensure player safety, and you must recognize when conditions arise that might threaten players' civil rights. In addition, if you are injured during an athletic event, you will need to have your own medical insurance because courts have generally held that officials cannot be covered for workers compensation. High school officials in some states are covered by a blanket policy administered by the National Federation of State High School Associations, which insures them for injuries sustained while officiating, and from

potential liability related to their decisions during an athletic contest. It is also possible to obtain automatic coverage for officials' liability because of injuries to others injured during contests and other events in which the official is a participant (plus other things such as loss of game stipends due to injury) through the National Association of Sports Officials' Sports Officials Security Program. Further details can be found on the NASO website at http://naso.org/benefits/benefits.htm.

JUDICIAL REVIEW OF OFFICIALS' GAME CALLS

When a sport official's game call is the result of an error in judgment or a misapplied game rule and it is challenged in court by a disgruntled team, player, or fan, the challenge is unlikely to be successful. Disagreements over a call are part of the game and should remain *on* the court, not *in* court. The only time someone might be able to challenge the decisions that an official makes during a game is when that person can show that the official was corrupt or acted in bad faith.

Judgment Calls

The genesis for the courts' view that sports officials' judgment calls are not subject to judicial review was the 1945 New York City Municipal Court case of *Shapiro v. Queens County Jockey Club* (184 Misc. 295 [N.Y. 1945]). In that case, only three of the six gates opened at the start of a horse race. The starter signaled an assistant a short distance down the track, who waved his recall flag. All the horses stopped, except

Player safety is a primary concern for every official.

a horse called Breezing Home. Breezing Home ran around the track for the full distance of the race and crossed the finish line. The race officials confirmed that it had been a false start.

A short while later, the race was run again and was won by another horse; Breezing Home finished fifth among the six horses. The plaintiff, who had bet on Breezing Home to win, argued that the first running of the race was an official race and that he should be paid his share of the winner's pool. He questioned the decisions of the starter and the race officials, but there was no proof that Breezing Home would have won if the false start had been a fair start.

Relying on the fact that horse racing is governed by the rules of the State Racing Commission and the race track, the court decided that judges should not substitute their determination "for that of those persons who were actually there at the time and who were specifically charged with the duty of determining the winners" (*Id.* at 300). When the officials declared a false start in the race, the court emphasized, "the plaintiff was bound by said decision. There was only one official race" (*Id.*

at 302). The court thus established a rule that has withstood analysis for 65 years and has become the general rule regarding officials of all sports—court judges will not substitute their judgments for the judgments of sports officials.

All competitive sports require umpires, referees, timekeepers, and other officials who are experienced, mentally alert, fair, and well qualified to make immediate decisions that are final and binding. Officials are truly judges of facts because they are closer to the situation and the players involved. Courts have found that on-site officials' immediate reactions and decisions during the conduct of a game should receive greater consideration than the remote observation by a court during litigation instigated by a disgruntled participant or spectator.

In 1982, in the *Snow v. New Hampshire Interscholastic Athletic Association* case, the Supreme Court of New Hampshire dealt with a challenge by a high school track star who participated in the 800-meter event in a state athletic association track meet (122 N.H. 735 [1982]). Plaintiff Snow alleged that he was one of the event leaders when he was cut off and physically brushed by another runner, resulting in his finishing seventh and failing to qualify for the statewide Meet of Champions. No track official was located near the spot where the alleged incident occurred. Consequently, when Snow filed a protest with the meet director, the director could not change the race result because he had no official's report. Snow filed a lawsuit to allow him to run in the Meet of Champions, and the trial court ruled for Snow. The Supreme Court then reversed the trial court's ruling, saying "the role of the courts in this area [judicial scrutiny of a sports official's decision] is exceedingly limited and we [do] not intend to merge the stadium bench and the judicial bench" (*Id.* at 737).

In *Bain v. Gillispie* in 1984, the Iowa Court of Appeals was faced with a claim by a merchandise company that a college sport official had made an incorrect game call, leading to lost sales of the company's products emblazoned with the losing team's logo (357 N.W.2d 47 [Ct. App. Iowa 1984]). Jim Bain was a veteran college basketball referee working a 1982 Big Ten Conference men's game between the University of Iowa and Purdue University. Near the end of the game, he determined that an Iowa player committed a foul, enabling a Purdue player to shoot two free throws that resulted in Purdue's winning the game. Following the game, the Gillispies, whose company was located in Iowa, began to sell T-shirts bearing a likeness of Bain with a rope around his neck and captioned "Jim Bain Fan Club." Bain filed for an injunction to stop the shirts from being sold and for monetary damages. In response, the Gillispies filed a counterclaim alleging that Bain's call was negligent and damaged their business, including the sale of items with the Iowa logo on them, because of Iowa's failure to advance to the national tournament. The Gillispies claimed that Bain had made a judgment error. The trial court granted Bain's motion for summary judgment and dismissed the Gillispies' counterclaim without a trial.

The court of appeals, relying in part on the National Association of Sports Officials' friend of the court brief on behalf of all sports officials, affirmed the dismissal of the counterclaim. It decided that a sport official owes no legal duty to a merchandiser for game calls. As in prior cases, the court reasoned that, in the absence of bad faith or corruption, a sport official's judgment-based game call is not subject to judicial review. The court adopted the strong policy considerations eloquently expressed by the Iowa trial court:

This is a case where the undisputed facts are of such a nature that a rational fact finder could only reach one conclusion—no foreseeability, no duty, no liability. Heaven knows what uncharted morass a court would find itself in if it were to hold that an athletic official subjects himself to liability every time he might make a questionable call. The possibilities are mind boggling. If there is a liability to a merchandiser like the Gillispies, why not to the thousands upon thousands of Iowa fans who bleed Hawkeye black and gold every time the whistle blows? It is bad enough when Iowa loses without transforming a loss into a litigation field day for "Monday Morning Quarterbacks" (Id. at 49).

Pagnotta v. Pennsylvania Interscholastic Athletic Association involved a high school wrestler, Randy Pagnotta, who was disqualified for allegedly illegally striking his opponent during

On-site officials' calls should not be subject to judicial review because of their proximity to the action.

a state tournament match (548 Pa. 629 [1997]). Pagnotta claimed that he should not have been disqualified by the referee because a similar incident had occurred in another match not involving him on the same day, and the other wrestler was not disqualified. The state wrestling rules for disqualification for intentionally striking an opponent and also stated, "On matters of judgment the referee shall have full control of the match and his decision shall be final." Regardless of this, Pagnotta was able to convince a judge that the referee had erred and was granted permission to wrestle in the next round. The athletic association immediately appealed, and the appellate court reversed, citing the prior precedent of nonintervention by courts regarding judgment calls by officials. Pagnotta thus did not wrestle again in the state tournament.

In *DelBuono v. Massachusetts Interscholastic Athletic Association* (2006 WL 1345563 [Mass. Super. 2006]), officials banned two high school hockey players from participating in the remainder of the 2006 Central Massachusetts Hockey Tournament because during the quarter-final game one player was assessed a penalty for being the "third man in" in a fight and the other was assessed a penalty for "spearing" with his hockey stick. Both players claimed that the officials had gotten the calls wrong. In denying the players' claims for a temporary restraining order stopping the association from enforcing the penalties, thus allowing them to participate in the tournament, the court stated that "this court is not in any position to review the penalty assessment decisions made by the referees at the time those decisions were made. . . [the court] is not the arena for contesting "bad calls" (*Id.* at *6). Furthermore, reinforcing the general concern of the courts discussed earlier, the court pointed out that if it were to review these types of claims from high school students who disagreed with the decisions of sports referees "The floodgates would open to a new wave of litigation that might severely damage the ability of schools to maintain competitive sports programs" (*Id.* at *7).

Rule Calls

The principle that a sport official's game calls are outside the jurisdiction of the courts was applied by the Supreme Court of Georgia in 1981 in a case involving a high school football

referee who admitted that he misapplied a rule. In *Georgia High School Association v. Waddell* (248 Ga. 542 [1981]), the court ruled that it did not possess authority to review the call of a high school football referee.

In a pre-state play-off football game between Osborne and Lithia Springs High Schools, Osborne had the ball and was ahead 7 to 6, with approximately seven minutes remaining in the game. On fourth down and 21 yards to go, Osborne punted, but a penalty for roughing the kicker was called on Lithia Springs. The referee assessed a 15-yard penalty but incorrectly declared that it was again fourth down with six yards to go. By rule, Osborne should have been awarded an automatic first down also. Osborne punted again, and Lithia Springs drove down the field to score a field goal. Later in the game, Lithia Springs scored again and won the game 16 to 7.

Osborne sued and the initial court agreed that the official had made an error and ordered that the game be replayed. Within a few days that decision was reversed by the Supreme

The Right Decision Is Sometimes Wrong

Sometimes officials must make difficult decisions and enforce the rules, even if the result is not a happy one. At the end of a state title wrestling match in New York in 2005, 12th-grader Frank Rodriquez was ahead by a 7-6 score. He threw his headgear in the air before the official handshake signaling that the match had ended. After the handshake, the head referee, who had not seen Rodriquez throw his headgear, was informed that it had been thrown and that Rodriquez had to be punished for unsporting conduct. Unfortunately for Rodriquez and for the referee involved, a 2-point penalty had to be assessed, and Rodriquez then lost the match. Rodriquez appealed to the protest committee, and when it would not overturn the decision, he took his dispute to court. Although the court sympathized with the athlete, it followed the cases discussed in this chapter and would not overturn the referee's decision. Rodriquez lost the state title because in his excitement he threw his headgear after the match.

Court of Georgia, which refused to review the referee's call, even though the referee made an error regarding a rule, declaring itself "without authority to review decisions of football referees because those decisions do not represent judicial controversies" (*Id.* at 543).

Bad Faith or Corruption

It has been rare in sports history for sports officials to act in bad faith or through corruption to influence the outcome of a contest. In these situations a court may intercede to correct the intentional wrong. Like the horse racing case that set the legal precedent for not overturning sports officials' judgment calls, another horse racing case set the precedent for the court's handling of corruption cases. In the 1897 case of *Wellington v. Monroe Trotting Park Co.* (90 Me. 495 [1897]), the Supreme Judicial Court of Maine declared several racing judges guilty of illegal behavior for deciding before a race to award a certain horse first place, when in fact another horse beat it to the wire. In this case the court demonstrated a willingness to overturn the decision because the officials were guilty of willfully influencing a contest, which could erode the public's confidence in the integrity of sports officials.

Perhaps the most recent example of a corrupt sport official is the scandal involving 13-year NBA referee Tim Donaghy. During the 2003-2004 season, he began to provide betting recommendations for NBA games, including games he officiated, to a friend, who then placed bets on Donaghy's behalf. Eventually, other gamblers became aware of Donaghy's bets and convinced him to work with them to provide picks using his access to private information including "the identity of the officiating crews for upcoming games, the interactions between certain referees and team personnel, and the physical condition of the players" (Pedowitz, 2008). Instead of betting his own money, Donaghy was paid a fee (of up to $5,000) for each correct pick. Soon after, the U.S. government became aware of the betting conspiracy, and Donaghy agreed to cooperate with the government's investigation. He pled guilty to conspiracy to commit wire fraud and to transmit wagering information in V.S. v. Donaghy (570 F. Supp. 2d 411 [E.D. NY 2008]).

After the Donaghy scandal, the NBA hired a New York law firm to review the league's officiating program and to report its findings to the league and the public. The report found no information showing that any other NBA referee was involved in betting on NBA games or leaking any confidential information to gamblers. However, the report did find that many other referees bet on other sports in violation of NBA rules. In the case of Donaghy, he repeatedly denied making any calls that would influence that outcome of an NBA game, a claim the government supported, and the report found no evidence to contradict this claim.

OFFICIALS' EMPLOYMENT STATUS

In 1974, during a children's baseball game in Palo Alto's Joe DiMaggio League, California baseball umpire Stan Feigenbaum turned to the state for help when he was struck in the head by a thrown ball. The boy who threw the ball had no liability insurance, and the California Umpires Association did not have workers compensation insurance. Feigenbaum filed a claim with the California Workers Compensation Uninsured Employers Fund, a state resource for injured employees. He was unsuccessful in his plea, because an independent contractor is not eligible for workers compensation.

The question of sports officials' status as employees or independent contractors has been debated for over four decades. Courts have generally found officials not to be employees, making employee benefits unavailable to them. In fact, according to NASO, 14 states have specifically ruled that amateur sports officials are independent contractors, with 8 states passing specific legislation to reflect this. Local officiating associations, school districts, and even state high school associations are not considered employers of sports officials, and as a result they have no obligation to maintain workers compensation insurance for officials.

The general test to determine whether a sport official is an employee or an independent contractor rests on whether the hiring entity has the right to control the official's performance. Basically, an organization that hires an official controls only the fact that the official is present; the official performs according to a standard that is not set by the contracting agent.

School Districts Are Not Employers

Beginning in 1956, state courts in almost every case have found that school districts are not officials' employers for workers compensation purposes. In a recent Colorado case, a referee broke his leg as he was officiating a high school football game. He sought to receive workers compensation benefits from the school district as an employee. The court reversed the decision of the Industrial Claims Appeals Panel and found that he was not an employee. Instead, the referee acted as an independent contractor because he was free from the control and direction of the school district when he was working as an umpire (Brighton School District v. Lyons, et al., 873 P.2d 26 [Ct. App. Col. 1993]).

Officials' Associations Are Not Employers

In 1973, a Maryland court decided that an injured umpire was not employed by his association. A player had struck umpire Donald Gale in the hip, neck, and leg with a bat. The court decided that, because Gale was not obliged to accept every assignment and could turn back games once they were assigned, he was indeed operating independently (Gale v. Greater Washington Softball Umpires Association, 19 Md. App. 481 [Ct. Sp. App. Mar. 1973]).

State High School Associations Are Not Employers

An Arizona wrestler, injured in a match, sued the referee and the state athletic association, and the association eventually settled the claim out of court. The insurance company that represented the association then attempted to sue the association to recover the money it paid in the settlement. In 1992, an Arizona appeals court determined that the state association was not the official's employer (Aetna Casualty & Surety Company v. Arizona Interscholastic Association, 173 Ariz. 260 [Ct. App. Ariz. 1992]). The short duration of work, limited control by the employer, and one-time method of payment for specific services were all factors in the court's decision.

College Conferences Are Not Employers

Although college conferences sometimes have a staff of officials, no workers compensation decisions have held them responsible when officials make claims for injury. By and large, officials must secure their own accident and medical insurance.

In 1987, the Collegiate Basketball Officials Association filed an unfair labor practice claim against the Big East Conference, because the conference would not bargain with the association over pay for Big East officials. Agreeing with the National Labor Relations Board's decision that officials could not collectively bargain for their pay rates because they were independent contractors and not employees, the court dismissed the case (Collegiate Basketball Officials Association v. NLRB, 836 F.2d 143 [3rd Cir. 1987]).

LIABILITY OF OFFICIALS FOR PLAYER INJURIES

As an official, you must be sure that games are played according to the rules and that rough and illegal plays are properly penalized. You can be held liable for injuries that result from repeated fouls that you fail to call. You can also be considered negligent if you did not curb baiting and taunting behavior that precipitated a fight. In general terms, negligence is a breach of a duty to another that causes the other harm. To demonstrate that an official was negligent, a plaintiff must show that (1) the official had a duty to the injured party (i.e., the official had the duty to make sure the playing rules were enforced), (2) the official breached this duty, (3) the plaintiff (player) was harmed, and (4) the official's breach of duty led to the harm to the plaintiff.

Your role as a sport official does not include administering first aid, unless a life-threatening situation exists. Instead, when a player is injured during a game, follow these steps:

1. Stop the game as soon as possible.
2. Report the injury to the player's coach.
3. Notify the game site administrator.
4. Stay near the player only to observe whether the player is conscious; then move aside to give attendants access to the player.

5. Permit other personnel to handle the injury and to move the player as necessary.

6. Hold up the game until the injured player is pronounced ready to play by authorized personnel or is removed from the area. (In some sports, players who are rendered unconscious via play action may not reenter the game without a doctor's permission).

7. Be patient; in many circumstances it may be necessary to wait for medical attendants to arrive and make decisions about removing the injured player.

Duty to Enforce Sport Safety Rules

Safety rules regarding game equipment are spelled out in each sport's rule publications. For example, metal standards such as volleyball net supports and football goalposts may need to be padded. Concrete hazards such as curbs and shot-put beams may need to be padded to avoid negligence when a field hockey, soccer, or football game is to be played. Player equipment also is subject to stringent specifications. Only certain kinds of footwear are permitted in each sport, and protective padding is defined by the rules, including the necessary width of slow-recovery absorbent materials. Mouth guards and kneepads are sometimes required. Certain kinds of support braces for leg joints may be permitted. You must know all these requirements and then inspect the site and the players to be sure of compliance. Overlooking vital equipment and its protective dimensions could result in your being held liable for negligence in an injury case.

Duty to Confirm Safe Weather Conditions

A Superior Court of New Jersey lawsuit involved a football player who became partially paralyzed when he fractured two vertebrae while trying to make a tackle. The player's suit, which named three high school football officials, among others, claimed that the field was unsafe because of heavy rain. The suit against the officials was dismissed. The court found that the officials controlled the game properly and did not make mistakes in judgment about the field conditions. But a similar case involving an injured football player and a rain-soaked field in Wisconsin was settled out of court; the officials were part of the settling group because they were found to be negligent in allowing the game to be played.

Inclement weather conditions can give rise to liability claims against sports officials. You have a duty to be sure that weather conditions are safe for play, and if weather deteriorates during a game—particularly if lightning starts—you should err on the side of caution and insist that players leave the premises for their safety.

However, officials are not always found to be liable for not stopping a game because inclement weather. In 2004, a father and son sued claiming that an official should have stopped an amateur rugby match once the National Weather Service issued a thunderstorm warning. The official did not stop the match, and the plaintiffs were struck by lightning. Noting that the plaintiffs were free to leave at any time, and that the plaintiffs could have also understood the potential danger of the storm, the court would not impose a duty on the official to warn and ruled that the official did not create a greater hazard than brought on by natural causes (Patton v. United States Football Rugby Union, 381 Md. 627 [Ct. App. Md. 2004]).

Rained *In?*

Indoor venues are not exempt from weather problems. In January 1986, NBA referee Mike Mathis halted a game at Seattle in the first half because rain was leaking onto the playing surface. A 1997 college basketball game at Walsh College in Ohio was terminated with 18 minutes remaining because of condensation forming on the playing floor, which was made of a plastic–foam composite. The humid atmosphere in the gym combined with frigid conditions outdoors to create an exceptionally slippery floor. A game administrator helped the officials arrive at the decision to call the game off.

Duty to Properly Inspect the Playing Surface

Rules impose an obligation on officials to note visible hazards—whether natural or artificial—and have them corrected before games.

Natural hazards include pitted fields, rocks, and mud holes. Artificial hazards include protruding sprinkler heads, protruding drainage conduits, curbing too close to the playing field, concrete runways not used in the game being played, goals for sports other than the one being played, debris, and loose bases or faulty pitcher's rubber. If the hazard or hazardous condition cannot be removed or secured, the hazard might be made safe by using added padding. Taking precautions will likely absolve you of negligence.

In 2000, a track athlete slipped on a wet track and injured his knee. National Federation requirements left the referees with primary responsibility for supervising the weather conditions and canceling a meet because of the hazardous weather conditions. Although it had been raining, the referees allowed the meet to continue, and the plaintiff was injured during the 110-meter hurdles. Finding that the referees' actions were, at most, negligent and so covered by New Jersey's limited liability statute, the court dismissed the claim against the referee. The court also noted that it could not determine whether the referees had exercised less than reasonable care because "[i]njury from a fall while running and jumping is inherent in the sport of hurdling and the extent to which that risk is enhanced by moisture on an all-weather track is not a matter of common understanding" (Harris & Harris v. Red Bank Regional High School, et. al., 2005 N.J. Super. Unpub. LEXIS 377 [N.J. App. Div. 2005]).

Duty to Protect Players' Civil and Religious Rights

Sports officials may also be targets of lawsuits alleging that they violated a player's civil or religious rights. Whether yarmulkes (skullcaps) worn by Orthodox Jewish players could be secured with hairpins was the problem in a California dispute. State commissioner Dean Crowley ruled that the clips were permissible, even though rules forbade metal objects such as jewelry worn on the head or neck. Game officials previously had given players the option of removing the head coverings or forfeiting a game. Other officials made players remove their yarmulkes halfway through a game.

A similar issue has arisen recently regarding female athletes who want to cover themselves out of respect for their Muslim faith.

Some Muslim women believe that they can only expose their faces, hands, and feet, and that the rest of their bodies must be covered, including covering their heads with veils or hijabs. Obviously, this much clothing can make participation in sport difficult. Although no court has yet addressed this issue, it is clear that similar to courts' reviews of the participation of Orthodox Jewish players, if an appropriate headpiece can be found, sports associations may have to allow these female athletes to play with some degree of excess clothing. In fact, several companies have recently developed special headwear designed to eliminate some of this excess clothing but keep the female athlete covered in accordance with the Muslim faith.

Legislative Efforts

In 1987, the National Association of Sports Officials designed limited-liability model legislation to curb the growing number of liability lawsuits against sports officials. The model legislation puts the burden of proof on the plaintiff to show that the official acted with gross negligence (i.e., failure to use any care in a way that shows reckless or willful disregard for the safety of others), and not ordinary negligence, as defined earlier in this chapter. To date, 21 states have adopted legislation similar to or based on this model, including Alabama, Arkansas, Delaware, Georgia, Hawaii, Illinois, Louisiana, Maryland, Massachusetts, Minnesota, Mississippi, Nevada, New Hampshire, New Jersey, New Mexico, North Carolina, North Dakota, Ohio, Pennsylvania, Rhode Island, and Tennessee. In 1997, the federal government also passed the Volunteer Protection Act, which provides additional limitations on liability for volunteers (including sports officials) who provide volunteer services on behalf of nonprofit organizations.

SUMMARY

You may not be aware of how you are legally responsible when you step onto a floor or field to work a contest. This chapter spelled out how the judicial system rules on officials' game calls. It also focused on officials' employment status as independent contractors, and liability of officials for player injuries. Now that you know your legal duties as an official, you are ready to learn about your rights and business responsibilities, which are addressed in chapter 12.

REVIEW QUESTIONS

1. Courts will review mistaken calls made by referees that affect the outcome of a game
   a. most of the time
   b. some of the time
   c. rarely
   d. never

2. Courts will review judgment calls made by officials
   a. never
   b. some of the time
   c. rarely
   d. most of the time

3. Referees can be subject to review by a court if it becomes clear that their calls were made because they had bet on the outcome of the contest.
   ___ True
   ___ False

4. Because officials are typically hired to work high school football contests, the school district that hires them can be considered their employer.
   ___ True
   ___ False

5. Officials are typically considered
   a. employees at will
   b. seasonal employees
   c. independent contractors
   d. part-time employees

6. Officials have a duty to protect the players they are officiating
   a. from hazardous weather conditions
   b. from unsafe field conditions
   c. from dangerous playing surfaces
   d. none of the above
   e. all of the above

7. Officials are immune from liability for the breach of their duties to the players only if they act
   a. recklessly
   b. intentionally
   c. negligently
   d. inattentively

8. States have been unwilling to provide protection for officials when they have acted negligently and caused a player's harm.
   a. No, states have enacted specific legislation to limit officials' liability for negligent actions that cause harm.
   b. Yes, states are unwilling to protect officials when athletes are harmed.
   c. It depends on the age of the athlete who is harmed; states do not want young athletes to be unable to recover if they are harmed.
   d. No, states have forced each official to buy insurance against negligence that results in harm to an athlete.

Answers on page 190

Chapter 12

Legal Rights and Business Responsibilities

Paul Anderson

This chapter addresses the following:

- Specific business practices important for officials as independent contractors
- Officials' potential rights to recover for violations of their civil rights and discriminatory conduct toward them
- The business structure and policies of sports officials' associations

Just as you need to ensure the well-being of players, so too do you need an umbrella of protection for yourself. First of all, you need to be a sound businessperson, because you are most likely in business for yourself. Some state and national officiating organizations have blanket insurance policies available for officials in the rare situations in which they are injured. But you need to be assured that if circumstances operate against you, opportunities for seeking justice are available. Some states have statutes to protect officials from physical harm by making it a crime to harm an official before, during, or immediately after a contest. As an official, you need to be aware of all avenues for impartial redress. Associations organized for the welfare of officials also need to have formal policies that ensure the fairness of their practices. This chapter explains these vital protective dimensions of athletic officiating.

INDEPENDENT CONTRACTOR STATUS

As a paid worker, you are essentially in business for yourself. As such, you need to observe the formalities of this setup. You will usually be issued a contract for game assignments. This contract is a simple written legal document that you sign showing that you agree to the specific details about your game assignments. If you fail to fulfill the stipulations of the contract, you may be obliged to pay a penalty, usually a game fee. Often, an individual represents a school or a league in procuring officials, and that individual may send several contracts for games. It is a good business practice to return contracts promptly. You should sign the contract, keep a copy, and send the other copy back to the party who issued the contract. Keep in mind that when schools are forced to break a contract, they do not always compensate the official, although they should.

Contracts usually indicate who your partners are. The contract's terms may or may not include stipends for meals and mileage, depending on the region in which you work and the customary policies of the school. It is important for you to keep a calendar of your officiating obligations, with times and locales clearly delineated. Unfortunately, at times officials get mixed up on starting times or cannot find the game site. Keep in mind that tardiness or failure to show up for a scheduled game is damaging to your reputation.

Sometimes you may have to give up a game assignment because of injury, job requirements, or a personal emergency. There is probably a policy in your geographic area for nullifying contracts. It is important for you to learn how to be relieved of an obligation. Often, local groups have replacement pools and standard practices for obtaining an acceptable substitute. Regardless, you are expected to cancel a game only for legitimate reasons, and working an alternate game is ordinarily frowned on as an excuse. Successful officiating rests on building a reputation for reliability and integrity.

Sometimes payments are made after games, sometimes at the end of a season. Whenever you are paid, you need to keep track of your income and expenses for tax purposes. You are obliged to report income, but you can also deduct expenses, including uniform purchases, mileage to games and meetings, clinic fees, and other outlays connected to your officiating. An accountant can tell you which tax deductions are permissible. If you are not a businessperson in your regular job, you need to become one when you start to officiate for pay.

OFFICIALS' CONSTITUTIONAL AND CIVIL RIGHTS

Sports officials have more vigorously asserted their civil rights during the past few decades. Cases have involved claims under federal and state civil rights and antidiscrimination laws.

Constitutional Rights

Federal constitutional rights should be protected in all situations in which a governmental entity attempts to infringe upon them. In fact, constitutional rights apply only in situations involving some governmental entity (e.g., a public school, public school district, state official). Oklahoma high school basketball referee Stanley Guffey deserves an ovation for standing up for the independence of sports officials.

On February 4, 1992, Officer Eldridge Wyatt was employed by Douglas High School to provide security during its Oklahoma City Conference Basketball Championship game against Star Spencer High School. With a few minutes left in the game, Officer Wyatt observed suspected gang members moving toward the court. Wyatt believed that the game's intensity might provoke a crowd problem. He approached the teams' coaches and asked them to calm their players during the vigorously played game.

Officer Wyatt also went onto the court and advised Guffey that the vigorous play had inflamed the spectators. He asked Guffey to "control the game so we can control the crowd." Officer Wyatt ordered Guffey to start calling more fouls. In response, Guffey stated, "I don't know who you are, but you don't have any business out here on the floor." Officer Wyatt then informed Guffey that he was under arrest and escorted him into a separate room away from the basketball court. After a brief period, Guffey was permitted to return and officiated the game to its conclusion.

Guffey filed a lawsuit alleging that his federal civil rights had been violated because Wyatt's actions constituted an arrest without probable cause and a violation of the Fourth Amendment to the U.S. Constitution, which prohibits illegal searches and seizures (Guffey v. Wyatt, 18 F.3d 869 [10th Cir. 1994]). Officer Wyatt argued that he had sufficient probable cause to arrest Guffey because of his failure to obey a lawful request for assistance from a police officer. Maintaining that he reasonably believed that a riot was imminent, Officer Wyatt contended that Guffey's refusal to act impeded Wyatt's ability to control the crowd and was an obstruction of justice under Oklahoma law. Guffey responded that neither the game nor the crowd was particularly unruly. Guffey likened Officer Wyatt's behavior to that of an irate fan and argued that Officer Wyatt never requested assistance but simply directed him to start "calling more fouls."

The Court of Appeals for the Tenth Circuit upheld the federal district court's decision not to dismiss this lawsuit. The court of appeals found that there was clearly a factual dispute, which should be left to the determination of a jury. The case was then tried in the district court, where the jury found in favor of Guffey and awarded him $4,000. The court then ordered that most of his attorneys' fees be paid by the defendant.

Regardless of the words used by Officer Wyatt, there does not appear to be justification for a police officer substituting his judgment for that of a game official by requesting the official to call fouls.

Antidiscrimination in Employment Laws

Title VII of the federal Civil Rights Act of 1964, other federal laws, and state antidiscrimination laws prohibit discrimination in employment based on certain protected categories, such as age, race, national origin, gender, and sexual preference.

Two former NFL officials divided $67,500 in back pay after a 1992 settlement reached by the NFL and the federal Equal Employment Opportunity Commission (EEOC). On behalf of ex-officials Jack Fette and Fred Silva, the EEOC filed an age-bias suit against the NFL. The EEOC found that the NFL discriminated against older officials because it "engaged in a policy of closer scrutiny" of the on-field work of officials aged 60 or older than of the work of younger officials, and that the NFL often forced the older officials to retire or to move to off-field positions.

In a more recent dispute concerning the age of an umpire, in 2007 Clark Davis sued the Atlantic League of Professional Baseball Clubs, claiming that the league discriminated against him in violation of the federal Age Discrimination in Employment Act and New Jersey's antidiscrimination laws (Davis v. The Atlantic League of Professional Baseball Clubs, Inc., 106 Fair Empl. Prac. [BNA] 807 [D.N.J. June 2, 2009]). Davis was 52 years old and claimed that his age caused the league to not assign him to a play-off game, and to not renew him for the following year. The court allowed Davis' claim to proceed because the league told him that he was not being assigned to a play-off game because he had "been doing it a lot of years, and we're going to give the younger guys a chance" (*Id.* at *2). Although no final decision has been reached in this case, this kind of decision presumably made in relation to an umpire's age can be found to be illegal.

In 1998, a New York federal district court jury awarded basketball referee Sandra Ortiz-Del Valle $850,000 compensatory and $7 million punitive damages in her sex discrimination lawsuit against the NBA (Ortiz-Del Valle v. NBA, 42 F. Supp. 2d 334 [S.D.N.Y. 1999]). Ortiz-Del Valle claimed that the NBA did not hire her to officiate because she is a woman. The NBA appealed the verdict (Ortiz-Del Valle v. NBA, 190 F.3d 598 [2nd Cir. 1999]).

Ortiz-Del Valle had officiated in the U.S. Basketball League in 1991, becoming the first woman to officiate any U.S. men's professional basketball game. She alleged that she was in line to be hired by the NBA and was passed over in favor of male officials of lower caliber. The NBA disagreed and argued that she did not possess the qualities to officiate in the NBA. A jury found that the NBA had discriminated against her and awarded her damages for lost income, mental pain, and emotional distress, along with additional punitive damages.

In 2003, African American umpire Milton Wadler sued the Eastern College Athletic Conference under Title VII claiming that it discriminated against him based on his race by reducing his schedule of games, not assigning him to play-off games, and eventually removing him from a list of available umpires (Wadler v. Eastern College Athletic Conference, et.al. 2003 U.S. Dist. LEXIS 14212 [S.D.N.Y. 2003]). Each member school paid the umpires and reimbursed them for travel, and although the conference controlled the umpire's work schedule, it did not pay any umpire directly. As a result, the court found that the umpire was an independent contractor and not an employee of the conference, and his Title VII claim was dismissed.

Americans With Disabilities Act

The Americans With Disabilities Act (ADA) is a federal law that prohibits discrimination against people with disabilities. A person with a disability is defined under the ADA as someone with a physical or mental impairment that substantially limits a major life activity or a person who has a record of this type of impairment or can be regarded as having an impairment. Among other categories, an impairment can be HIV positive status or having AIDS, a hearing impairment, mental illness, or a physical disability.

Although far-reaching in its scope, the provisions of the ADA that apply most directly to sports officials are those applicable to employers, defined as "a person engaged in an industry affecting commerce who has 15 or more employees for each working day in each of 20 or more calendar weeks in the current or preceding calendar year" (42 U.S.C. §12111[5] [A], 2010). Exempted from this definition is a "bona fide private membership club that is exempt from taxation under Section 501(c) of the Internal Revenue Code of 1986" (*Id.* §12111[5][B][ii]). An employee is defined as "an individual employed by an employer" (*Id.* §12111[4]).

In 1994, a court in Alabama was faced with the issue of whether a local baseball umpires' association was subject to the ADA. Umpire David Jones sued the Southeast Alabama Baseball Umpires Association (SABUA), alleging that he had been discriminated against in his level of assignments because of a leg

prosthesis that he wears as a result of an amputation (Jones v. Southeast Alabama Baseball Umpires Association, 864 F.Supp. 1135 [M.Dist. Ala. 1994]). The court refused to dismiss Jones' claim because it disagreed with the association's defense that it was neither an employer nor an employment agency and, therefore, that it was not a "covered entity" under the ADA.

The SABUA supervises the hiring of baseball umpires for high schools in Houston County, Alabama, and the surrounding area. From 1989 to 1992, the SABUA assigned Jones to work high school junior varsity baseball games. Occasionally, he was assigned to work varsity games. In 1992, Jones notified the SABUA that he no longer desired to umpire only junior varsity games, but rather believed that he was good enough to be assigned solely to varsity-level games. In March 1992, the SABUA informed Jones that they had rejected his request because, as a result of his leg prosthesis, it believed that he did not have the mobility to umpire effectively on a regular

A disability should not limit your ability to be an official.

basis at the varsity level. The SABUA further based its determination on its perception that his disability presented a safety problem and potential injury to him and participants in the games in which he would umpire.

A recent issue that has arisen under the ADA is whether officiating is a major life activity and thus whether the inability to officiate is proof of a disability. In 1997, an Illinois court dismissed football official Lorenzo Clemons' lawsuit against the Big Ten Conference claiming that his supervisor perceived that he was disabled because he weighed 285 pounds (Clemons v. The Big Ten Conference, 73 Fair Emp. Prac. Cas. [BNA] 466 [N.D. Ill. 1997]).

When Clemons was hired, he weighed 235 pounds, but he continued to gain weight. In 1990, the conference implemented a rating system for football officials, and Clemons rated 36th out of 44 officials. In 1991, he was rated 49th out of 49. At the conclusion of both seasons, his supervisor discussed Clemons' weight and its effect on his performance. In 1993, Clemons was rated 43rd out of 45 officials, and his written evaluation pointed out that his weight—277 pounds at the beginning of the 1993 season and 280 at its conclusion—affected his performance. During the season, he had made 12 errors in judgment, the most of any conference official. Clemons was told to lose 10 pounds and placed on probation. He then reported to the pre-1994 season clinic at 285 pounds, and his contract for the 1994 season was terminated.

In reviewing his claim, the court agreed with the conference and found that he did not meet the ADA's definition of being disabled. To prevail on his claim, Clemons had to show that he had an impairment that substantially limited a major life activity. One such major life activity under the ADA is working. However, as defined by the law, the inability to perform a single, particular job does not constitute a substantial limitation on working. In addition, the regulations interpreting the ADA note that "except in rare circumstances, obesity is not considered a disabling impairment" (*Id.* at *17). The court found that Clemons could not have been perceived to be disabled because he was not permitted to work as a referee only for 11 days, and he could and did work at his regular job. Therefore, he was not substantially limited in the major life activity of working.

If followed by other courts, this decision implies that at least football officials, and perhaps all nonprofessional officials, will not be able to use inability to officiate as proof of a disability under the ADA. In addition, because officiating is often an avocation, it may not be within the ADA's definition of a major life activity. However, an official may still be able to succeed on such a claim under certain states' laws against discrimination that do not have such definitional limitations.

Joan Schmitz umpired numerous softball games for the City of Eau Claire Parks and Recreation Department from 1998 to 2001. In 2001, Schmitz was in a car accident, and she had to have her left arm and leg amputated. As a result of her limited mobility, she was assigned a partner to umpire a limited number of softball games and was not chosen to umpire the year-end tournament in 2002. In 2003, Schmitz was evaluated by a neutral evaluator,

Sex Does Not Matter

Under Title VII, employees can sue employers when the employers act in way that discriminates against them based on sex. However, courts have recently reminded female high school officials that they cannot recover for this alleged discrimination because they are not employees. Tamika Covington and Jude Davis both sued officials' associations (the International Association of Approved Basketball Officials and the New York Sports Officials' Council and Soccer Officials' Association, respectively) claiming that these groups assigned them to fewer games and in other ways lessened their ability to officiate, all because they are women. Unfortunately for them, the New Jersey and New York courts do not agree. Agreeing with the principles laid out earlier in this chapter, both courts found that these women were not employees of the associations, and so they cannot bring sexual discrimination claims against them (Davis v. The New York Sports Officials' Council, et al., 2010 U.S. Dist. LEXIS 104631 [N.D.N.Y. 2010] and Covington v. International Association of Approved Basketball Officials, 2010 U.S. Dist. LEXIS 88088 [D. N.J. 2010]).

who determined that she could umpire games by herself. Following several complaints from players who said she had made questionable, confusing calls and made derogatory comments to players, she was given warnings by the superintendent of recreation that she had to change her behavior. After additional incidents, she was not rehired for the 2004 season. Schmitz filed a retaliation claim with the city's Equal Rights Division claiming that she was not rehired because of her disability. Although the court did not reach a conclusion as to whether Schmitz was actually fired as a result of her disability, it was willing to consider that the recreation department had illegally discriminated against her as a result of her disability (Schmitz v. City of Eau Claire, 2007 U.S. Dist. LEXIS 78941 [W. Dist. Wis. 2007]).

SPORTS OFFICIALS' ASSOCIATIONS

More than 4,000 local sports officials' associations operate in the United States. As officiating has grown as a profession, so has the manner in which sports officials' associations conduct their business. Many of these groups are voluntary nonprofit membership organizations, whereas others are profit-making businesses. Both types train and assign their officials to games.

Business Structure

Most officials' associations operate as profit corporations, sole proprietorships, unincorporated associations, or nonprofit corporations. For voluntary membership groups, the best form of business is a nonprofit corporation organized for educational purposes. This is easily accomplished by filing articles or a certificate of incorporation with the state and is relatively inexpensive. The filing fees and attorneys' fees are approximately $100 to $1,500, depending on the state. This is not expensive when compared with the liability of individual members should the association be sued.

The most important reason for incorporation is to protect the association's officers and members from liability for contractual or injury claims. If an association incorporates, only the corporation, not the officials involved in the corporation, has potential liability. For

example, what happens if a member is authorized by an association to buy jackets for all officials but fails to pay for them? If the local association is unincorporated, every member could be individually liable for the full cost of the jackets. However, if the association is a corporation, then it is required to pay the debt if the store sues and obtains a judgment.

Similarly, if a member is sued by a player who claims that she was injured by the official's negligence, the association will likely be joined in the lawsuit as a defendant. The claim will be that the association failed to train the official properly. If the association is not a corporation, each official and officer may be responsible to pay any judgment, legal fees, and costs awarded to the player.

The Russ Fendley Sports Officials' Association in California discovered this problem. It was an unincorporated association of umpires. At this time, one of its members was sued by the City of Long Beach, which had been sued by a player in a recreational baseball game whose leg was injured by the base spike when sliding into second base. The city attempted to recover the damages it paid by going after the umpire it believed was responsible for the injury.

Corporate Bylaws

In conjunction with incorporation, an officials' association should also adopt bylaws, the operating rules of the group. One of the most unpleasant tasks sports officials' groups must occasionally perform is disciplining their members. A disciplinary procedure that is not well planned or not performed properly may create serious legal problems for a local association. An Ohio wrongful expulsion lawsuit brought by an umpire against his association focused attention on how officials' groups may discipline their members. In that case, the umpire alleged that he was expelled from membership for bad-faith reasons and in violation of his constitutional, procedural due-process rights by not being given an appropriate hearing. The judge dismissed the suit, ruling that the association acted properly and within the scope of its constitution (Sorge v. The Greater Parma Umpires Association, 1979 Ohio App. LEXIS 9051 [Ct. App. Ohio 1979]).

Losing such a case can be avoided by providing appropriate provisions in the bylaws. Unacceptable behavior should be clearly defined so that members are aware of required and prohibited activities. For example, violations of a game-assigning system, specific conduct unbecoming an official, the requirement of taking and passing an annual written rules test, and meeting attendance requirements should be specified. Each member should be given a copy of the bylaws.

In addition to listing required and prohibited activities, the bylaws should also include the procedure for handling violations. The penalties that might be imposed, such as fines, suspension, or expulsion, for various violations should also be included in the bylaws. The key elements to keep in mind in drafting these provisions are that they must provide the member reasonable notice of the alleged violation, a reasonable opportunity to present his or her side of the story, reasonable notice of the possible penalty, and a right to appeal.

Notice of a violation should be given to a member in writing by certified mail, return receipt requested. The notice should include a brief explanation of the alleged violation, the date of the violation, the names of the people who filed the allegation, the possible penalty, and a reference to the bylaw provision that provides the procedure for the member to be heard and to present her version of the incident.

The member must then be given the opportunity to present her account by appearing with any witnesses and documentary evidence to support her side before the appropriate committee for the group. The proceeding should begin with the presentation of the charge, the possible penalty, and evidence against the member. People who have knowledge about the incident should also tell their stories. All this should be done with the accused member present so that she may ask questions if desired. The accused member then should be permitted to present her side with witnesses and documents. The committee should make its decision, including any penalty, and communicate it in writing to the member by certified mail, return receipt requested.

Group members should have an opportunity to appeal an adverse decision. The bylaws should include a provision that a member may appeal to the executive board by requesting an appeal within a certain number of days after the decision has been rendered. The executive board can then schedule a meeting to consider the appeal or can decide to hold another full hearing. The decision of the executive board should also be communicated in writing to the member.

The group should keep and retain accurate records of all proceedings concerning the disciplining of members. The group should keep copies of all letters sent and received and minutes of all general membership meetings and executive board meetings so that a complete record will be available if needed. An officer should retain these records in a specific location and pass them on when there is a change of administration. It is not unusual for a lawsuit to be filed a year or more after the relevant events took place.

The key to well-written bylaws is that they be reasonable and fair. Courts have generally upheld provisions if those prerequisites are followed. Bylaws not only protect a group from future legal problems in the disciplining of members, but also help a group to function in an evenhanded manner.

Kurz and Carter were umpires for the Federation of Petanque, U.S.A. (FPUSA). An entry form for a FPUSA tournament in Sacramento included language prohibiting smoking and drinking of alcoholic beverages on or off the court while playing. Kurz noticed the language and posted a message on the Internet. Carter responded and told him it was not a FPUSA rule, and then Kurz responded saying that if Carter were to umpire the tournament, he should not enforce the rule. The FPUSA Disciplinary Committee notified Kurz and Carter that they were looking into whether they violated a rule that stated that all umpires are to conduct themselves in a manner that reflects well on all FPUSA umpires. Kurz and Carter were allowed to provide a written defense. FPUSA suspended their umpire credentials for one year, after which they were to undergo a two-year probationary period.

Kurz and Carter sued in 2005, claiming that California law, which addresses how nonprofit corporations may expel or suspend members, applied and that FPUSA had to follow its own rules as laid out in its bylaws. The court ruled that FPUSA was not required to follow its rules regarding discipline imposed on members because the decision involved only the suspension of umpire credentials (Kurz v. Federation of Petanque, 146 Cal. App. 4th 136 [Ct. App. Cal. 2006]).

Sample Bylaws

The following sections provide some sample clauses that might be found in the corporate bylaws of an officials' association.

1. Membership

Any person desiring to become a member of the Association must present his or her application to the Association office with the appropriate application fee, as well as a completed history background check form.

Qualifications for membership are as follows:

a. Current registration with the Association

b. Submission of an acceptable history background check form with the Association

c. Membership in good standing in a recognized association or board in any one sport

To annually retain membership in the Association, an official must do the following:

a. Complete the Association's online rules clinic

b. Pass the annual approved test in the sport officiated with a score of ___ or higher

c. Meet the meeting requirements of the local association

Only officials certified by the Association may be assigned to varsity or postseason contests

2. Dues

The annual dues for each registered official will be determined by the Association's Executive Committee.

3. Meetings

Section 1. Number. There shall be a minimum of seven (7) meetings between October and April of each year.

Section 2. Notice. Notices shall be sent out by the secretary-treasurer prior to October of each year.

Section 3. Attendance. Active members must attend at least four (4) meetings between October and April of each year, one of which must be a rules interpretation meeting.

4. Tests and Examinations

Officials must annually take and pass the approved rules test with a score of ___ or higher to be certified. In addition, prior to the start of each sport season, completion of the Association's online rules clinic is required of each official who plans to officiate a varsity or postseason contest.

5. Conduct

All members shall conduct themselves at all times while engaged in officiating duties and officiating-related duties in a manner becoming to an official and according to the Code of Ethics of the National Federation of State High Schools (see Appendix A).

6. Discipline of Members

Section 1. Grounds for discipline. Any of the following forms of misconduct can be grounds for an official facing discipline. The following list is merely illustrative. The Association has the sole discretion to deem conduct by an official to be misconduct subject to discipline.

1. Using abusive language or distasteful gestures

2. Degrading fellow Association members or Association staff

3. Using substances (i.e., alcohol or drugs) the day of a contest that could impair the official's ability to perform his or her duties as an official

4. Failing to show up for a contest that the official has been assigned to officiate

5. Violating any section of the Association's Bylaws or rules

6. Deviating from the proper enforcement of NFHS sports rules or Association rules

7. Being charged or convicted of a criminal act

8. Abusing a player or coach

9. Obligating themselves to any person not affiliated with any contest they might be assigned to officiate

Section 2. Appeal. Any member suspended by the Board shall have the right of appeal to the Executive Committee.

Section 3. Right to a fair hearing. A member charged with any violation shall have the right to be heard in person or by written statement made by the member in his or her own defense. Such right shall be afforded prior to the imposition of any fine, penalty, or any other disciplinary action, and thereupon a member may seek a personal hearing if the member makes a request in writing to the member who sent the notification of a violation within fourteen (14) days of the date of the notification. A member may then appeal the determination to the Executive Committee by giving the Executive Committee written notice within seven (7) days of the receipt of the determination. The Executive Committee may then decide the matter on the facts and determination previously made or by asking the member to appear personally.

Section 4. Discipline notice. When a member is suspended or expelled, the Executive Committee shall notify all concerned that such a member is no longer able to accept assignments or officiate as a member of this Board. No active member shall officiate knowingly with a suspended or expelled member.

7. Amendments

Amendments to these Bylaws can be made by a majority vote of the Association's Executive Committee at any regularly scheduled annual meeting.

Insurance

Local officials' associations, as well as all individual members, should have liability insurance. This insurance pays attorneys' fees and costs should the association or its members be sued for negligence, defamation, civil rights violations, or other related claims. Two types of policies must be purchased: one for the association and the other by each member individually. Both types of policies are available from several sources, including the National Association of Sports Officials through its Sports Officials Security Program, and the National Federation of State High School Associations. An association should also have a directors' and officers' liability policy to cover it for claims regarding decisions and official policies of the association and its committees.

Contracts

Officials' associations should, as a good business practice, prepare and require each member official and hiring school to complete a written contract for each game. Such a contract helps avoid misunderstandings and lawsuits. Provisions that are important to include are game date and place, official's legal status, payment, and what happens if the game is cancelled or postponed. Keep in mind that this type of event-specific contract does not change the relationship between the official and the association; that is, the official is still an independent contractor and not an employee.

SUMMARY

The keys to avoiding legal problems for officials and officials' associations are awareness of potential liability claims and good business practices. Because officials may not be aware of the law, properly constructed officials' association bylaws may protect them when they step on a floor or field to work a contest. This chapter provided several cases that illustrate how the law may protect your employment, constitutional, and civil rights. Officiating associations should also take steps to ensure fairness as they strive to serve both schools and member officials.

Because sports officiating requires additional commitments from individuals, chapter 13 describes ways to organize time effectively.

REVIEW QUESTIONS

1. An official's civil rights could be affected by which of the following entities?

   a. Public school

   b. City school district

   c. Private vocational school

   d. All of the above

   e. Only *a* and *b*

2. An official's association can limit the games officiated by members over the age of 60.

   a. True

   b. Possibly true if the decision is not based on the person's eyesight

   c. False

   d. Possibly true if the decision is not based on the person's age

3. Overweight umpires can sue under the ADA if they are barred from umpiring.

   a. True

   b. False

4. Why would an officials' organization seek to become incorporated?

   a. To make a profit

   b. To sell merchandise

   c. To protect members from individual liability

   d. To avoid taxes

5. What type of information should be included in the bylaws of an officials' organization?

   a. Disciplinary procedures for members

   b. Membership requirements

   c. Appeal procedures related to discipline

   d. All of the above

   e. Some of the above

Answers on page 190

Chapter 13

Time Management

Jerry Grunska

This chapter addresses the following:

- The importance of managing time well
- The causes of poor time management
- How to evaluate your time management skills
- How to improve your time management
- How time commitments expand as you advance as an official

Anytime you add an activity to your life, you must make accommodations for it. Finding the time needed to perform competently as an official takes a special kind of planning. Sports officiating often necessitates covering games in the evening and on weekends, times that many people usually consider free time. This chapter shows the types of time commitments necessary for succeeding as an official, illustrates the problems of arranging for that time, and offers advice about how to meet your time commitments.

OFFICIALS AS TIME MANAGERS

If your life is busy, a commitment to officiating requires your wedging in blocks of time to ensure that your sports enterprise will be of a high caliber. If you take a casual approach, showing only partial dedication to becoming a

top-flight performer, you are not likely to rise above mediocrity.

Because you no doubt need to accommodate the requirements of officiating along with those of your primary career and other obligations, such as family commitments, time is a precious commodity that should not be wasted. As an official, you will need to address the following seven types of additional time commitments, none of which you can afford to overlook.

1. *Time for games.* Contests usually last from one to three hours, depending on the sport, and often you'll be asked to officiate several games in succession, particularly at the high school underclass level. Schools ordinarily schedule varsity games on Friday nights and Saturdays, but some varsity sports and many underclass programs can take place any weekday, usually after school around 4:00 p.m. In metropolitan areas, where schools and recreation centers may be relatively close together, many top-flight (varsity) games are likely to be scheduled for weekday evenings, particularly indoor games such as basketball and volleyball. Because ice arenas usually have many groups competing for space, they may schedule games at odd times, such as early morning or late at night.

2. *Time for travel.* If you live an hour away from a game site, plan for three hours of travel time: two hours there and back, plus an extra half hour before and after the game.

3. *Time for on-site game preparation.* In many sports, officials wear special uniforms and are expected to be at a site in time to change and even to warm up. Also, many sports require

Officials should strive for a good working relationship with players without fraternizing.

officials to conduct pregame inspections such as checking score books and equipment. Some rule books insist that officials observe player warm-ups a half hour before the start of games.

4. *Time for on-site mental preparation.* Several sports require pregame conferences for officials, so that they can exchange ideas about preferred techniques, agree on crew synchrony, and review key rules to prepare for the upcoming contest. If the crew travels together, this orienting can take place on the way to the game, but sometimes this opportunity is not available.

5. *Time for book learning.* The rules of each sport and their myriad applications are intricate, difficult to digest, and require study. Some sources recommend reading a single rule at a time or spending 15 to 20 minutes a day in diligent perusal. Often, a good way to solidify learning is to discuss ramifications of rules with fellow officials or to participate in formal class discussions.

6. *Time for practical learning.* Few officials feel comfortable going into a season cold, so

they customarily attend clinics in the off-season for simulations, walk-through experiences, and game tips. Also, school coaches frequently ask officials to handle preseason scrimmages, which are excellent opportunities to review and practice officiating skills before the season.

7. *Time for meetings.* Officials' associations are charged with the task of introducing new rules and upgrading officiating knowledge. Not all local groups are organized to perform these tasks, serving instead as social gatherings and assigning forums, but a fortunate number of associations strive to fulfill a training function. Often, officiating groups meet several times before the season and weekly thereafter.

Common Errors in Managing Time

Selectivity and careful planning are key in managing time. Squandering is the opposite of making conscious choices. No one likes to have vital plans interrupted or derailed. Specific steps for making sure that you allocate your time carefully are explained later, but first we identify some common pitfalls.

Certain habits and behaviors can cause you literally to lose time and can deprive you of valuable opportunities. This doesn't mean that you must have your nose to the grindstone continually or give up leisure pleasures entirely, but it does mean that you should think positively about using your time well and establishing priorities. Consider whether you have any of the following habits.

Relying on Mythical Time to Fulfill Obligations

Some people permit a task to draw out, believing that they can finish later, when in fact the time left for completion diminishes. You might be less efficient than you presume, be thrown off schedule by interruptions, or improperly estimate the time needed for preliminary tasks. Therefore, anticipated time is an illusion that fades away, resulting in a project that may be hurried, poorly finished, or incomplete because you calculated the time requirements inaccurately. You may intend to study the rules on a regular basis, for example, but the time never comes; as a result, you start the season with gaps in your preparation.

Putting Things Off

We often push aside our least appealing responsibilities, with the result that the time needed for working on the task disappears. For example, you may vow to notify the assigner of availability but miss the deadline and therefore are deprived of a decent game schedule.

Task Hopping

Failure to complete one task before undertaking another often results in having too many things going at once and not doing a thorough job with any of them. People guilty of this practice fail to meet deadlines and end up doing a shoddy job because they are behind, and their mistakes are often costly. Some officials work so many games, sometimes even shifting from one sport to another on a given day, that they become officiating vagabonds, hurrying from venue to venue in perpetual motion. It is impossible for them to be good at what they are attempting.

Faulty Concentration

In their primary occupations, people with poor concentration may procrastinate or be sidetracked by distractions such as doodling, a trip to the water cooler, or chatting with colleagues. The inability to zero in on necessary tasks is caused by a failure to prioritize and results in a lack of follow-through—that is, not finishing what you start. Though a lack of concentration during a game can cause the quality of your officiating to suffer, it also creates problems before and after games because it prevents you from making the most efficient use of your time.

Ignoring Reality

Sometimes we are unaware of overloading ourselves with commitments. Taking on an extra chore may indicate that you're willing to extend yourself, but you may not have time to meet that additional obligation.

EVALUATING YOUR TIME MANAGEMENT SKILLS

You can estimate your effectiveness in managing time by completing the following self-evaluation questionnaire. Circle your answers or jot them on a separate sheet of paper and add them up for your total.

If you have been honest with yourself, you can tell from the questionnaire (table 13.1 on page 174) which areas need improvement. If you scored worse than you would like, consult the guidelines for improving your time management skills in the next section, Improving Your Time Management Skills.

IMPROVING YOUR TIME MANAGEMENT SKILLS

You can always improve the way you manage your time. Even if you're satisfied with your efficiency level, take a look at the list that follows. It will help you organize your tasks without feeling overwhelmed by them.

- Set aside time for planning your tasks. Isolate yourself, if possible, to concentrate on step-by-step approaches to getting things done. Planning will save time in the long run, because it gives you a chance to prioritize your tasks before you begin them.

- Define your goals on paper, preferably each week, so that you can review them daily and check them off when you reach them. Writing down your weekly goals gives you a chance to see and evaluate what you plan to accomplish. Break down weekly goals into daily goals to make them more manageable.

- Establish tentative time frames for task completion. Having done a specific task before will help you determine realistic guidelines. Simply having a time estimate will also make you more conscious of how you spend your time, which will likely result in spending it more efficiently.

- Identify onerous tasks and place them in the priority list. Be sure to earmark responsibilities that require immediate attention.

- Establish a routine; do not dilute or neglect everyday duties.

- Adhere to deadlines, and monitor your success in this regard. Reward yourself for meeting your goals.

- Delegate whenever possible, and do not let your ego stand in the way of turning over responsibility and praising others for their accomplishments.

- Don't let others waste your time, and don't waste colleagues' time. Practice termi-

Table 13.1 Time Management Self-Assessment

1. To what extent do I plan my time?				
1 always	2 frequently	3 sometimes	4 seldom	5 never

2. To what extent do I set and stick to priorities?				
1 always	2 frequently	3 sometimes	4 seldom	5 never

3. To what extent do I waste time on such things as chatter, indulgences, and diversions?				
1 never	2 seldom	3 sometimes	4 frequently	5 always

4. To what extent do I permit telephone interruptions?				
1 never	2 seldom	3 sometimes	4 frequently	5 always

5. To what extent do I waste time in meetings (by my own choice)?				
1 never	2 seldom	3 sometimes	4 frequently	5 always

6. To what extent do I lose time due to inefficient paperwork processing?				
1 never	2 seldom	3 sometimes	4 frequently	5 always

7. To what extent do I overcommit to obligations?				
1 never	2 seldom	3 sometimes	4 frequently	5 always

8. To what extent do I procrastinate and avoid immersing myself in a task?				
1 never	2 seldom	3 sometimes	4 frequently	5 always

9. To what extent do I delegate work and share responsibilities?				
1 always	2 frequently	3 sometimes	4 seldom	5 never

10. To what extent do I engage in "task hopping," leaving projects unfinished?				
1 never	2 seldom	3 sometimes	4 frequently	5 always

Total your score and compare it with the scale below.				
Range	Rating			
10–15	Outstanding			
16–20	Superior			
21–25	Good			
26–30	Mediocre			
31–50	Weak			

nating conversations gently but firmly in person and over the phone.

- Learn to make rapid and smooth transitions between tasks, and monitor your own progress in this endeavor.

- Monitor the degree of stress you are experiencing in completing tasks. Strive to be upbeat about digging into challenges. Talk yourself into being a happy worker. State of mind is largely a chosen attitude.

- When others place burdens on you or when tasks seem overwhelming, take a mental break and reestablish your goals. Make sure that your original goals are flexible enough to deal with unforeseen circumstances. Try not to let surprises upset you.

- Try to erase from your mind the responsibilities of work when you are away from it, and seize time for enjoyment. Make a private vow that you will not feel guilty for maintaining your emotional stability.

INCREASED TIME COMMITMENTS AT ADVANCED LEVELS

Randy McCall, athletic director at Cherry Creek High School, a prominent institution in suburban Denver, had the good fortune of being selected to work the NCAA Final Four in basketball as a top-notch college referee. His selection had an unfortunate result, however: His local community became alarmed when the Cherry Creek school board questioned the extent of his time commitment to his primary career position.

Athletic directors are ordinarily expected to be on hand for many school sports activities, both boys' and girls'. Seasons overlap to some degree, but even more critical, games often take place simultaneously—for example, a boys' soccer game may be going on during a girls' field hockey contest at an alternate venue. McCall's practice was undoubtedly to delegate responsibilities to assistants, but his superiors questioned his dedication to what they considered his main job, the one he was contracted for, with an attendant job description about his presence at events.

McCall's experience, while extreme (only a small number of people will be chosen to work the Final Four in a given year), highlights the possible conflicts that can occur when an official advances up the ladder of an avocation to the point when time becomes squeezed between a primary career and an appealing sideline.

The epitome of an avocation is one thing (the honor of being chosen), but the road upward is also fraught with dangers related to the allocation of time. To become a candidate to officiate at the college level, one must devote many hours and whole days (sometimes weeks) of striving to be recognized. College commissioners hold weeklong clinics in the off-season, where aspirants can handle practice scrimmages and games by teams that work out in the postseason. Evening and weekend study groups are also expectations at higher levels of college officiating in several sports.

Travel is another issue. Division I officials in both football and basketball frequently must take long plane flights to the outer limits of a person's realistic geographical extensions. An official from Boston can officiate a game in Memphis, stay overnight, and be home the next day. However, expecting a referee in Tampa to be at a game in Salt Lake City and return the

Bonding Time

Former Super Bowl referee Jerry Markbreit, presently a trainer and supervisor of professional referees, said that after film sessions and pregame preparations on Saturdays during the season, his crew went to dinner where football talk was taboo and family issues were shared instead. The purpose of this was to cement relationships with crew members, knowing that they'd have to be exceptionally united in tense action the next day. Sunday morning, Markbreit's crew attended a church service, with each member selecting a church on a rotating basis.

Although they don't ordinarily gather in a religious setting, many high school crews also make it a point to gather periodically, either to prepare for the season or to assess their own performances once the season is underway. They have the same purpose as Markbreit's crew: to synchronize their approach and to solidify their companionship.

next day to get on another flight for the next assignment may be asking too much. Division I basketball officials, despite savoring their status as arbiters at the pinnacle of success, often lament their existence as vagabonds for nearly half a year: in Detroit one night, in Milwaukee the next night.

Some professional sports hire, train, and maintain officials on a full-time basis: Hockey, baseball, and basketball are prime examples. In addition to working the regular seasons, these officials are obliged to extend their commitments into preseason exhibition games, after-season rookie leagues, and off-season look-see operations in which veterans are on rehab assignments and minor league performers are showcased. True, some of the travel is exotic (e.g., overseas games), and major league umpires, through collective bargaining, have secured two-week vacations at home during the regular season. Nevertheless, officials at this level experience immense time pressure, a literal appropriating of their free time.

The National Football League, theoretically at least, does not hire full-time officials. The word *theoretically* means that officiating personnel can pursue regular careers, but in practice much of their free time is dedicated to things such as review and training. First of all, they must be in the city of their game a day early, and if their assignment is on a Sunday or Monday night, they will journey home a day later. Then there are e-mail and phone conferences with crew chiefs on an almost daily basis, plus the film clips received via the Internet at midweek that show missed calls and errant flags (league administrators view every game in minute detail, and officials get a grade on every play). "Sometimes Wednesdays are pretty anxious days," NFL official Kent Payne of Aurora, Colorado, mused.

Life at the top can indeed become tense and time-consuming, and in football to be sure, the college game differs little. Many Division I college coordinators have adopted NFL tactics in terms of expectations of officials. Doug Rhoads said that his officials also are graded on every play. The goal is to strive for perfection. His officials also meet regionally in the off-season for discussion, rules review, and film study. "Then there are spring scrimmages and games at respective universities, talks with teams about rules (another NFL practice), and at least two summer clinics," Rhoads said. "We expect

Time and Tide

At one time, college and professional football officials viewed their previous games' films the day before their next game, at the upcoming site. Currently, with the advent of sophisticated electronic imagery (i.e., replays, slow motion, and stop-action, all recorded by as many as a dozen video cameras), game action is captured more thoroughly and in much more detail.

Doug Rhoads, coordinator of Football Officials for the Atlantic Coast Collegiate Conference, spends 14 hours each Sunday with his assistant, Ben Tario, and other replay technical advisers, analyzing each conference game from the previous day. On Monday, they select isolated clips of superior calls and coverage along with illustrations of questionable officiating, and on Tuesday, Rhoads prepares a voice-over training video that game officials download on their computers on Wednesday.

This comprehensive, integrated system permits officials to review and discuss with crew members via Internet hookups the precise elements of officiating responses in the prior weekend. Outtakes of these game videos are inventoried and stored for subsequent use in clinics. Most major college conferences and professional leagues do the same.

our officials to take their involvement very seriously" (*Referee, op. cit.* April, 2011 pp. 58-59).

This is the way time is eaten up at the highest levels. A prep school official, although not under the same kind of pressure, can still extend commitments beyond reasonable expectations. Some officials, for example, wear several hats. They may work a volleyball match in the afternoon and a basketball game that night. They are itinerants of a different sort, on the go, often determined to make a living in a striped shirt. At least their skeptical fellow officials usually look on them that way. Other determined officials are so obsessed with moving to higher levels that they spend hours e-mailing supervisors and more hours schmoozing with people they believe can promote them.

The point is that you can obsess at any level. You can wear yourself to a frazzle trying to advance or fill up a schedule to overflowing. Conversely, you can also balance your life with measured energies and useful time. As the adage goes, you can't create extra time; the best you can do is settle for a swap.

SUMMARY

If you took stock of how you spend your time on a given day, you may be surprised at how many interruptions you are forced to deal with. Few people plan for such things as intrusions via telephone. You may be startled to discover how much time you spend on personal chats.

This chapter highlights seven necessary time commitments in officiating. If you find yourself continually pressed for time, examine the probable causes of faulty time management. The self-assessment tool in this chapter can show you the personal habits you may need to change to make effective use of your time. We also offered ways to make those changes.

REVIEW QUESTIONS

1. Ice arenas, where many organizations may compete for time slots, may schedule games
   a. in the early morning or late at night
   b. on grass fields outside the building
   c. with four teams playing on the same rink
   d. six to twelve months in advance

2. One time factor that officials must account for is
   a. how to fit in a nutritious meal
   b. where to go after the game
   c. a pregame officials' conference
   d. writing a game report

3. Perhaps the best way to study a sports rule book is to
   a. set aside a day to read the entire contents
   b. memorize large batches of text
   c. have someone read aloud to you
   d. read short segments at a time

4. One good way to prepare for the season is to
   a. check in with the coaches of the teams you'll meet
   b. imagine game situations in the off-season
   c. clear the mind by focusing on things other than sports
   d. work a scrimmage or intrasquad practice

5. Which of the following is a detrimental and nonproductive use of time?
   a. sticking with a project until it is done
   b. task hopping (moving from one duty to another without completing any of them)
   c. getting lost on highways and city streets
   d. listening to favorite tunes while at work

6. One effective way to achieve goals is to
   a. put them down on paper
   b. let them happen naturally
   c. share them with others
   d. set unrealistic goals

7. One effective way to approach obligations is to
   a. do the most difficult or least desirable one first
   b. get other people involved
   c. stretch out requirements to fill in the time
   d. hop from one task to another, hoping to complete them all at once

8. Which of the following is a prominent time waster?
   a. worrying about financial obligations
   b. outlining how a task should be done
   c. permitting intrusions and holding extensive social conversations
   d. starting a project too late in the day

9. Professional officials
   a. usually neglect their families
   b. can easily gain a sense of arrogance about their infallibility
   c. often have much of their time taken up with preparation and game reviews
   d. have special systems for using their down time effectively

10. One way to advance to the college level is to
   a. write an essay to a college commissioner explaining your philosophy
   b. attend weekend or weeklong clinics under the auspices of college officials coordinators
   c. send repeat e-mails to a college commissioner containing your high school game schedule for review
   d. make repeated phone calls to a college commissioner to establish name recognition

Answers on page 190

APPENDIX A

SPORTS OFFICIALS CODE OF ETHICS

The National Association of Sports Officials (NASO) believes the duty of sports officials is to act as impartial judges of sports competitions. We believe this duty carries with it an obligation to perform with accuracy, fairness, and objectivity through an overriding sense of integrity.

Although the vast majority of sports officials work contests played by amateur athletes, it is vital that every official approach each assignment in a professional manner. Because of their authority and autonomy, officials must have a high degree of commitment and expertise. NASO believes these facts impose on sports officials the higher ethical standard by which true professionals are judged.

Officials who are professionals voluntarily observe a high level of conduct, not because they fear a penalty but because of their own personal character. They accept responsibility for their actions. This conduct has as its foundation a deep sense of moral values and use of reason that substantiates the belief a given conduct is proper simply because it is.

The Code

The purposes of the National Association of Sports Officials Code of Ethics are briefly summarized through the following three provisions:

1. To provide our members a meaningful set of guidelines for their professional conduct and to provide them with agreed-upon standards of practice;

2. To provide to other sports officials these same guidelines and standards of practice for their consideration;

3. To provide to others (i.e., players, coaches, administrators, fans, media) criteria by which to judge our actions as professionals.

NASO has adopted this code and strongly urges its members and officials in general to adhere to its principles. By doing so, notice is given that we recognize the need to preserve and encourage confidence in the professionalism of officiating. This confidence must first be fostered within the community of officials and then within the public generally.

NASO believes the integrity of officiating rests on the integrity and ethical conduct of each individual official. This integrity and conduct are the very basis of the future and well-being of organized sports and the effectiveness of this association. NASO shall, by programs of education and other means, encourage acceptance and implementation of the articles named below. To these ends NASO declares acceptance of the following code:

Article I Sports officials must be free of obligation to any interest other than the impartial and fair judging of sports competitions. Without equivocation, game decisions slanted by personal bias are dishonest and unacceptable.

Article II Sports officials recognize that anything that may lead to a conflict of interest, either real or apparent, must be avoided. Gifts, favors, special treatment, privileges, employment, or a personal relationship with a school or team that can compromise the perceived impartiality of officiating must be avoided.

Article III Sports officials are obligated to treat other officials with professional dignity and courtesy and recognize that it is inappropriate to criticize other officials publicly.

Article IV Sports officials have a responsibility to continuously seek self-improvement through study of the game, rules, mechanics, and the techniques of game management. They have a responsibility to accurately represent their qualifications and abilities when requesting or accepting officiating assignments.

Article V Sports officials shall protect the public (including fans, administrators, coaches, and players) from inappropriate conduct and shall attempt to eliminate from the officiating avocation and profession all practices that bring discredit to the profession.

Article VI Sports officials shall not be party to actions designed to unfairly limit or restrain access to officiating, officiating assignments, or association membership. This includes selection for positions of leadership based on economic factors, race, creed, color, age, sex, physical handicap, country, or national origin.

APPENDIX B

STATE HIGH SCHOOL ASSOCIATIONS AND CALIFORNIA INTERSCHOLASTIC FEDERATION (CIF) SECTIONS

Alabama High School Athletic Association
7325 Halcyon Summit Drive
Montgomery, AL 36117
334-263-6994
Fax: 334-387-0075
www.ahsaa.com

Alaska School Activities Association
4120 Laurel Street, Suite 102
Anchorage, AK 99508
907-563-3723
Fax: 907-561-0720
www.asaa.org/

Arizona Interscholastic Association, Inc.
7007 North 18th Street
Phoenix, AZ 85020-5552
602-385-3810
Fax: 602-385-3779
www.aiaonline.org

Arkansas Activities Association
3920 Richards Road
North Little Rock, AR 72117
501-955-2500
Fax: 501-955-2600
www.ahsaa.org

California Interscholastic Federation
4658 Duckhorn Drive
Sacramento, CA 95834
916-239-4477
Fax: 916-239-4478
www.cifstate.org

Colorado High School Activities Association
14855 E. Second Avenue
Aurora, CO 80011
303-344-5050
Fax: 303-367-4101
www.chsaa.org

Connecticut Interscholastic Athletic Conference, Inc.
30 Realty Drive
Cheshire, CT 06410
203-250-1111
Fax: 203-250-1345
www.casciac.org

Delaware Interscholastic Athletic Association
35 Commerce Way, Suite 1
Dover, DE 19904
302-857-3365
Fax: 302-739-1769

DC Interscholastic Athletic Association
1401 Brentwood Parkway NE
Washington, DC 20002
202-698-3326
Fax: 202-698-6397

Florida High School Athletic Association
1801 NW 80th Boulevard
Gainesville, FL 32606
352-372-9551
Fax: 352-373-1528
www.fhsaa.org

Georgia High School Association
151 S. Bethel Street
Thomaston, GA 30286
706-647-7473
Fax: 706-647-2638
www.ghsa.net

Hawaii High School Athletic Association
P. O. Box 62029
Honolulu, HI 62029
808-587-4495
Fax: 808-587-4496
www.sportshigh.com

Idaho High School Activities Association
8011 Ustick Road
Boise, ID 83704
208-375-7027
Fax: 208-322-5505
www.idhsaa.org

Illinois High School Association
2715 McGraw Drive
Bloomington, IL 61702-2715
309-663-6377
Fax: 309-663-7479
www.ihsa.org

Indiana High School Athletic Association
9150 N. Meridian Street
Indianapolis, IN 46260
317-846-6601
Fax: 317-575-4244
www.ihsaa.org

Iowa High School Athletic Association
1605 South Story Street
Boone, IA 50036
515-432-2011
Fax: 515-432-2961
www.iahsaa.org

Kansas State High School Activities Association
601 SW Commerce Place
Topeka, KS 66615
785-273-5329
Fax: 785-271-0236
www.kshsaa.org

Kentucky High School Athletic Association
2280 Executive Drive
Lexington, KY 40505
859-299-5472
Fax: 859-293-5999
www.khsaa.org

Louisiana High School Athletic Association
3029 S. Sherwood Forest Blvd.
Baton Rouge, LA 70879
225-296-5882
Fax: 225-296-5919
www.lhsaa.org

Maine Principals' Association
50 Industrial Drive
Augusta, ME 04338
207-622-0217
Fax: 207-622-1513
www.mpa.cc

Maryland Public Secondary Schools Athletic Association
200 W. Baltimore Street
Baltimore, MD 21201
410-767-0555
Fax: 410-333-3111
www.mpssaa.org

Massachusetts Interscholastic Athletic Association
33 Forge Parkway
Franklin, MA 02038
508-541-7997
Fax: 508-541-9888
www.miaa.net

Michigan High School Athletic Association
1661 Ramblewood Drive
East Lansing, MI 48823
517-332-5046
Fax: 517-332-4071
www.mhsaa.com

Minnesota State High School League
2100 Freeway Boulevard
Brooklyn Center, MN 55430
612-560-2262
Fax: 612-569-0499
www.mshsl.org

Mississippi High School Activities Association, Inc.
1201 Clinton-Raymond Road
Clinton, MS 39056
601-924-6400
Fax: 601-924-1725
www.misshsaa.com

Missouri State High School Activities Association
1 North Keene Street
Columbia, MO 65201
573-875-4880
Fax: 573-875-1450
www.mshsaa.org

Montana High School Association
1 South Dakota Avenue
Helena, MT 59601
406-442-6010
Fax: 406-442-8250
www.mhsa.org

Nebraska School Activities Association
500 Charleston Street
Lincoln, NE 68510
402-489-0386
Fax: 402-489-0934
www.nsaahome.org

Nevada Interscholastic Activities Association
549 Court Street
Reno, NV 89501
775-453-1012
Fax: 775-453-1016
www.niaa.com

New Hampshire Interscholastic Athletic Association
251 Clinton Street
Concord, NH 03301
603-228-8671
Fax: 603-225-7978
www.nhiaa.org

New Jersey State Interscholastic Athletic Association
P. O. Box 487
Robbinsville, NJ 08691
609-259-2776
Fax: 609-259-3047
www.njsiaa.org

New Mexico Activities Association
6600 Palomas NE
Albuquerque, NM 87109
505-821-1887
Fax: 505-821-2441
www.nmact.org

New York State Public High School Athletic Association
8 Airport Park Boulevard
Latham, NY 12110
518-690-0771
Fax: 518-690-0775
www.nysphsaa.org

North Carolina High School Athletic Association
222 Finley Golf Course Road
Chapel Hill, NC 27517
919-962-2345
Fax: 919-962-1686
www.nchsaa.org

North Dakota High School Activities Association
P.O. Box 817
Valley City, ND 58072
701-845-3953
Fax: 701-845-4935
www.ndhsaa.com

Ohio High School Athletic Association
4080 Roselea Place
Columbus, OH 43214
614-267-2502
Fax: 614-267-1677
www.ohsaa.org

Oklahoma Secondary School Activities Association
7300 North Broadway Extension
Oklahoma City, OK 73116
405-840-1116
Fax: 405-840-9559
www.ossaa.com

Oregon School Activities Association
25200 SW Parkway Avenue
Wilsonville, OR 97070
503-682-6722
Fax: 503-682-0960
www.osaa.org

Pennsylvania Interscholastic Athletic Association, Inc.
550 Gettysburg Road
Mechanicsburg, PA 17055
717-697-0374
Fax: 717-697-7721
www.piaa.org

Rhode Island Interscholastic League
Bldg. #6 R.I. College Campus
600 Mt. Pleasant Avenue
Providence, RI 02908
401-272-9844
Fax: 401-272-9838
www.riil.org

South Carolina High School League
121 Westpark Boulevard
Columbia, SC 29210
803-798-0120
Fax: 803-731-9679
www.schsl.org

South Dakota High School Activities Association
804 North Euclid, Suite 102
Pierre, SD 57501
605-224-9261
Fax: 605-224-9262
www.sdhsaa.com

Tennessee Secondary School Athletic Association
3333 Lebanon Road
Hermitage, TN 37076
615-889-6740
Fax: 615-889-0544
www.tssaa.org

Texas University Interscholastic League
1701 Manor Road
Austin, TX 78713
512-471-5883
Fax: 512-471-5908
www.uiltexas.org

Utah High School Activities Association
199 East 7200 South
Midvale, UT 84047
801-566-0681
Fax: 801-566-0633
www.uhsaa.org

Vermont Principals' Association
Two Prospect Street
Montpelier, VT 05602
802-229-0547
Fax: 802-229-4801
www.vpaonline.org

Virginia High School League
1642 State Farm Boulevard
Charlottesville, VA 22911
804-977-8475
Fax: 804-977-5943
www.vhsl.org

Washington Interscholastic Activities Association
435 Maine Avenue South
Renton, WA 98055
425-687-8585
Fax: 425-687-9476
www.wiaa.com

West Virginia Secondary School Activities Commission
2875 Staunton Turnpike
Parkersburg, WV 26104
304-485-5494
Fax: 304-428-5431
www.wvssac.org

Wisconsin Interscholastic Athletic Association
5516 Vern Holmes Drive
Stevens Point, WI 54481
715-344-8580
Fax: 715-344-4241
www.wiaawi.org

Wyoming High School Activities Association
731 E. 2nd Street
Casper, WY 82601
307-577-0614
Fax: 307-577-0637
www.whsaa.org

CIF—Central Section
P.O. Box 1567
Porterville, CA 93258
559-781-7586
Fax: 559-781-7033
www.cifcs.org

CIF—Central Coast Section
6830 Via Del Oro, Suite 103
San Jose, CA 95119
408-224-2994
Fax: 408-224-0476
www.cifccs.org

CIF—Los Angeles City Section
1545 Wilshire Boulevard, Suite 200
P.O. Box 330
Los Angeles, CA 90017
213-207-2200
Fax: 213-207-2209
www.cif-la.org

CIF—North Coast Section
12925 Alcosta Boulevard, Suite 8
San Ramon, CA 94583
925-866-8400
Fax: 925-866-7100
www.cifncs.org

CIF—Northern Section
2241 St. George Lane, Suite 2
Chico, CA 95928
530-343-7285
Fax: 530-343-5619
www.cifns.org

CIF—Oakland Section
Oakland City Schools
900 High Street
Oakland, CA 94601
510-879-8311
Fax: 510-879-1835
www.cifstate.org

CIF—San Diego Section
6401 Linda Vista Road, Room 504
San Diego, CA 92111
858-292-8165
Fax: 858-292-1375
www.cifsds.org

CIF—San Francisco Section
555 Portola Drive, Room 250
San Francisco, CA 94131
415-920-5185
Fax: 415-920-5189
www.cifsf.org

CIF—San Joaquin Section
1368 East Turner Road, Suite A
Lodi, CA 95240
209-334-5900
Fax: 209-334-0300
www.cifsjs.org

CIF—Southern Section
10932 Pine Street
Los Alamitos, CA 90720
562-493-9500
Fax: 562-493-6266
www.cifss.org

APPENDIX C

OTHER GOVERNING BODIES

Amateur Baseball Umpires' Association (ABUA)
200 S. Wilcox Street #508
Castle Rock, CO 80104
303-290-7411
www.umpire.org

American Youth Soccer Organization (AYSO)
12501 South Isis Avenue
Hawthorne, CA 90250
800-872-2976
Fax: 310-643-5310
www.soccer.org/home.aspx

Arena Football League (AFL)
75 E. Wacker #400
Chicago, IL 60601
312-332-5510
www.arenafootball.com

Babe Ruth League, Inc.
1770 Brunswick Pike
Trenton, NJ 08638
609-695-1434
www.baberuthleague.org

Continental Basketball Association (CBA)
Two Arizona Center
400 N. 5th St. #1425
Phoenix, AZ 85004
602-254-6677
www.cblhoopsonline.com

Little League Baseball, Inc.
P.O. Box 3485
Williamsport, PA 17701
570-326-1921
www.littleleague.org

National Alliance for Youth Sports
2050 Vista Parkway
West Palm Beach, FL 33411
561-684-1141
www.nays.org

National Association for Girls and Women in Sports (NAGWS)
1900 Association Drive
Reston, VA 22091
703-476-3452
www.aahperd.org/nagws

National Association of Intercollegiate Athletics (NAIA)
6120 South Yale Avenue #1450
Tulsa, OK 74136
918-494-8828
www.naia.cstv.com

National Association of Sports Officials (NASO)
2017 Lathrop Avenue
Racine, WI 53405
414-632-8855
Fax: 414-632-5460
www.naso.org

National Basketball Association (NBA)
Olympic Tower
645 Fifth Avenue
New York, NY 10022
212-407-8000
www.nba.org

National Collegiate Athletic Association (NCAA)
700 W. Washington Street
P.O. Box 6222
Indianapolis, IN 46206
317-917-6222
Fax: 317-917-6888
www.ncaa.com

National Federation of State High School Associations
11724 NW Plaza Circle
Kansas City, MO 64195
816-464-5400
www.nfhs.org

National Football League (NFL)
280 Park Avenue
New York, NY 10017
212-450-2000
www.nfl.com

National Intercollegiate Soccer Officials Association (NISOA)
541 Woodview Drive
Longwood, FL 32779
407-862-3305
www.nisoa.com

National Junior College Athletic Association (NJCAA)
P.O. Box 7305
Colorado Springs, CO 80933
719-590-9788
www.njcaa.org

Pony Baseball and Softball
P.O. Box 225
Washington, PA 15301
412-225-1060
www.pony.org

Pop Warner Football
586 Middletown Boulevard, Suite C-100
Langhorne, PA 19047
215-752-2691
www.popwarner.com

Soccer Association for Youth (SAY)
4050 Executive Park Drive, Suite #100
Cincinnati, OH 45241
800-233-7291
513-769-0500
www.saysoccer.org

Soccer in the Streets (SITS)
149 S. McDonough Street, Suite 270
Jonesboro, GA 30236
770-477-0354
770-478-1862
www.soccerstreets.org

USA Hockey
1775 Bob Johnson Drive
Colorado Springs, CO 80906
www.usahockey.com

USA Volleyball
One Olympic Plaza
Colorado Springs, CO 80910
719-637-8300
www.usavolleyball.org

United States Olympic Committee
One Olympic Plaza
Colorado Springs, CO 80909
www.teamusa.org

United States Soccer Federation (USSF)
1801-1811 South Prairie Avenue
Chicago, IL 60616
312-808-1300
Fax: 312-808-1301
www.ussoccer.com

Women's National Basketball Association (WNBA)
Olympic Tower
645 Fifth Avenue
New York, NY 10022
212-688-9622
www.wnba.com

APPENDIX D

ANSWERS TO PROBLEMS AND REVIEW QUESTIONS

This appendix contains the answers to all the problems and review questions listed at the end of each chapter. However, you should make a genuine effort to answer each question before referring to this appendix—use it only to check your answers. Several different answers may exist for the short answer questions.

CHAPTER 1

1. b
2. d
3. c
4. d
5. d
6. b
7. c
8. c
9. b
10. d

CHAPTER 2

1. False
2. True
3. False
4. True
5. False
6. True
7. False
8. True
9. True
10. True

CHAPTER 3

1. Naturally, the best officials are those who have a deep sense of what the game is all about. There are times when it is necessary to be strict and other times when leniency is called for. For instance, a game played between youngsters who are just learning might call for an official to understand their lack of technical proficiency and be lenient. On the other hand, a game played between two high-caliber teams might call for a stricter hand. Some rules, however, do not permit any deviance. The clearest examples are the rules regarding the boundary lines that confine a sport and define its critical areas. When a ball possessed by a runner crosses the plane of the goal line in football, it is a touchdown, with no room for equivocation. When a batted ball hits a base in softball or baseball, it is a fair ball. When a basketball bounces on a sideline, it is out of bounds. Accurate judgement (which is not always easy) is the determining factor in these cases. In addition, officials should always be strict when safety is an issue.

2. b
3. c
4. d
5. d
6. b
7. c
8. c
9. d

CHAPTER 4

1. d
2. d
3. e
4. a
5. d
6. d
7. b

CHAPTER 5

1. We cannot *not* communicate. We are always sending some sort of message.

2. What might be acceptable in one context or situation might not be acceptable in another.

3. Concerns, panic, random thoughts, defensiveness, or anything running through the mind of the listener are all examples.

4. To gain information, to empathize, to anticipate responding, to make judgments, and to simply be entertained are three examples.

5. It is important to understand the frustrations or stress levels of the speaker; officials also need to be aware of what the speaker's expressions and gestures mean.

6. Barriers include erroneously anticipating the speaker's response, tuning out or letting one's mind wander, and letting emotions interfere with listening.

7. Denotative meanings are the dictionary meanings; connotative meanings are what words mean in context.

8. Officials must speak clearly in all situations but especially when explaining calls and rules.

9. Poor word choices, even those that may seem so trivial in more casual or personal contexts, can greatly affect professionalism.

10. Nonverbal communication constitutes most of the message sent; verbal communication involves only words.

11. Monitoring your own behavior is the first step to improvement. Enlist the help of others to get objective feedback on your nonverbal communication. Also, performing a body language drill in front of a mirror is a great way to evaluate and improve nonverbal communication.

CHAPTER 6

1. Careless or frivolous breaches of the game's tempo may annoy participants, coaches, and spectators. Their impatience may result in complaints, moans of anguish over routine calls, and even outcries of disagreement.

2. Perhaps the best way for a beginner to learn the rules and their implications is to attend a class in which the sport's jargon is introduced and discussed. Going over rules with an acquaintance is also useful, but the best system is to have a knowledgeable person, such as an experienced official, explain the facets of seemingly simple definitions. Also, the rules should be absorbed over time, with the official studying and learning only a small section of the rule book at a time.

3. Many answers exist for this question. For example, football players may sometimes run with the ball after picking it up from the ground, but at other times, they may not. A basketball player may retain possession of the ball after falling down in some very specific and carefully described circumstances. A baseball or softball player may run out of a baseline when certain conditions exist.

4. Many peculiar things happen in sports and an official needs to know the appropriate steps to take in these instances. For instance, a ball lodges in an unexpected place during a baseball game, or a football player comes off the sidelines to tackle a runner. The rules generally specify the ruling should these events occur, and officials should have these rules memorized.

5. If you know the language of your sport, you have a better chance of getting rulings right consistently. Moreover, it's important to be fluent in your sport's language so that you can convey rulings appropriately to players and coaches.

6. Different sports have different responsibilities for officials depending on the situations and rotations. It's important for officials to look off of the ball or object to see fouls, unsportsmanlike conduct, or anything pertinent to an official that might weigh in on the outcome of a game.

7. Player safety is one of the biggest concerns for officials, and with so much going on in contact sports, it's vital for an official to have an intricate knowledge of the rules in order to know what's legal or illegal.

8. Pregame imaging is one way that top-flight officials practice good tactics by imagining scenarios in their minds, mentally creating game situations—particular phases that pose problems with judgment, execution, and difficult people—and rehearsing how they would respond to these moments in a game. Imaging or inward rehearsing is an effective method for enhancing performance.

9. There are several ways to accommodate a fellow official. Here are a few: An official may help his colleague with an on-field ruling if his judgment is sought. Also, officials can help clarify mechanics and proper placement—this is especially true for younger officials. Finally, officials can be a cooperating friend and record the game from high in the stands to capture them in action. A game video can be an extremely valuable resource for improvement.

10. Any number of examples could be correct: A call on the bases in baseball or softball, a shooting foul in basketball, or an illegal block in football are all examples of plays in which an official should expect a partner to make a call without input.

CHAPTER 7

1. a
2. a
3. d
4. d
5. a
6. b
7. b
8. a

CHAPTER 8

1. a
2. a
3. d
4. d
5. a

6. Coaches may complain in an effort to gain a presumed edge from officials. They believe that if they get on the officials about one call, maybe the next one will go in their favor. In addition, when they think their teams are too lethargic, some coaches yell at the officials to fire the team up. Coaches can also get frustrated because they believe (mistakenly, in most instances, as has been discussed) that officials aren't accountable.

7. Use the quiet word when you notice something that could develop into a larger problem. When the quiet word doesn't work, sometimes a louder word does. Be firm and strong, but don't ever yell or curse. When the quiet word and the louder word don't work, use a visual warning. Use a stop gesture—fingers upward and palm extended to the offender—to show all around that you've heard enough and have issued an informal warning.

8. A curse word clearly audible to others, trash talk to an opponent, and a coach on the court or field arguing with an official are all examples requiring a formal warning.

9. First, always treat everyone with respect and don't treat anyone as inferior. That being said, it is your job to hear complaints from a head coach, not with complaints from assistants or players. They should be treated with respect but with little leniency.

10. Crossing your arms in front of your chest will appear too aggressive. Also avoid an aggressive hands-on-hips stance with your chest thrust out. When an argument ensues, consider placing your hands behind your back. Stand tall and strong while doing so, never slouch. Standing tall does not appear confrontational yet shows you're in control. Avoid pointing at a player or coach. That gesture appears too aggressive and almost always gets a heated response, such as, "Get your finger out of my face!" Make solid eye contact. If your eyes wander or your head moves around, you give the impression that you're intimidated by the coach or not sure of your position.

CHAPTER 9

1. The minimum recommendation is 150 minutes and an even greater health benefit (most notably for adults who must perform physical tasks such as officiating) is derived from an increase in aerobic activity up to 300 minutes (5 hours) per week and more than 2 days of muscle-strengthening activities.

2. Moderate-intensity activities are those that raise your heart rate and cause you to break a sweat (such as brisk walking, bicycling on level ground, playing doubles tennis, even gardening and yard work) and more vigorous-intensity activities are ones that raise your heart rate, produce sweat, and increase your breathing rate to the point that you cannot say more than a few words. In fact, an easy way to remember the difference between moderate-intensity and vigorous intensity activities is commonly known as the talk test. That is, if you can carry on a conversation while exercising, then the activity is probably moderate.

3. Ideally, you should eat a variety of dark green vegetables, such as spinach and broccoli, red vegetables, such as peppers, and orange vegetables, such as carrots and sweet potatoes.

4. b

5. a

CHAPTER 10

1. After your body's temperature is raised, your body is more conducive to a series of stretching exercises that will further help prepare it for activity and reduce the chance of injury.

2. One reason for assessing waist circumference is to better determine fat distribution. That is, even someone who is highly muscled would still not want to have a large waist. Excess body fat stored around the abdominal region is also known as android (apple shaped) obesity and is a risk factor for coronary artery disease, stroke, hypertension, high cholesterol and triglycerides, and type 2 diabetes.

3. The four components or RICE are rest, ice, compression, and elevation.

4. d

5. b

CHAPTER 11

1. d
2. a
3. True
4. False
5. c
6. e
7. c
8. a

CHAPTER 12

1. e
2. d
3. b
4. c
5. d

CHAPTER 13

1. a
2. c
3. d
4. d
5. b
6. a
7. a
8. c
9. c
10. b

REFERENCES

AAHPERD. 1999. *Physical Education for Life long fitness: The Physical Best Teacher's Guide.* Champaign, IL: Human Kinetics.

Adler, Ronald B., and Jeanne Marquardt Elmhorst. 2008. *Communicating at Work: Principles and Practices for Business and the Professions.* New York: McGraw-Hill.

American Dietetic Association. 2010. "It's About Eating Right." www.eatright.org/Public/.

Bell, Keith. 1983. Championship Thinking. Englewood Cliffs, NJ: Prentice Hall.

Blumenthal, Karen. 2005. *Let Me Play.* New York: Atheneum Books for Young Readers.

Burton, Damon, and Cheryl Weiss. 2008. "The Fundamental Goal Concept: The Path to Process and Performance Success." In *Advances in Sport Psychology.* 3d ed. Champaign, IL: Human Kinetics.

Folkesson, P., C. Nyberg, T. Archer, and T. Norlander. 2002. "Soccer Referees' Experience of Threat and Aggression: Effects of Age, Experience, and Life Orientation on Outcome of Coping Strategy." *Aggressive Behavior* 28 (4): 317-27.

Guttman, Allen. 1991. *Women's Sports: A History.* New York: Columbia University Press.

Heim, Pat. *Invisible Rules: Men, Women & Teams.* CorVision Media. www.trainingabc.com/invisible-rules-men-women-and-teams-p-16322.html.

Kelly, Marylin S. 2006. *Communication at Work.* Upper Saddle River, NJ: Pearson Education.

Locke, E.A., K.N. Shaw, L.M. Saari, and G.P. Latham, GP. 1981. "Goal Setting and Task Performance." *Psychological Bulletin* 90: 125-52.

Locke, E. and Latham, G. *A theory of goal setting and task performance.* Prentice Hall. Englewood Cliffs, New Jersey. 1990.

Locke, E. and Latham, G. "New directions in goal-setting theory." *Current Directions in Psychological Science,* (2006) 15: 265-268.

Pedowitz, L.B. et al. 2008, Oct. 1. *Report to the Board of Governors of the National Basketball Association.*

Rooff-Steffen, Kay. 2004. "Trigger Words: Watch Your Language." *Teaching for Success.* 16(6).

Snyder, E., and D. Purdy. 1987. "Social Control in Sport: An Analysis of Basketball Officiating." *Sociology of Sport Journal* 4: 392-402.

Steitz, Edward. 1976. *Illustrated Basketball Rules.* New York: Dolphin Books.

Stern, Jeffrey. 2010, January. "26 hrs with an NFL Crew." Referee.

The University of Idaho Intramural Sports Official Handbook. 2009-10.

Thayer, J. and Johnsen, B. "Sex differences in judgement of facial affect: A multivariate analysis of recognition errors." *Scandinavian Journal of Psychology,* (2000) 41: 243–246.

Tunney, J. 1987, July. "They Said It Couldn't Be Done." *Referee.*

University of Idaho Intramural Sports Official Handbook, 2009-2010.

U.S. Department of Health and Human Services. 2008. *Physical Activity Guidelines for Americans.* www.health.gov/paguidelines/adultguide/default.aspx.

Weinberg, Robert, and Daniel Gould. 2011. *Foundations of Sport and Exercise Psychology.* 5th ed. Champaign, IL: Human Kinetics.

Weinberg, R., and P. Richardson. 1990. *Psychology of Officiating.* Champaign, IL: Human Kinetics.

World Book Encyclopedia. 2010. Chicago: Scott Fetzer Company.

INDEX

ABOUT THE CONTRIBUTORS

Paul M. Anderson is the associate director of the National Sports Law Institute and an adjunct professor of law. He earned a BA in economics and philosophy (cum laude and Phi Beta Kappa) and a law degree from Marquette University, where he received the first Joseph E. O'Neill scholarship for sports ethics. Professor Anderson teaches workshops on legal and business issues in collegiate athletics; legal issues in youth, high school, and recreational sports; and advanced legal research-sport law. He also teaches selected topics in Sports Law Seminar and Entertainment Law. He coteaches the seminar in the economics of sport in the College of Business Administration. He is the founder and chair of the Sports Law Alumni Association and received the 2003 Sports Law Alumnus of the Year Award. Professor Anderson is a former editor in chief and current faculty coadvisor to the *Marquette Sports Law Review,* former editor of the *Journal of Legal Aspects of Sport,* and former Managing Editor of the *Journal of Sport and Social Issues.* He is the author of numerous articles and several books, including *Introduction to Sports Law* (2009, with Spengler, Connaughton, and Baker), and is chair of the Sports and Entertainment Law section of the State Bar of Wisconsin. Under his supervision, the National Sports Law Institute has provided focused seminars on officials and liability issues in sports and has developed training programs for high school coaches, administrators, and officials. He has also worked with the National Association of Sports Officials on its *Assaults of Sports Officials Reports* and worked with the National Council of Youth Sports providing expert guidance on liability issues involving volunteers, officials, and coaches.

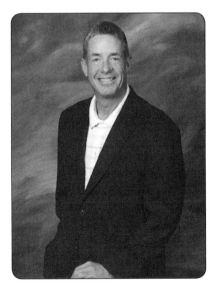

Jon Bible has been a professor of business law at Texas State University since 1986. Before that, he served as an assistant attorney general of Texas. His specialties are employment and constitutional law. He has coauthored two books and numerous legal articles. He has also written columns on baseball umpiring and football officiating for *Referee* magazine since 1978.

He has also been a sports official for over 40 years. He umpired baseball professionally for four years and has been working at the college level since 1974. He has 25 NCAA Division I postseason regional tournaments and seven College World Series to his credit. He began officiating football in 1970 and worked in the Southwest Conference from 1987 to 1994, NFL from 1994 to 1996, and Big XII Conference from 1997 to 2008. In 2009 he joined the new professional United Football League, where he serves as a referee. In his college career he worked several bowl games and conference championships, and he worked the Division I National Championship games in 1993 (Alabama-Miami) and 2007 (Ohio State-LSU).

Jerry Grunska received a BS degree in English and physical education from LaCrosse State College Wisconsin and earned an MA in English from Colorado State College. Grunska also earned his PhD in English from Northwestern University. Jerry had a 37-year career as an English instructor. He coached intermittently for 16 years in three sports (baseball, basketball, and football) while also officiating for 45 years in various sports (baseball, basketball, football, and softball). In 2004 he was elected to the Colorado Officials Hall of Fame.

Jerry has had a well-published career; he wrote sporadically for almost 20 years, including columns for *Referee* magazine and contributions to articles for multiple English journals and regional magazines. The first football officiating book he wrote was published in 1984. He's had more than 200 sports officiating articles published and 24 books—8 as sole author and the others as coauthor, contributor, and editor. Jerry is now retired from teaching and lives with his wife in Colorado. He has four adult children.

Kathleen Poole is an associate professor at Radford University in Virginia. She received her BS and MS from Virginia Tech and her PhD from the University of Utah. **Jon Poole** is a professor also at Radford University. He received his BS from Colorado State University and his MS and EdD from Virginia Tech.

Since 1996, they have worked with NFL officials to enhance overall health and officiating performance. They have conducted agility testing and assessed cardiorespiratory fitness, body composition, and flexibility on an annual basis. They have also worked one on one with officials to develop nutrition, weight management, strength training, and cardiorespiratory fitness programs. During the 2003 and 2004 seasons, they conducted a 10-game study to examine the physiological demands of officiating in the NFL. The results of this study were presented at the American College of Sports Medicine Conference in Indianapolis, Indiana, in 2004.

During the summer of 2009 and 2010, the Pooles conducted body composition testing with several college officiating conferences, including the Big 12 Conference, Southland Conference, Western Athletic Conference, Mountain West Conference, and Conference USA.

Kay Rooff-Steffen, MA, has chaired the communication and humanities department at Eastern Iowa Community Colleges since 1991. A former full-time and still occasional communication consultant, she wrote articles for *Referee* magazine for several years and contributed a similar chapter to the first *Successful Sports Officiating*. She teaches topics related to professional communication, managing conflict, responding to change, and public speaking. Kay is also a life coach and continues to write for various professional journals and trade magazines. She lives near the Iowa Quad Cities.

Robert Weinberg received a BS degree from Brooklyn College in physical education and received both an MA in psychology and MS in kinesiology from UCLA. In addition, he earned his PhD in psychology at UCLA and was a postdoctoral scholar in psychology at UCLA. Currently, he is a professor in the department of kinesiology and health at Miami University. He has published over 140 journal articles as well as 9 books (including the most popular textbook in the field, titled *Foundations of Sport and Exercise Psychology*, and 40 book chapters). He was editor in chief of the *Journal of Applied Sport Psychology* and serves on the editorial board of 7 sport and exercise psychology journals. He served as president of AASP and NASPSPA and chair of the AAHPERD Sport Psychology Academy.

Robert was voted a distinguished scholar and the outstanding faculty member in the School of Education and Allied Professions at Miami University. He is a certified consultant of AASP and a member of the U.S. Olympic Committee's Sport Psychology Registry. With coauthor Peggy Richardson he published one of the few books focusing on the mental aspects of officiating, titled *The Psychology of Officiating*. He has published several articles regarding the mental aspects of officiating and was an official in several sports. In addition, he has been a varsity athlete and coach in tennis, football, and basketball.

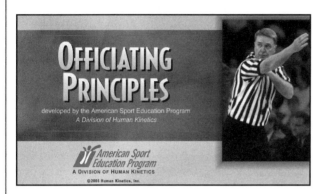